MADE IN JAPAN
AND OTHER JAPANESE
"BUSINESS NOVELS"

MADE IN JAPAN
AND OTHER JAPANESE "BUSINESS NOVELS"

TRANSLATOR AND EDITOR
TAMAE K. PRINDLE

An East Gate Book

M. E. Sharpe, Inc.
Armonk, New York
London, England

An East Gate Book

Copyright © 1989 by M. E. Sharpe, Inc.

All rights reserved. No part of this book may be reproduced in any
form without written permission from the publisher, M. E. Sharpe, Inc.,
80 Business Park Drive, Armonk, New York 10504

Available in the United Kingdom and Europe from M. E. Sharpe,
Publishers, 3 Henrietta Street, London WC2E 8LU.

Library of Congress Cataloging-in-Publication Data

Made in Japan and other Japanese business novels / translated and
   edited by Tamae K. Prindle.
       p.   cm.
   Translation of 7 Japanese short stories.
   ISBN 0-87332-529-X
   1. Short stories, Japanese—Translations into English. 2. Short
stories, English—Translations from Japanese. 3. Business
enterprises—Fiction. I. Prindle, Tamae K., 1944– . II. Title:
Japanese business novels.
   PL782.E8M34   1989   89-4218
   891.73 ′01 ′08—dc19   CIP

Printed in the United States of America

∞

BB 10 9 8 7 6 5 4 3 2 1

To Peter, Tiffany, Kazan,
and Japanese and American businessmen

Contents

Acknowledgments

I wish to thank the authors, Saburō Shiroyama, Ikkō Shimizu, Ryō Takasugi, Taichi Sakaiya, and Takeshi Kaikō, for discussing their works with me and for giving me permission to translate their fascinating publications. I thank my husband Peter Prindle, and my friends Bob Gillespie, Grace Von Tobel, Frances Parker, Frederick Ruder, Judd Jones, Lin Poyer, Jean Sanborn, and Garry Leonard for their helpful comments. I am also indebted to critic Makoto Sataka for generously offering me his publications and introducing me to many business novel writers. Professors Brett de Bary, Karen Brazell, T. J. Pempel, Hotsuki Ozaki, Carol Greenhouse, and others also assisted me at the dissertation writing stage which gave the impetus for this translation.

T.K.P.

Introduction

The term "business novel" is a translation of the Japanese word *kēzai shōsetsu*, which may be translated literally as "economy novel." Critic Makoto Sataka first used the word "business" in place of "economy" in his monograph *How to Read Business Novels* (1980).[1] Business novels are "popular novels" *(taishū bungaku)* widely read by Japanese businessmen, their wives, students, and other professionals. Many of these novels are given subcategorical names such as "enterprise novels" *(kigyō shōsetsu)*, "bank novels" *(ginkō shōsetsu)*, or "information novels" *(jōhō shōsetsu)*.[2]

Business novels were recognized as a "field" or a literary sub-genre in the late 1950s. It was Saburō Shiroyama's *Export* (Yushutsu) (1957), if not his *Kinjō the Corporate Bouncer* (Sōkaiya Kinjō) (1959), which marshalled their enormous popularity. A breathtaking number of writers took up their pens in the 1960s and 1970s. The topics they covered extended to banks, the stock market, the automobile industry, steel, textiles, transportation, medicine, construction, shipbuilding, electronics, chemicals, service industries, and ecology—in short, all realms of business. Well-known business novel writers, besides the five introduced in this book, include: Yūsuke Fukada, Toyoko Yamasaki, Toshiyuki Kajiyama, Niki Hirose, Tomohiko Yamada, Seiichi Morimura, Kazuo Watanabe, Tōru Miyoshi, Shirō Kunimitsu, Eiji Ohshita, Kan Sakiyama, Jirō Yasuda, Naoki Kojima, Yōzō Maki, Katsuya Sasago, Yasuaki Kadota, Ryōzō Saki, Shizuko Natsuki, Toshio Ohta, Yoshie Hotta, Hideo Akimoto, Eisuke Nakazono, Kan Muromachi, and Jirō Odakane. Ikkō Shimizu, one of the authors represented in this collection, predicts that business novels will become more psychologically oriented in the future.[3] In addition, according to the critic Hotsuki Ozaki, they will be recognized as a means to convey detailed technical and scientific information.[4]

The seven short works in this collection represent prototypes of the business novel. Their distinctive features are that business activities motivate plot developments, although psycho-socio-cultural elements are tightly interwoven. Dry economic theories are given flesh and blood by literary explorations. An encounter with business novels, hence, is a double-edged experience in which humanity is felt and objective theories are understood. The width and depth of individuals' psychological complexity are trimmed down to meet the size of the theory or the exposition of economic activities. This tendency is particularly prominent in short business stories. The emphasis on economics pulls the human dramas toward the pole of cultural "verisimilitude," or closeness to reality, rather than to that of biographic truism. That is, most characters in these novels are more typical than real. This is why, on principle, Saburō Shiroyama tries not to meet the real-life subjects of his novels prior to his writing. In discussing the case of his *Bureaucrats' Summer* (Kanryō-tachi no natsu) (1974) (whose protagonist is modeled after businessman Shigeru Sahashi), Shiroyama confesses, "I was glad that I hadn't met him during my research. If I had, the image of my protagonist would have been squelched by [Mr. Sahashi's] powerful personality."[5]

About the authors

Saburō Shiroyama was born in 1927 in Aichi Prefecture. He graduated from the economics department of the Tokyo University of Commerce (Tokyo Shōdai)[6] and taught economic theory at Nagoya Gakugei University. He later joined the navy to be trained as a special leader cadet, but the war ended before he was sent overseas. Shiroyama explains why he decided to write business novels:

> I had a smothering desire to overcome the terrible war experience our generation had to go through. Something I would call a militaristic mentality had settled over us. I had to write that down.
>
> At the same time, I always felt that Japan had become an economic giant, and had built an economically oriented society, but Japanese novels have been written outside the economic culture. If novels are to question people's ways of living, how to live in this economic environment and what kind of relationships people have therein should be their serious concern. I could not compromise with novels which ignored these problems.[7]

As is obvious from this quotation and statements made elsewhere, Shiroyama's focus is on the relationship between the socioeconomic structure and the people involved. Shiroyama's novels explain the rationale and motivations behind people's behavior; war experiences often provide one of the hidden incentives. Because of this, the author is almost always sympathetic towards his fictional heroes.

The Literary Circle New Face Prize *(Bungakukai Shinjin-shō)* awarded for his "Export" and the prestigious Naoki Prize given for "Kinjō the Sokaiya" reflect the popularity of this author's literary style. Some of his full-length novels are: *War Criminal: The Life and Death of Hirota Kōki* (Rakujitsu moyu) (1974),[8] a biography of the wartime Prime Minister Kōki Hirota; *Bank of Japan, a Novel* (Shōsetsu Nihon Ginkō) (1962), which describes the economic devastation during the postwar period; *3:00 P.M. in the Board Room* (Yakuin-shitsu Gogo Sanji) (1974), which deals with the tragic displacement of the owner-president at a textile company; *Bureaucrats' Summer* (Kanryōtachi no Natsu) (1975), an exploration of the political environment of the Ministry of International Trade and Industry (MITI), and *Every Day Is Sunday* (Mainichi ga Nichiyōbi) (1976), which studies the cultural shock children experience when they return to Japan after an extended stay in the United States.

Ikkō Shimizu was born in Tokyo in 1931. Literature was one of his keen interests as a student at Waseda University; the other was economics. His favorite authors were Sartre and Camus. The marriage of literature and economics gave birth to his first career as a journalist with the *Weekly Bunshun* (Shūkan Bunshun). But before long, Shimizu became a "freelancer" and produced excellent articles on the stock market. His debut as a business novel writer with *Kabutochō, a Novel* (Shōsetsu Shima) (1966) was backed by five years of solid experience at Kabutochō, Japan's Wall Street.

While Shiroyama aims to give a cinematic picture of businesses and historical moments, many of Shimizu's book-length works are sharply focused on particular incidents or individuals, often in scandalous settings. This is why Shimizu is called a pioneer of inside storytelling, or exposé. His data collecting is extensive, and his description of characters can be importunate. In addition to studying "lots of people who are directly involved in businesses," Shimizu expresses his other goal as:

. . . giving serious thought to breaking down business and industry novels into a pornographic or sensuous narrative. I would like to write a novel in which the abominable fraud of the economic world looms up from something like a woman's recondite and soppy monologue.[9]

In several of Shimuzu's novels, quite effective attempts have been made to blend women, or women's voices and sentiments, into the narration. *The Artery Archipelago* (Dōmyaku rettō) (1980), *Bloody River* (Chi no kawa) (1981), and *A Woman Executive* (Onna jūyaku) (1985) see women take over the narration and color the theme of the stories. In two of Shimizu's short stories, *Arbitrage* (Kyōjin sōba) (1970) and *Silver Sanctuary* (Gin no seiiki) (1969), female characters are the framework on which Shimizu builds the severe reality of the business world.

Shimizu is one of the most prolific and knowledgeable writers of stock market novels, which include: *Kabutochō, a Novel* (1966), *Cornering* (Kaijime) (1966), *Tokyo Stock Exchange, the Second Session* (Tōshō dai nibu) (1966), *Gamble* (Kake) (1968), *Crash* (Gara) (1968), *Investment Area* (Tōki chitai) (1974), *Speculator* (Sōbashi) (1980), and *The Tale of Kabutochō* (Kabutochō Monogatari) (1985). Besides these, Shimizu has written novels on banks, the automobile industry, construction companies, pollution, school teachers, and a variety of other subjects. His *The Artery Archipelago* received the Japanese Suspense Novel Writers' Association Prize of 1975 and was made into a film by Tōhō Studio (1975).

Ryō Takasugi was born in Tokyo in 1939. After majoring in Japanese literature at Waseda University, Takasugi became a journalist specializing in the petrochemical industry. He was a chief editor when he fell victim to acute nephritis and was hospitalized for about a year. It was during his convalescence period that Takasugi wrote his first novel. In a friend's words, Takasugi "is the kind of person who becomes engrossed no matter what he tries."[10]

Takasugi is now at the leading edge of business novel writing in both popularity and productivity. In addition to doing research, he produces about 200 pages a month. His specialty is the description of middle-rank businessmen. His publications place "the relationship between companies and individuals in a three-dimensional perspective, using the sorrow and anger of the middle echelon employees as their base notes.''[11] And within the economic sphere, they ''carve in a realistic relief the substance of enterprises. Companies in his novels are given organic life by his sound and substantial research.''[12]

Takasugi's major works are: *A Brilliant Retirement* (Azayakana tainin) (1979), a novel about factionalism in a large electronics company; *Change of Power* (Dai-gyakuten) (1980), which monitors the attempted merger of the Mitsubishi Bank and the First Bank; *My Burning Life* (Seimei moyu) (1983), the story of an engineer who spent his life in the petrochemical industry; *Disciplinary Lay-off* (Chōkai kaiko) (1985), about the dismissal of an ''elitist'' businessman and his reaction; *Flaming Manager* (Honoo no keiei-sha) (1986), the biography of a man who expanded a town factory into a first-rate company; and *A Reanimated Firm* (Kaisha sosei) (1987), about a lawyer's unfaltering effort to restore a company which has filed for bankruptcy.

Taichi Sakaiya was born in 1935 and pursued an ''elitist career,'' starting with the University of Tokyo, continuing through MITI, and finally as a novelist and economics commentator. He is well known and frequently appears on television talk shows. Sakaiya is the pioneer of a new type of business novel called ''prediction novels'' *(yosoku shō-setsu)* or ''near-future novels'' *(kin-mirai shōsetsu)*, whose range is usually within a decade. He uses a Markov chain formula, which incorporates current events and historical patterns, to predict their future outcomes. Sakaiya's research staff feeds information on basic propositions to the computer, which then sorts the data into numerous possibilities, and finally boils these down to a limited set of the strongest probabilities.

Some of his futuresque novels are: *Oil Shock/Carelessness* (Yudan) (1975),[13] which predicts an oil shortage in Japan; *The Breaking Point* (Hadankai) (1976), which draws a pessimistic picture of Japan's future; *The Baby Boom Generation* (Dankai no sedai) (1980), which describes problems facing the postwar ''baby boom generation''; and *The Cracked Rainbow* (Hibiwareta niji) (1977), which investigates the U.S.-Japan trade relationship.

Sakaiya uses a similar method for his historical works, which go farther back into antiquity than Shiroyama's works about wartime and postwar Japan. *Figures on the Mountain Ridge* (Tōge no gunzō) (1982), Sakaiya's ambitious work of 1,357 pages, is about the famous feudal-era Akō family whose forty-six retainers avenged their master's death by assassinating Kira, their master's political foe. The author's job is to edit the by-now-retold-dramatized-and-filmed historical incident from a modern politico-economic perspective that gives characters legitimate reasons to act the way they do. Sakaiya's essay *We Can See Japan from the Mountain Ridge* (Tōge kara Nihon ga mieru) (1982) backs up this novel by way of investigating Japan's political and economic trends. Another research-based historical work is *Hidenaga Toyotomi* (Toyotomi Hidenaga) (1985), which discloses the hardships born by the brother (and first assistant) of a sixteenth-century autocrat (Toyotomi Hideyoshi). These works may be safely ranked as being somewhere between historical fiction and socioeconomic analyses.

Takeshi Kaikō was born in 1930 in Osaka. His father, a headmaster at the Osaka Tsuruhashi Second National School, died when Kaikō was thirteen years old, and Kaikō had to support his family by taking up a variety of part-time jobs while going to school. Later on, while studying law at Osaka City University, he found more interesting and remunerative jobs, such as tutoring the child of a wealthy family, translating fan letters to foreign stars into English, and teaching English to businessmen. While in school, Kaikō joined a literary circle and published stories. After graduation, he worked for a foreign book importer for a year and then was employed by Kotobukiya, the maker of Suntory Whiskey. With the coining of numerous commercial phrases, Kaikō created a "golden age" of advertising for Suntory and introduced the whisky to middle-class Japanese homes.

This diversified background later helped strengthen Kaikō's writing. His "Emperor's New Clothes" (Hadaka no ōsama) (1957)—a short story in which child psychology and adult psychology are contrasted by a private art teacher—won the respected Akutagawa Prize, and *Into A Black Sun* (Kagayakeru yami) (1968)—a novel about the Vietnam war—won the Mainichi Newspaper Publication Cultural Award. Most recently, he won the 19th Shinchō Prize for *Ear Stories, Parts I and II* (Mimi no monogatari I, II) (1987).

Kaikō is not usually regarded as a business novel writer, but his "Giants and Toys" (Kyojin to omocha) (1957) has all the qualities of one, and is included in *Selected Business Novels* (Keizai shōsetsu meisaku-sen) (1980), compiled by Saburō Shiroyama.

What we see in the seven short works in this collection is a cross section of business novels. "Silver Sanctuary" disguises the essence of the banker personality in a melodramatic mask. "Kinjō the Corporate

Bouncer'' is monumental both as the father of Japanese business novels and as an exposé of the traditional business psychology. ''In Los Angeles'' reveals that the time has passed for the kamikaze-type businessman, stressing that a new, milder breed must take charge, particularly in international trade. ''Made in Japan'' is an attempt to break down the elements of the Japanese success drive into an action-oriented drama within a business context. ''From Paris'' gives us a glimpse of the mechanism governing staff rotations, where the determining factor is neither the candidate's caliber nor his seniors' favoritism. ''The Baby Boom Generation'' studies both logically and statistically the problems haunting this generation. ''Giants and Toys'' is an attempt by an author of so-called ''genuine literature'' *(jun bungaku)* to integrate business activities into his writing.

Vignette-style short works are few, and somewhat restricted to the earlier stages of the development of business novels. Nevertheless, the seven stories presented here are valuable in that they attest to the ABCs of the Japanese business culture. It is also noteworthy that the themes of some of these works overlap with those in longer ones. For instance, the effects of the war experiences explored in Shiroyama's ''Made in Japan'' influence protagonists in Shiroyama's *Smashing Prices* (Kakaku hakai) (1969), Shimizu's *Phony Capital* (Gisei shihon) (1983), and Yūsuke Fukada's Naoki Prize-winning novel *Merchants in the Tropics* (Ennetsu shōnin) (1982), to name a few. Essentially, Japanese business novels are reproductions of the Japanese business culture, and the short works translated here are their microcosms.

Notes

1. Makoto Sataka, *Keizai shōsetsu no yomikata/How to Read Business Novels* (Tokyo: Kou Business, 1980). This book has Japanese and English titles, although the contents are entirely in Japanese.

2. What Japanese casually call *shōsetsu* include novels and short stories.

3. Mr. Shimizu told me during an interview in 1984 that business topics will be more deeply imbedded in other so-called genuine literature *(junbungaku)*.

4. My interview with Professor Ozaki in January 1984.

5. Mr. Shiroyama's comments appeared in the *Weekly Asahi* (December 6, 1974), and are quoted in Sataka's *The Drama of Reality and Unreality* (Jitsu to kyo no dorama) (Tokyo: Nihon Keizai Shinbun-sha, 1983), p. 9.

6. This university is now called Hitotsubashi University.

7. Mr. Shiroyama's comment in *Financial World* (Zaikai) (May 15 and June 1, 1973), quoted in *How to Read Business Novels*, p. 22. Henceforth, all translations of Japanese texts are mine.

8. The English translation of this novel was published by Kodansha International.

9. Quoted from *Asahi Journal* (November 15, 1985): 10.

10. Quoted from Kengo Ohtake's "Editorial" (Kaisetsu) in Takasugi's *White Rebellion* (Shiroi hanran) (Tokyo: Shūei-sha Bunko, 1983), p. 346.

11. Quoted from Makoto Sataka's "Editorial" in *A Fake Castle* (Kyokō no shiro) (Tokyo: Kōdansha Bunko, 1981), p. 339.

12. Quoted from Kengo Ohtake, p. 342.

13. The word *"yudan"* means "carelessness," but it is written with the Chinese ideographs meaning "oil" and "cut off."

MADE IN JAPAN
AND OTHER JAPANESE
"BUSINESS NOVELS"

Made in Japan

Saburō Shiroyama

I

Fujishita's hands trembled when he ripped open the telegram.

"Ippatsuya[1] did it again. . . ." He turned in disgust, and bit his thick lower lip. The telegraph from the D-Trading Company in Calcutta cancelled the order of 80 thousand thermometers, some of which had already been packaged for shipment. Japanese discount items had undoubtedly caught up with the export channel of the Galaxy Thermometer Company and invaded the Calcutta market.

"I wonder if Mase-san[2] has any bearing on this." Manager Ohshima's sympathetic voice spoke from behind Fujishita.

"I don't know, but I wouldn't be surprised if he does," said Fujishita, envisioning Bumpei Mase's camelbacked silhouette against the factory wall where sparks of fire danced. His hands still trembled.

"Bad news?" Mayer lifted his eyes from a stopwatch without getting up. His stocky body squatted in the dead heat of the factory. As his ruddy cheeks glowed in the light of the fire arrows, his red hair looked ready to burst into flame.

Fujishita found the situation embarrassing. He would rather keep the problem to himself, were it not for Mayer's sincere stare.

"Market robbers. It seems that some cheapies took over the market our thermometers opened up."

"Which market?"

"India. The same with Brazil and Hong Kong as well. This time it's India." Things were getting out of hand. The hard-earned

Hong Kong market had shut him out two years ago, and Brazil, six months ago. A pattern was set by now: inferior products, like the Mase Thermometer, took over Galaxy's hard-earned markets. In the aftermath of the price war, low quality products flooded the market. They destroyed the reputation of Japanese thermometers as a whole. Consumers were led to believe that MADE IN JAPAN stood for bad quality. Although the saying goes, "bad coins drive away good coins," inferior merchandise brought about a ban on Japanese goods altogether. New markets were rooted out one by one by fellow traders who sought short-term profits.

"Prices are sacred. Dumping destroys markets," lectured Mayer, as if remonstrating.

"Absolutely. But your country, where we fellow traders have agreed not to dump, is now preparing to raise the tariff. We have enemies in the West and the East."

Mayer broke into an exaggeratedly apologetic smile.

"It's not decided yet. I'm in no better position than you. I import blanks[3] and sell them finished. Let's fight it out together." Mayer recorded in his notebook the time marked on his stopwatch. His eyes examined in detail the process and number of steps needed for production. His data would determine the market price.

Fujishita looked away. His own words, "enemies in the West and the East," brought home an unpleasant reality. Without focusing, his eyes gazed at the many streaks of fire arrows flying in disorder.

The 500° centigrade furnace roared with heat, and some fifteen young workers ceaselessly ran about, carrying the bright red glass balls which had just been pulled from the furnace. The sound, for some reason, had dropped. The noise was sealed off by the enthusiasm of the young workers. Even the heat of the factory was overpowered by the energy of the workers. Every now and then, the electric furnace, which gaped as if it were ready to swallow the whole factory, squirted out sheets of blinding scarlet glass. The fireballs which sprang out flew vertically and horizontally across Fujishita's vision, but they didn't look hot. In search of maximum efficiency of the flying fire arrows, Fujishita had spent three years carefully studying the movements of the best-skilled workers, measuring precisely the width and speed of their paces, and he had trained the rest of his workers to shuttle forward, backward, and sideways in the same rhythm. During each movement, the fireball, as large as a human fist, was transformed into a 100-foot-long fire arrow, then cooled into glass, and cut into 80-centimeter-long tubes to make five thermometer cylinders. Ordinarily, Fujishita saw the entire movement as a mechanical geometric design, but now there was no order in their irregular pulses. They even looked ready to lunge at him without warning.

"Akira-san. I hear that you picked the more expensive one of the two American lawyers." A grating voice caught Fujishita's ears by surprise. The strained air of the factory lapsed into a vacant yawn. There was only one man to ever call the president of the Galaxy Thermometer Company "Akira-san." It was Bumpei Mase. Bumpei pushed past Manager Ohshima and pressed his ashen face toward Fujishita. The rasping breath was the result of running up to Fujishita after fighting himself free from the obstructing guard. This was the third time Bumpei had marched into the factory under the pretext of business. He surveyed the interior of the furnace shop from the corner of his eyes as he talked to Fujishita.

Fujishita was also the head of the Thermometer Export Association. This function gave him the privilege of choosing a lawyer to defend Japanese businesses against the American move to raise the tariff.

"I decided to hire Attorney Dubridge. He charges more, but after some inquiries I found out that Dubridge is better trusted, and he's said to be brighter."

"It's wonderful that he's bright, but he charges twice as much as the less expensive lawyer, Mr. Saves."

"Yes, exactly twice as much. Twenty thousand dollars."

"Twenty thousand dollars? That's more than seven million yen. Don't you think it's more than we can afford?"

"Mase-san, I would like to use Lawyer Saves if possible, because you recommended him, and because he charges less, but the lawyer is going to be the only person we can depend on in the entire United States. It's imperative that we have a man of the highest caliber."

"It's up to you. The Thermometer Association has given you the exclusive right to select a lawyer, Akira-san, but twenty thousand dollars is . . . I suppose you'll be needing all kinds of spending money when you get to the United States."

Mase's rhetoric and silent pause hinted at a poisonous suspicion that Fujishita would embezzle part of the twenty thousand dollars.

"I'm talking about the lawyer's fee. It has nothing to do with my . . ." Fujishita's tone became defensive.

Bumpei shook his gray hair, "It's a lot of money, no matter what you say. I hate to repeat myself, but what if we humbly give in and apply for a voluntary quota?"

"Let's not sell ourselves short. Hasn't the association voted to fight to the bitter end?"

"It wasn't a vote, Akira-san. You used your leadership and forced the decision on the members, that's all. You never tried to take a vote, from the very beginning."

Fujishita couldn't come up with a good rebuttal. It was true that he had not given his fellow members a chance to vote. He knew too well that the association preferred to compromise with the voluntary quota system rather than confront the tariff hike.

Bumpei's eyes scanned Fujishita's silent face. "It's good if it works out. But how are you going to bear the blame if you spend twenty thousand dollars, lose the case, and the tariff goes up?"

"We must at least try, even if it costs us twenty thousand dollars. There's no reason for Japan to step down."

"There goes your bluff."

"Faintheartedness takes you nowhere. It only makes the market smaller. Let's extend credit to Lawyer Dubridge and do our best."

Fujishita's words drifted over Bumpei's head again. Bumpei's eyes had been following the movements of the young workers who ran with the fireballs.

Manager Ohshima caught on to the real purpose of Bumpei's visit and stood in front of him. "It's too distracting here. Let's move to the office."

Fujishita joined Ohshima's effort to lead his guest to the office. His tall body came in useful.

"So, you wear the workers' uniform to give them orders. What devotion!" Bumpei spoke sarcastically, his eyes swinging from Fujishita to Ohshima. Those eyes, however, suddenly flashed another light. They seemed to have landed for the first time on Mayer, who squatted down and took notes. Bumpei jerked his chin at the American. "Is that your buyer?"

Mayer, who was hidden behind Fujishita until then, was also clad in the Galaxy Thermometer work uniform, a navy-blue jacket.

Fujishita had to introduce Mayer to Bumpei. Bumpei tediously repeated in his broken English how he wanted Mayer to visit Mase Thermometer as well.

"Why don't you take him sightseeing or something? This is no place

for a foreigner,'' Bumpei sniped at Fujishita. "If you want, I can show
him around.''

"It doesn't work. He isn't interested in anything other than the
factory. I've offered to show him to the Imperial Palace, but he told me
he had no big desire to see somebody else's residence.''

Mayer waved with his large hand and squatted down again, as if to
endorse what Fujishita had said.

"If you have the largesse to allow a buyer to take notes, why can't
you let us, fellow Japanese, do the same?''

"I certainly will, if you become our subsidiary company.''

As they talked, Fujishita and Ohshima sandwiched Bumpei and
walked him out of the furnace shop. Bumpei kept looking back even
after he was led outdoors.

"I've heard that the average age of the Galaxy employees is nineteen
years old. I must have heard it right. That's how you keep wages low.''

While being guided by the two men, Bumpei kept a sharp eye on the
walkway. His eyes below the visor looked for the secret of Galaxy's
production process in every unswept piece of scrap glass lying around
along the walkway.

Galaxy Thermometer was one of Japan's three largest thermometer
makers. It employed 421 people. Before World War II, it was the maker
of a digestive medicine, "Galaxy.'' But since the company lost its
major market, China, it switched to thermometer production under the
leadership of the young president, Akira Fujishita. Up until the time
Fujishita took over, the company was a mere cottage industry sustained
by the dexterity of trained workers. It was Fujishita who thoroughly
measured and analyzed the work process. This radical and maximal
mechanization made the work manageable for young people. It made
possible the production of thermometers that were priced modestly
relative to their quality. Bumpei Mase, who used to work for Galaxy as
a general sales manager in China, followed Fujishita's path upon his
return from the continent as another thermometer maker. He now
exported inexpensive and low quality products.

Fujishita and Ohshima finally hauled the intruder back to the front
office. Bumpei wiped his balding pate with a thin Japanese towel,
spending an obnoxiously long time.

Fujishita signaled to Ohshima with his eyes to leave, and said blunt-
ly, "Mase-san, you did it again in India.''

"What did I do?'' Bumpei responded innocently but kept his eyes
away from Fujishita.

"Why make light of our markets?" Fujishita's rage, dammed up since Bumpei first walked in the shop, finally exploded.

"How can you stop less expensive goods from being made?"

"You know they aren't just less expensive. They're cheap and crummy."

"Well then, why don't you teach us how to make better ones?" Bumpei retorted aggressively. "India is just a small market. The biggie is the United States. We're counting on your success in the United States."

"That's how Ippatsuya wipes out our markets. You must realize that our markets elsewhere make our position in the United States stronger."

Bumpei lifted the sweaty towel up against the sun, as if to screen out Fujishita's words, then flapped it down with a snap, and folded it into quarters. The sound of the motor from inside the factory returned to their ears like the sound of rising waves.

"Akira-san, won't you let me arrange your lodging in New York?" Bumpei's eyes suddenly looked as mellow as those of old people. "I'm the vice-president of the export association, although I may not be living up to the title. I've trusted everything with you, as you know, but I want to be helpful, too. At least with regards to your hotel and things."

Fujishita hesitated, trying to verify Bumpei's sincerity before responding.

Bumpei continued in his hoarse voice. "My daughter Tomoko goes to a university in New York. She's been there for three years now. You still remember her, don't you?" He directed a scathing look toward Fujishita.

"Oh, yes." Fujishita left it ambiguous.

"Your father and I made a marriage agreement . . . but agreements are there to break these days. Breaking them is easy, but it's hard to be on the betrayed side of the game. That's why she chose to move to the United States."

In silence, Fujishita stared at Bumpei's deeply wrinkled neck. The last time he saw Tomoko was during the summer vacation of the year she entered a Japanese women's college in Peking. Bumpei brought her to Fujishita's house. Her white sailor's collar and round eyes surfaced in his memory. Bumpei, standing next to her, wore the nationalist uniform and carried souvenirs in both hands.

"I'm sure Tomoko can arrange for your hotel. She says that she has rented a car from somebody. You can use her as a chauffeur and a secretary.''

Fujishita nodded noncommittally. There was no reason to turn down the offer. Also, he was rather curious as to how New York might have changed Tomoko.

Bumpei noticed the change in Fujishita's countenance. "It'll be a good change of air for Akira-san. But it's going to be hard for Tomoko. . . .'' He hurriedly corrected himself. "Be sure to take advantage of Tomoko's help.''

Fujishita lowered his clouded face. Distrust of the Mase family surged through his head.

Bumpei looked equally troubled. "You don't even treat for a cup of tea here. I guess I'd better be going.''

Bumpei took a step away from his old friend's son, who made no gesture of calling him back. He yelled on his way out, "Twenty thousand dollars is a lot of money. It's not something you can lose without embarrassment.''

II

The May sun streamed in from a glass wall, turning the marble staircase into a whirlpool of light. The stone steps, polished so smoothly that people might slip, gleamed with the texture of ivory. They reminded Fujishita of a luxurious palace corridor which admitted no commoners.

Fujishita sprinted ahead two steps at a time up the stairs of the United States Tariff Committee Building on Constitution Avenue in the Northeast District of Washington, D.C.

"You sure have a valiant way of walking up stairs!'' Tomoko's voice followed him from behind. The tone was very much like Bumpei's.

Turning back, while his mind played with the idea of the father-daughter bond, Fujishita saw Tomoko's smile flickering like flower petals in the light.

"I haven't gotten rid of the habit from my navy days. In the navy, we walked up two steps at a time.''

"Navy? Wasn't that more than ten years ago?'' Tomoko, who caught up with Fujishita, filled his eyes with her smile.

The sunbeams ceaselessly danced and blinded Fujishita as if with golden sand. Fujishita resumed his climb as soon as Tomoko came up to his level. Although less hastily than before, he continued skipping every other step. Grinning disapprovingly of his own habit, he kept up the pace all the way to the top.

"Can't you get rid of that habit?" Tomoko's voice, trailing from below, gradually gained a condemnatory tone.

"There's no reason to get rid of good habits."

"You call it a good habit? Why hurry so much? If you are so pressed for time, we could have taken an elevator."

"Why are you so concerned about my habits?" Fujishita wanted to twist off the spearhead of Tomoko's accusation.

"Because a person who hangs on to a habit so long is repulsive. I have no habit so dear that I can't get rid of. Absolutely none!" declared Tomoko.

Beyond the linoleum tile landing, there was a wall-to-wall shaggy gray carpet. Passing below the neon "NO SMOKING" sign and opening the third door as they had been instructed, they found the public hearing hall. The large stars and stripes banner in front gave the illusion of cloaking the attendants. Gray, brown, and green eyes of various hues scanned Fujishita intently while he stood motionless in a daze. These were the eyes of the auditors, the tariff-hike advocators. Fujishita felt caged in, immobilized by their whispers and stares. It seemed that there were about thirty people in the hall.

Somebody called from the other side of this cluster of eyes. It was ruddy-faced Mayer smiling at him. Mayer must have flown directly from Wisconsin. Fujishita recognized his two other clients and a Japanese embassy employee. The auditors on the Japanese side consisted of six persons, including Fujishita and Tomoko.

Fujishita introduced Tomoko Mase. After exchanging handshakes, scorched by the hot stares of the tax-hike auditors, Mayer hit fast in a loud voice: "You've gotten a hotel in a lousy area of New York. You're close to Broadway all right, but you're in a notorious crime district. Aren't you scared?"

Fujishita's back instantly straightened, as if to intercept Mayer's voice from reaching Tomoko. The paved cement passageway leading to his hotel saw no sunlight, like a valley in the shadow of a steep mountain range. Rows of theaters, cheap hotels, and grimy office buildings lined the neighborhood of the four-story hotel to which Tomoko had taken Fujishita. The building was flanked by a cigarette shop and a flea circus. The railing on the balcony was wiggly and the plaster walls had several cracks. In front, there was a signboard one yard wide with white letters, "Rooms for Rent, $1.50."

"Well, you see, I didn't plan to spend much on hotels," Fujishita answered, recalling the signboard.

"I don't know who took you there, but it's the last place I'd want to stay. I wish I'd been there to help you. Maybe it's not too late," Mayer said with enough volume to speak over factory noise.

"The meeting is starting." Tomoko interrupted before Fujishita could answer Mayer. "Those people look surprised to find how few of us are here." The sangfroid of her voice came out of her effort to change the subject. Fujishita marked Tomoko as cunning, in a corner of his mind.

"Japanese filled the hall when the tableware and fabric industries were brought to the court. I've seen their pictures, all lined up with headbands on."

"The more the better, right?" said Fujishita with not much feeling.

"Yes, Americans think that Japanese always come in great numbers. Our adversaries must have expected us to be that way today, too," Mayer joined in.

At the Thermometer Association meeting, Fujishita had insisted that he, as the president of the association, would go to the United States and campaign alone. He had preached that sending a great number of people, as other businesses did, would only antagonize the other party. This decision was based on his calculation that it would be more effective to spend the budget on a good lawyer and competent lobbyists. Surprisingly, nobody in the meeting objected, partly because Vice-President Mase, who usually countered Fujishita at every opportunity, had for once held the rest of the members in check.

Fujishita put every trust in Dubridge's ability. He had talked with the lawyer more than enough and had contacted two or three lobbyists under Dubridge's supervision. All he had to do now was to reaffirm with his lips shut tight that he had made the right decision and cast defiant eyes on the tariff-hike advocators. Lawyers for each camp took their seats. And at ten o'clock sharp, five tax officers entered the hall. Each stripe of the American flag behind the officers pierced Fujishita's eyes.

A court clerk started reading the prospectus.

"As a result of the concession made in the Trade Treaty to allow for the import of finished and/or unfinished thermometers, Japanese imports have inflicted serious problems, or are threatening to cause serious damage to American industries. As a relief measure, we demand the revocation of the tariff concession policy and demand that the tariff be brought back to the pre-revision level."

The current tariff rate was 42.5 percent, which was plenty high from the exporters' standpoint. The pre-revision level meant 85 percent.

After reading the prospectus, the advocators' lawyer briefly explained the reason why this proposal was brought to the court. Following this explanation, the center doors swung open to admit expert witnesses who were summoned by the committee at the request of the advocators and protesters. While the advocators brought thirteen of their people, Dubridge brought only one. The difference in the number relieved the advocators from tension noticeably. A few of them cast inquisitive glances at the Japanese camp, as if to ask, "Have you given up already?" "Have you decided to put a voluntary quota on your exports?"

"Is one expert witness enough?" Tomoko spoke in a voice of anxiety and disbelief. Her eyes mirrored Bumpei's train of reasoning: *Does Lawyer Dubridge think he's done his job now that he's gotten his twenty thousand dollars? If this is how American lawyers work, we should have hired the less expensive one.*

Fujishita didn't answer.

The first expert witness stood on the stand and swore with his hand on the Bible. He was a watery-eyed elderly man with the title of Secretary of Weights and Measures. He testified, in response to the advocator's lawyer:

> 1. The prices of the materials for thermometers as well as the workers' wages have gone up. For example, the price of mercury has risen by four dollars per pound in the last three years. But the price of the finished product has gone down from 90ᶜ to 80ᶜ because of the pressure from the lower-priced Japanese products.
>
> 2. One-third of the blanks distributed in the United States are made in Japan.
>
> 3. For these two reasons, the American thermometer industry is endangered.

Lawyer Dubridge stood up for a cross-examination. His blond hair was of a pallid hue, and the area rising from the firm bridge of his nose to his broad forehead reflected the lights. He was nearing the age of 60, but his voice and movements were resilient. The lawyer first challenged the Weights and Measures' testimony concerning the price of the thermometers, by calling his attention to the existence of three-dollar thermometers. Their brand names were cited. The testifier nodded in agreement. Dubridge then asked where the figure "one-third," as the percentage of blank thermometers, came from. The old man cited a person's name in an inaudibly faint voice, mumbling that he was confident that this figure was reliable.

The second expert witness was a thermometer manufacturer by the name of H. H's brawny square jaw and sensitively sharp eyes spoke for his highly competitive personality. He affirmed almost in one breath, with a voice loud enough to bounce against the wall behind the auditors, that thermometer production required a special skill, that the workers trained at a tremendous cost were not transferable to other professions, but that the increase of Japanese imports had caused the closing down of fellow thermometer makers, and that this in turn caused serious unemployment problems.

A window in the Tariff Committee Building commanded a panoramic view of the thick clump of Capitol Hill, with the Capitol Building dome peeking from a side. Fujishita took a deep breath as he faced the hill. He couldn't buy the earlier half of the testimony. There was a basic fallacy in the beliefs of not only this testifier but also Bumpei Mase and many other Japanese thermometer makers. None of these people had overhauled the work process. None was aware that most work was manageable by teenage boys and girls. He recalled with fondness his young workers, moving busily among hot glass tubes.

Lawyer Dubridge stood up. In a tone of talking to a close friend, he asked which companies had to close down. The expert witness proudly cited the names of S-Thermometer and G-Instrument. For the first time, the frown on Dubridge's thick eyebrows slackened. He looked at the Japanese camp from the corner of his eyes and winked. He cited the dates of both incidents and argued that S-Thermometer's business license was revoked for manufacturing below standard products and that G-Instrument had closed down before the Japanese imports increased. The testifier reluctantly acquiesced.

The third expert witness was a thermometer maker who had flown in from the West Coast. He was short, his hair was the color of dirty snow, and his face an equally unhealthy shade. He started with a preface that his testimony concerned his own company, then went on to complain that his business had steadily declined since 1955 on account of the pressure from Japanese imports. From his brown briefcase he removed a folder, which apparently contained a document of proof, and started reading off the declining sales figures month by month. The hushed gallery of the advocator-audience finally took a breath of relief. Again, piercing eyes turned toward the Japanese camp.

This witness's deposition was so endless that he was admonished twice by the chairman of the hearing. The manufacturer's appeal, made with the ring of a tongue-tied peasant, had the ironic effect of authenticity that sent a heavy air toward the Japanese camp and warmed the hearts of the advocators.

Dubridge got on his feet immediately after the tariff-hike defender had asked questions. With a sheet of paper in his hand flapping in the air, he reviewed the witness's major points. Having done this, he asked if the witness's company hadn't had a three-month strike. The man answered yes, and blushed as he footnoted that its effect was minimal. Dubridge let slide the opportunity to ask for qualifications and turned to the paper he had been letting swim in the air. He leaned forward, showed it to the expert witness, and said reprovingly, "This is a letter you sent in the spring of 1957. It says that your orders are so booked up that you cannot possibly take another one."

Groans of admiration and sighs of disappointment came from the auditors of both camps. Fujishita wondered how Dubridge had managed to obtain a letter written by a small-scale thermometer maker living on the West Coast. Dubridge must have really meant it each time he said with a smile that he had done his homework. No wonder he didn't invite more than one witness to support his interests. It looked more convincing to overturn his opponents' testimonies than to make his own witness prove his point. The single task entrusted to his testifier was to give some structure to the points dragged out of earlier witnesses.

Before he knew it, Fujishita was counting the number of stars on the American flag. The oath of the fourth witness sounded as if it was from a distant dreamland. Fujishita had toyed with the expression "an able lawyer" many times before. And what he had now was the culminating moment when the word "able" finally gained some weight. It was a pleasant feeling. It was a feeling of victory over Japanese manufacturers like Mase, who set no store in Dubridge, to say nothing of the tariff-hike advocators. The word "able" transcended nationalities and professions. It touched his heart.

His eyes raised, Fujishita saw the trees of Capitol Hill scintillating in the sky of early summer as if they were hemmed with a piece of gold thread. The vast expanse of the capital below the window was inactively silent. Only the traffic on Pennsylvania Avenue, beyond the hill, hummed low.

Inside the hall, a potbellied, ruddy-faced man was prattling on, with the gesture of stroking over the entire hall with his hands. Fujishita leaned forward to catch the man's strongly trilled speech. This was also a way to keep his unburdened mind from drifting.

III

Back in New York, milk-white weary dusk was setting on the mammoth city which had done a day's work. The sound of the five o'clock time-to-go-home siren brayed in the polluted blurry air. Already, small jewel-like lights along the Manhattan skyline had multiplied.

Tomoko had parked her 1953 model sedan by the cement wall along the bank of the East River. She was waiting for someone. Another siren from the Mullenbaum Glass Company jolted her from behind. She turned around and saw the front gate of the factory swing wide open, exposing to view the long belt of green lawn inside. She could see on the lawn rows of roofs which looked like airport hangars in formation, like a fleet at berth.

Fujishita had gone in to see the factory manager some time ago. Tomoko was patient. Chauffeuring him all over the area for the last several days, she had gotten used to waiting—in front of the Japanese Consulate, in front of a political arbiter's office, in front of Japanese trading companies and banks which were spread throughout New York, and in front of the thirty-five-story glass-walled Mullenbaum Glass Company building. Each trip made it increasingly obvious how much more desperate Fujishita was. This Mullenbaum Glass by the East River was his last resort. The decision of the president of the United States was supposed to come out within a couple of days.

Tomoko waited, holding back words which hovered on the very tip of her tongue. "Don't give up Akira-san!" But down deep, she actually hated Fujishita. So much so that she could kill him. This was why she had taken him to that hotel. She also kept a brown bottle in her pocketbook. She had obtained the bottle for their trip to Washington, D.C., and had tried to catch Fujishita off guard. Such occasions had been numerous in the last several days.

The tariff committee hearing had lasted for three days, and the committee's decision was brought into the open two days afterward. By three to two, the committee decided to recommend the tariff hike to the president of the United States. Officially, this was Japan's defeat. But there were precedents for reversing the committee decisions; that is, although Japanese cotton goods, tableware, and plywood industries had lost their cases by five to none, all the tariff-hike recommendations had been pigeonholed by the president of the United States in a deferral of the ruling or for reexamination. And partly because Japanese industries volunteered to set a modest quota on their exports, perhaps, the tariff hike never materialized. Compared to these precedents, the hydrometer case, which was voted down by the narrow margin of three to two, looked more promising. Fujishita guessed that the U.S. president would pass it. As far as he was concerned, he had already scored a victory.

What came in pursuit of Fujishita, who happily returned to New York, was a call to "voluntarily control exports." Telegrams from Japanese fellow manufacturers and the Ministry of International Trade and Industry, words of caution from the Foreign Service, newspapers, trade-related parties, and all the rest in New York gave the same warning. Fujishita responded to each and all of these by plugging his ears with his fingers. Tomoko found this prank amusing only the first couple of times, but after the third time, she joined her father in urging Fujishita to support the quota.

It was when Lawyer Dubridge made an unsolicited call that Fujishita finally began to feel apprehensive. Dubridge's message was that an executive of Mullenbaum Glass had gone to Washington, D.C., possibly to make approaches to the president of the United States. Mullenbaum Glass happens to be the largest glass company in the United States, perhaps the world's largest. It operates on a capital of 2.2 billion dollars and employs 170,000 people. Apparently, this company started politicking at the request of its client thermometer companies.

The only way for Japanese industries to compete with this economic and political giant, and to appeal to the White House, was to offer to adopt a voluntary quota. This realization, however, left no lasting mark on Fujishita's mind. After two days' deep thinking, he started looking for an escape hatch in a quarter unbelievable to Tomoko and others.

"Why should we be confined to our house? If Mullenbaum is worried about a drop in business, I can buy glass from them in the place of American thermometer makers. Even imported glass will make it pay. Our hard work will make it pay."

Listening to Fujishita speak in this vein, Tomoko let out a scream inside herself. She was tempted to make a wry remark, "What's the capital of your company, and how many people do you employ?'' She could see how her father abhorred Fujishita as a deadly enemy.

With a bravura plan to persuade the head of the company, Fujishita had paid many visits to the Mullenbaum building in central downtown. Executives did not bother to answer his calls. The man who received him had a suspicious look on his face: *Why should a Japanese hydrometer maker bring such a ludicrous deal?* Tomoko had to drive Fujishita from the main office to the factory.

Cars honked in the factory ground. One hundred and twenty thousand people were going home from this factory alone. Their cars emerged from the right and left. The central lawn was now practically invisible. The number of overtaking vehicles increased in the flurry as if riding on top of the ones in front. Before long, the entire factory grounds became covered with numerous kinds of cars of all colors. They poured out in six lines after converging at the gate.

The volume of honking rose, just as Tomoko stretched to see if Fujishita was coming. A tall man leaped out from behind a gate post into the river of cars. He bounced up and down, making people wonder if his soles had springs. The lines of cars veered around the obstacle, forming a vortex, like a herd of lost sheep. The man turned out to be Fujishita. His body and nerves seemed to be made of steel springs. This reminded Tomoko of Fujishita jumping two steps at a time in the Tariff Committee Building. This time, Fujishita brought the honking with him.

"How did you make out?"

"No luck. No agreement." In spite of his words, his face showed no sign of disappointment. "I'll go to the main office tomorrow again."

"But what about the president's decision?"

"I'll keep trying until the very moment it comes out. It's still possible to impede Mullenbaum."

"Good grief, you're a poor loser. The game is over. It's obvious."

Without answering, Fujishita took a fresh look at the stream of cars behind him.

"My god, there are a lot of cars!"

"You cut across so recklessly. Good thing you weren't run over."

"How can one hit and run in front of this many witnesses? The more cars, the safer it is." Fujishita lit a cigarette.

Tomoko's heart was slowly charred by revulsion. "So, this factory has over one hundred thousand workers. How many times your company's size is that? You said yours has 421. How many times does that make?''

Fujishita did not look at Tomoko, who spoke wryly.

"The numbers don't mean much. If you want to compare, you should compare the mean quality of workers and managers."

"You're saying that Galaxy Thermometer is not inferior."

"No question about it." Fujishita turned his eyes directly upon Tomoko. "Tomoko-san, may I see your hand?"

Tomoko's hand was already in Fujishita's thick palm by the time she shrieked in surprise. His body temperature penetrated through the meshes of her thin lace glove. Her body felt heated.

"You have gloves on."

"Yes." Blood drained out of her face after answering. She had put on gloves out of the tedium of waiting. She had bought them only recently as a precaution for not leaving fingerprints when she put poison in Fujishita's drink. She jerked up her face directly toward Fujishita in an effort to hide her bewilderment.

Fujishita transferred his cigarette to his mouth, and started pulling off her glove with both hands, as gently as peeling off a sheer wafer. Her little finger emerged. Even without nail polish, it was salmon pink to the tip of the nail. Tomoko didn't have the courage to pull her hand back. Fujishita's cigarette smoke sent off the scent of man.

"Take good care of your hands."

Fujishita's muttering confused Tomoko again. *What does he mean by that? Did he see through my plan to hide my fingerprints?* Her expression hardened, she searched Fujishita's eyes. His eyes, on the other side of his glasses, were more impassioned than she had ever known. Animosity or suspicion were absent; they emitted warmth like hot spring water.

"Why? What are you up to?" Tomoko panted. All the nerves in her body had moved to her right hand. Her entire nervous system ached, as though two naked bodies touched, when the tips of her ungloved fingers came in contact with the man's palm.

He must feel for me, after all those years, and I, too. . . . Even the rims of her eyes glowed with embarrassment and passion. Fujishita's face faded out of her vision.

Fujishita's hands stroked her fingers one at a time. Pain shot in a flash from the skin to the core of her body. The next time their eyes met, Fujishita had her index finger between his thumb and two fingers.

"Tender fingers. Only Japanese women have these limber fingers," said Fujishita.

"What?" With a cry, Tomoko drew back her hand. Her heart beat wildly. "Akira-san, you've been . . ." Her quivering voice could not finish the sentence.

Fujishita tapped the cigarette ash. "No matter how good Mullenbaum's workers may be, when it comes to thermometer making, they can't outdo our well-trained girls. In thermometer making, the United States cannot get ahead of Japan, even if the country turns itself inside out."

Tomoko pulled away from Fujishita, noisily kicking her shoes.

Over her head, Fujishita saw the darkening dusk of Manhattan. "I've been looking at people's hands ever since I came to this country. Here, even women have peasant-like, coarse hands, hands like boiled lobsters, scabby hands, bear-furred hands. . . . Those hands don't know what to do with themselves. Machines cannot make them do delicate work. Only trained, lissome Japanese fingers can use delicate machines."

Tomoko had nothing to say. Sounds from other cars on the highway faded and rumbled in the distance. She recovered her voice at the sign of Fujishita's next commentary. "Your wife must have nice fingers, too; too nice to keep as a mere housewife."

"Yes, they used to be, but they've hardened. I like unmarried girls' fingers the best."

"So, my fingers are great for factory work. I may as well be employed by Galaxy." Tomoko meant to plague Fujishita, but her words did more harm to herself than him. Tears dampened her eyes. She put an arm on the railing at an angle to hide her face. The Staten Island Ferry glided below her eyes. Lights on its deck glimmered on the water. Ahead of it, an ocean liner wedged through the violet night, in search of a place to moor. Tomoko started to feel that the twenty-odd years she had spent in Peking, Japan, and New York contributed only to this miserable scene of being put to shame by Fujishita. Her exodus to the States was meant to be an escape from this Fujishita and from her father, who had made a shambles of her life by engaging her to him. *See where I am now!* She tried to steady her mind by focusing it on Fujishita's hotel with the broken railing, and on the brown bottle in her pocketbook.

"Wow, am I tired!" Fujishita's voice was loud. He crossed his arms behind his head and stretched out. His arched body looked like a shadow play on the river bank.

I must not show my weakness. I must free myself from Fuji-shita.

Tomoko put together a resilient voice. "A voluntary export quota would have solved your problems easy as pie."

Fujishita shot an angry glance at her. "Not on my life! No matter how many times you bring that up!"

"The problem isn't just yours, you know. The survival of the whole industry depends on it."

"That's why I won't give in. A voluntary quota will lock up the future of our industry. It's like tying your own legs together. Nothing is more absurd than voluntarily trimming exports by 30 or even 40 percent."

"Why does everyone urge you to do so, then?"

"Who do you mean by 'everyone'?" Fujishita asked petulantly.

Tomoko did not wince. "My father, for instance."

"Excuse me for saying this to you, but Mase-san is a trickster. He has no confidence in cost cutting and quality improvement which he will have to implement after the tariff hike. All he knows is that he can snatch a large export quota from his fellow companies. He's stronger against fellow companies than against Americans. Actually, it's injuring others, not fighting a battle, that he is good at. Mase-san is not the only one of this kind. There are too many of them in Japan. Why don't they train Japanese fingers, nimble fingers and arms that can use machines?"

Tomoko was again shaken by Fujishita's insult of her father.

"Here comes another lecture. Why don't you worship the Thousand-Armed Buddha in your factory?"

"You've said it. We have the god of harvest now, but I'm seriously thinking of replacing it with a Thousand-Armed Buddha." Fujishita looked serious.

"You're kidding!" Tomoko was the one to burst out. With the momentum of laughter, teardrops trickled down her cheeks from the corners of her eyes. "Give it a sleeve strap with the design of the rising sun."[4]

The evening glow of an ivory sky and golden arrows had given way to a violet night. Beyond the docks and the port, a chain of skyscrapers had drawn a light blue skyline.

They returned to their car and switched on the overhead light. Fujishita took the back seat.

"Wouldn't you like to go out drinking? I'd be glad to take you to a pub," proposed Tomoko.

"Thank you, but I'd better wait till the game is over. You keep telling me every night to go drinking. Why don't you go by yourself?"

Tomoko looked at the rear view mirror. It was filled with Fujishita's handsome, suntanned face. The reflection on his glasses made it impossible to tell where he was looking. Her own face, looking up, was on the edge of the mirror. Tracks of her old tears showed. Her face looked small, as it seemed in her high school days. She opened her compact and bent over it.

"I'm concerned about you. I thought you might want to relax and forget your troubles." She stuck out her tongue at the round mirror.

"How can I get drunk in the middle of a battle? Are you quite so eager to get me drunk?"

"Yes, I am," said Tomoko coquettishly and added to herself, *I want you to get drunk and drop dead.*

They drove back to his hotel on 49th Street. A tall woman with heavy makeup stood at the corner of 8th Avenue and winked at passersby. Fujishita and Tomoko saw several cars parked diagonal to the curb below the white neon sign "Rooms for Rent, $1.50." People got out of two or three of them and rushed up just as Tomoko's sedan halted. They were Japanese newswriters stationed in New York. Fujishita, still seated, but with his door open, was showered with their questions.

"The president's decision has come out. The tariff will be raised. What are your plans now?"

"Why didn't you volunteer to regulate exports?"

"Don't you think you were overconfident?"

Fujishita silently surveyed their faces first, then asked, "Are you sure? When did the announcement come out? Do you have the official statement?"

One of the newsmen showed him a copy of teletype. Fujishita held it in one hand and poked at Tomoko's back with the other.

"Drive! Let's get out of here!"

The car kicked off. It ran at full speed, twisting right and left with abrasive squeals of the tires. Heavy traffic got rid of the pursuers in five minutes.

"There's nothing I can do for those guys. I'd rather drink with you. Take me to a bar," Fujishita said, unconsciously clouting his forehead with his fist. He added in a cheerful voice, "The game is over. I'm going to drink my heart out."

Tomoko made a small nod and kept driving. *If you lose, you'll have no face to show us.* Bumpei's words echoed as Fujishita stared at Tomoko's back.

"I didn't lose!" Fujishita found himself shouting. He snickered at the loudness of his own voice.

Tomoko took a quick glance at the rear view mirror and drove on without a word.

Fujishita didn't consider himself a poor loser. *So, the tariff will go up. That's how it's going to be, I see.* He made up his mind to face it. The sense of defeat was not there. He slumped deeper into the seat and folded his arms. A high tariff of 85 percent! As a first repercussion, there would be a major standstill in exports. This was not a simple matter. Still, there was room for effort. One of the ways to cut production costs was to upgrade the technology. Japanese thermometers must be made superior to American varieties. The time had come for a new, treacherous, but worthy battle to replace the senseless one with Mullenbaum. The battle with Mullenbaum was very much like wrestling with a phantom. The new battle would bear no resemblance to a demeaning imposition such as the voluntary export control. A man never fails until he stops trying.

Tomoko drove her car without a word. Against the neon-lit evening sky, Fujishita saw the fire arrows carried by his boys, and also the rows of his girls' white fingers working at the mercury filling system. He wanted to sing to them, "We didn't lose." An urge welled up to smile at the newswriters, at fellow manufacturers like Mase, and at rows of other worried, stormy faces.

The car jerked twice and stopped.

"I don't know many classy bars." Tomoko started walking ahead of Fujishita. "Let's stop talking about your battles. It makes me sick." Her flat voice battered Fujishita's eardrums.

They stepped into a brightly tiled bar. Beyond the wall with pictures of boxers and horse racers, the din of slot machines resonated. On the counter, hard-boiled eggs were jammed in a glass jar. A wooden placard saying, "Free to regulars; 5ᶜ to irregulars," rested against it.

Fujishita surveyed the face of the woman who was once engaged to him. Her large eyes were overflowing; her pretty lips were shut tight ever since her car was chased by the newswriters; a girlish curve ran from her cheeks to her jaw. The pang and the pity of an elder brother, who had unfairly ignored his younger sister, overtook him. But the tender feeling lasted no more than a second. His eyes focused on hers, like examination lenses. As Bumpei had put it, this woman was very useful as a secretary, driver, and assistant. She had good sense, and occasionally presented something like her own opinions. Had he married this woman instead of his homey housewife, who does nothing other than raising two children, would it have improved his life as a manager of a company? No! A wife's brilliance added little to a man's work. What mattered more to him was Bumpei's influence on Tomoko.

The cocktail he hadn't tasted since he arrived in the United States burned his tongue. Tomoko drank only Coke, and talked with a bartender she seemed to know, playing with a boiled egg between her palms. *What are you going to do if you spend the twenty thousand dollars and lose the case, too?* Bumpei's voice resounded. *The biggie is the United States. We're counting on your success.*

Fujishita left the bar and wandered into a nearby building that seemed to be a nightclub. Tomoko followed him. An amateurish band played a conga. A hired dancer came swimming over the wood chip covered floor. Tomoko refused to dance, insisting that she didn't know how. She had searching eyes.

"Why do you look at me like that?" asked Fujishita.

Instead of answering, the corners of her eyes smiled.

Fujishita felt for her again. "What are you thinking?"

"Oh, nothing much. Would you like another glass?"

Fujishita told Tomoko to go home without him, since she wasn't going to drink anyhow. She shook her head and didn't get up. A wish to get rid of her and a longing for her alternated back and forth in his head.

They went back to Broadway. The stream of lights like jewel dust, the pale glow of neon lights, a shadowless street . . . ; the Broadway region went on with its endless activities. Fujishita's body, pressed against a bar wall, could hear golden roars. A mysterious vigor permeated his body. It invited him to drink one more and yet another.

How much did he drink? It was past three in the morning when he got back to his hotel on 8th Avenue. Tomoko, who usually hesitated to go beyond the lobby, pressed forward along the filthy linoleum floor, ahead of Fujishita. There was a staircase. Fujishita tried to skip every other step, but faltered. After that, the alcohol suddenly roused him. He gathered twice the force of before and lunged forth two steps at a time. Tomoko yelled and ran ahead of him, her body curled forward. The landing led to a balcony. Tomoko stood there, her arms outstretched, blocking his way. She was pale.

"This balcony doesn't have a railing!"

A door from Fujishita's room also led to the same balcony. From there, he had seen Tomoko's car go off, or had enjoyed the view of Broadway with a cigarette in his mouth. Tomoko entered his room and stood with her back to the door.

"Please don't go out from this door."

"Don't worry." Fujishita tried to push Tomoko aside.

"Please listen. Someone has fallen from here and died." She clung to his waist.

"All right. I got it. I got it, so please go home." Fujishita lit a cigarette.

Tomoko's eyes were set in a hard stare. Her body remained perfectly still.

"What are you doing there, with those big eyes?"

"I'm not going home until I see you fall asleep." Tomoko spoke as she pulled up the collar of her white raincoat. Her face looked paler than her raincoat.

Fujishita took a shower to sober up, put on a gown, and came back to the bedroom. Tomoko's small body sat snugly on a chair by the door. Her dark eyes sparkled. Fujishita's feet passed through the bedding and stuck out toward the chair Tomoko sat on.

Tomoko silently wept into her arms. The lines of tears glistened in the light that streamed in from outside. Fujishita naively assumed that she was being sentimental and did not bother to ask why she cried.

A green net of lights flashed on the two faces at rhythmic intervals. It was from the leftover neon lights of the flea circus next door to the hotel.

IV

The Export Association staff meeting in Tokyo had an air of blood-thirstiness from the outset. Fujishita was taken there straight from Haneda Airport on the pretext of discussing emergency measures, but the meeting was actually more like Fujishita's trial.

Fujishita first apologized and explained the process whereby the tariff was raised and what he had tried to do at Mullenbaum. But Bumpei Mase bellowed, "Enough of your excuses. How can a glass company be so powerful? Where do you have the proof? Or are you saying that your twenty thousand dollar lawyer Dubridge was just a nosy detective?"

Fujishita wished that Tomoko were there. She could have described the closing time at Mullenbaum, the six lines of cars and everything else. *So, this factory has over one hundred thousand workers. How many times your company's size is that?* Tomoko's caustic voice echoed in his ears. Fujishita realized, with a tight grin, that father and daughter shared only stubbornness. He didn't waste energy on Bumpei. He went on with the report.

Exchanges of sake and dishes sounded noisily. The participants in the meeting had already been drinking when Fujishita arrived. During Fujishita's chairmanship, the committee had refrained from drinking. The noise of cups and bottles was a declaration of their rebellion.

"Why did you ignore all the telegrams we sent to you?" Another voice cut into Fujishita's explanation.

"Because we decided against the voluntary control before I left for the States." Fujishita lost his temper.

"It was your decision, not ours!"

"Look at other industries. The voluntary quota saved them from a tariff hike."

Fujishita slowly glanced around at the members, giving them a chance to hold back their shouting. "I want to make this clear to you. I frankly think it's fortunate that we have the higher tariff, instead of the voluntary quota. Applying for the quota at the first threat of the United States' import control and tariff hike is tantamount to admitting with an apology, *I'm sorry we've exported too much.* You must understand that a voluntary quota will make us devour each other as though we were made to combat inside a small cage. No doubt the 85 percent wall is very high, but walls are there to climb over. Even if the import tax goes up, once Americans learn that Japanese goods are expensive but excellent, exports can grow. All depends on our efforts to trim costs. Remember, walls are there to climb over!" Fujishita kept his voice controlled the best he could. "Excellent but inexpensive goods will help Americans, too. Only a handful of Japanese manufacturers will stumble over the new law. Why do you think it's necessary to protect the few inefficient manufacturers, and raise the tariff between the two countries in a technological age when people are talking about going to the moon?"

"To whom are you referring?" Bumpei blustered, to take the wind out of Fujishita's sails. But he toned down. "It's all right for you. Your factory is big and you have new technology."

"You could do the same if you tried harder."

"Akira-san's place will probably do all right." Bumpei sounded bitter. "You murder us, and do business by yourself. You want all of us to be absorbed by Galaxy, am I wrong?"

"You are twisting things around. It's true that it takes time to improve facilities. Why don't we first team up and ask the importers to shoulder part of our new tax? Our thermometers are called halfway finished, but in reality, they are 80 to 90 percent complete. They are virtually finished products. We sell them for 15ᶜ. They add some finishing touches, and sell them for a dollar. They ought to be able to bear part of the tax."

"We'd better not talk about the 'finished product' so loud. After all, a finished product needs the label MADE IN JAPAN." Bumpei's voice pounded.

The words MADE IN JAPAN echoed bleakly through the room. It had a dreadful connotation. Since MADE IN JAPAN was believed to be synonymous with "poor quality," it was a 95 percent assurance that the merchandise would not sell. A hush fell over the manufacturers, as if they were strangled.

"Why not go ahead and put MADE IN JAPAN?" Fujishita talked back, but his voice lacked conviction. It fizzled out before reaching anyone's ears. "I can be proud of my products even if they are branded MADE IN JAPAN. At least I am manufacturing them with that in mind. I am not one of you Ippatsuya."

"What do you mean by 'you Ippatsuya'?" A man stood up in anger.

Bumpei held the man back. "Japan altogether is an Ippatsuya. Look at the government and the foreign services. Not just us!"

The air in the room froze right there. The sound MADE IN JAPAN left an uncanny resonance in the manufacturers' ears. It twanged in Fujishita's ears as well.

Thanks to a consensus among the members of the Thermometer Association, the Japanese manufacturers managed to persuade the American companies, as Fujishita had insisted, to shoulder a half of the raised tariff. The drop in exports was milder than feared, but two manufacturers lost their businesses and became Galaxy's subdivisions. Bumpei Mase proposed that production techniques be shared, but Fujishita didn't comply. The uncompromising situation was analogous to hurdles breaking the legs of slow runners. Many changes needed to be made: technical improvements, cost cutting, and so on. Fujishita and Manager Ohshima worked long hours in the factory in their navy-blue work uniforms.

But this economic lull was short-lived. The last and highest wall was put up by the United States against the Japanese products which poured in over the first wall. The second wall was a nasty one which had once hushed the manufacturers, namely, mandating the stamping of MADE IN JAPAN on the thermometers. The new law was issued by a state on the West Coast but in no time spread to several others.

"Mayer Trading Company has sent a telegram of cancellation, too." Manager Ohshima, who came in with bowed head, spoke without looking at Fujishita's face. "But it says that it would resume the contract if we change our mind, and agree to stamp MADE IN JAPAN only on the extra long portion."

That Mayer, too. . . . Fujishita gazed into space, thinking back on how he had trusted Mayer—the man who didn't want to take sightseeing tours, who squatted in front of the furnace with a stopwatch.

"No thanks. I refuse to make myself an Ippatsuya," said Fujishita sharply.

The enforcement of the law to stamp MADE IN JAPAN impeded the export of thermometers to the United States. But Bumpei soon found a way around it. He made his thermometers about one centimeter longer than necessary, stamped MADE IN JAPAN on the protruding portion, and had the American importers cut it off. Mase Thermometer expanded its business in this manner. It was a strategic victory, taking chances and outsmarting the law. This became a common practice throughout the industry. Renewed orders mandated the apocryphal stamping. But Fujishita's Galaxy Thermometer did not resort to this trick. New orders stopped coming, and more and more standing orders were called off.

"At this rate, we will have to reduce production by 30 percent," said Ohshima in a low voice. He looked up at Fujishita. "We will have to lay off one hundred more workers before next month."

The 421 workers had already been reduced to 300; 100 more need to be laid off. . . .

"I'm not putting up with all this nonsense just because I made that speech at our meeting, or to prove my will power. I do this only for the conviction that Ippatsuya cannot win. No matter how difficult it is, we've got to teach Americans that Japanese goods are good. I swear they'll understand someday. We must be patient until that time." Fujishita spoke in the manner of consoling Ohshima.

Ohshima listened silently but raised his thick silver brows. "Yes, I understand. Still, I beg you to let us make our thermometers long and to stamp the tips of them.''

Fujishita was torn. He said only ''No'' and looked away.

''After I've asked you this earnestly? Please let me leave the company, then.''

''Leave?'' Fujishita tried to raise his head.

''Please don't fall prey to harassments and blackmailing. Your belief is noble. It's best if you live by it. But having come this far, there's nothing more I can do for you. With my salary, you can keep five workers. That will serve Galaxy better than my presence.'' Ohshima spoke determinedly.

''But Manager, you . . .''

''I have enough savings to get by. I've heard somewhere that many managers in olden times gave up their private properties when their companies fell in trouble. I regret that I can only resign.''

Fujishita couldn't think of a proper reply.

''This is partly my fault. . . . Perhaps I should have told you to ask for the voluntary quota.''

At this moment, the face of this simple, peasant-like man of few words looked exactly like those of the other manufacturers.

''You think so, too.'' Murmuring, Fujishita made fast calculations. He had little work to do for the association now; he could devote the released time to company business. He never dreamed of Ohshima's resignation, but as Ohshima himself had figured, it might in fact help.

''If you are so resolved, I'm very sorry, but maybe I'll accept your resignation, or rather, I'll have you rest. I'm sorry I cannot pay your retirement benefit . . . but I'll come get you someday. Please count on it.'' Fujishita's voice trembled, but he said once more, ''I promise to come get you.''

V

It drizzled in Tokyo Harbor near the end of the year. The five smoke-stacks and the oil tank, in the shape of an upside-down silver bowl, smoldered gray in the direction of Toyosu and Harumi. There was hardly a person on the wharf. The scent of the waves, dampened by the rain, drifted slowly. The freighter *Ohkura Maru*, anchored alongside the cliff by the Shibaura pier, belched white water from its hawsehole.

Fujishita, in a raincoat with his shoulders hunched, walked up the gangway two steps at a time. The steps were wet and slippery.

It was December 26th. Fujishita had driven his car to the port to see with his own eyes the last shipment of the year. At the top, he ran into a descending shadow. Their shoulders just missed.

"Oh, it's you Akira-san." "Akira-san."

The overlapping voices startled him to look up. The shadows were those of Bumpei and an unexpected Tomoko.

"When did you come back?" asked Fujishita.

"Your cargo is really small this time," interrupted Bumpei. His dry lips smiled. "Your special client Mr. Mayer—we got orders from him, too—thanks to him, we have five times your cargo. This is the first time we got ahead of Galaxy. This is not a stylish victory, but if you stay so stubborn, we just have to go find our own way."

"What did you do about the MADE IN JAPAN stamp?"

"I stamped them."

"On the products?"

"I'll let you guess." Bumpei kept his smile. "You are as heartless as ever. I hear that you got rid of Manager Ohshima without any retirement benefit."

"I didn't get rid of him."

"Well, if you say so. But Ohshima is a loyal man. He refuses to work for Mase, no matter how much I offer."

Was Ohshima still counting on Fujishita's promise, *I'll come get you,* and waiting for that moment? The sight of Bumpei irritated Fujishita unbearably.

"To hell with Ippatsuya!" He pushed aside Bumpei's hand which held an umbrella and ran to the deck.

"Akira-san!" Tomoko called.

Fujishita didn't turn back. Cold rain streaked down his cheeks.

The packaged Galaxy thermometers lay timidly in a corner of the hold. Mase thermometers were piled high next to them. Bumpei's description of "five times" was no exaggeration.

The rain was stronger back on the rock wall. Fujishita put up the collar of his raincoat and ran. A woman jumped out from behind the bonded warehouse, offering her umbrella. It was Tomoko. She spoke as she ran up, "I'm glad I came. I thought I might have a chance to see you."

"When did you come back?"

"My sister died about three weeks ago. . . . I'm going back soon."

"Going back? To the States?"

"Yes. I have no attachment to Japan. I can live more comfortably there. People are easygoing. I wonder if it's because there aren't what you call Ippatsuya out there.''

"And your father?"

"He's given up. My sister is dead. If I'm not around, he can bring his mistress home.''

Fujishita heard the low putt-putt of a tugboat, and saw it move, raising white wakes.

Tomoko peered into Fujishita's face, "Can you guess why I wanted to see you? Do you think it's because I want to be asked again to your hotel with the broken balcony?'' She smiled only with her eyes. "To be honest with you, there's one thing I wanted to tell you. Without telling you, I feel indebted to you and to Japan.'' Tomoko took a deep breath and directed her moist eyes straight at Fujishita.

"I was planning to kill you in New York.''

The shock bolted Fujishita on the spot. Tomoko started walking, and the cold rain beat horizontally into Fujishita's face.

"Mr. Mayer almost read the reason why I took you to that hotel. To drop you off the balcony with a broken railing—that was my first attempt. That's why I reserved a room leading to the balcony. I thought of getting you drunk and letting you fall, without my being there at all. I had poison with me, too. If only people found out why you went to the States, they could surmise that you had good reason to take poison. I looked for a chance to kill you every day until that night of the tariff hike announcement.''

"Why did you want to kill me?''

"First of all, I wanted to clear my debt with you.''

"Your debt?''

"Yes. I grew up hearing about you ever since I can remember. You were put in front of my path, during my Peking Japanese Elementary School days, and during my women's high school days. I was haunted by dreams about you. I was forced to dream only about a person named Akira. The dream didn't go away even after I came back to Japan and found out that you were already married. By then, I couldn't think of another man. That's why I decided to go to the States. I couldn't stand the idea that you and your wife were living in the same country as I. Do you understand how cruel it is to monopolize the throne in a woman's heart for such a long, long time?''

Fujishita turned his face away. "It's not my fault.''

"I'm not asking whose fault it was. My father was hurt, too. Our fathers made something like a promise before Galaxy became big. But your father's business boomed. He made my father travel abroad, and didn't call him back. Only once, my father invited himself to your house, with me as a high school student. Your father passed away after the war. You as the successor had a wife and children, and were totally immersed in the thermometer business. You railed at my father when he asked you to rehire him.''

"Railed?"

"I still remember. You said, 'A company isn't a charity organization; one drowns if he tries to save another.'"

"I may have." Fujishita dissembled enigmatically.

"I should imagine Manager What's-his-name was thrown out the same way. My father decided to beat you in the same thermometer business. He madly saved money. I'm sure he played some dirty tricks, too. At one point, he was called by four police stations in one day. My parents feigned nonchalance and said, 'The police are a cinch compared to what we've been through in Manchuria and China. They won't take our lives.' But the fatigue from that kind of living took my mother's life. She contracted pneumonia and died only two days later.''

Fujishita put a stop to her talking. "Why didn't you kill me, then?"

"Because I reached the conclusion that it's no use killing you. You don't even have a shadow of my father or me in your mind. You took my hand as if you were checking one of your girl workers' hands. If I kill you, the anguish will turn back on me. I will be the one to get hurt. I came to feel that I would be haunted by your ghost for the rest of my life. That's something I should be able to avoid, after taking the trouble of running away from Japan, your habitat. You take such pride in your work. You kept saying that you weren't beaten. I was afraid that your self-respect would glow, even after I killed you. When I thought that I would hurt myself, and won't even be able to trip you. . . .''

Unconsciously, Fujishita was guided by Tomoko to skirt along the edge of the cliff. Below the cliff, the livid ocean, which rocked straw pieces and scrap vegetables, extended far. The rain hammered in round ripples on the flat surface.

"You are lucky." Fujishita spoke out of his honest heart.

"Why?"

"You are lucky to be able to hate a person so thoroughly."

"I think you are lucky. Hatred and agony cast no shadows on your life.''

"That makes both of us lucky," Fujishita laughed. "In my opinion, hating each other is no solution. To me, depth of hatred has no other meaning than its own. Maybe it's because I went through such a hardship during the war. All I want to do now is to get to the top of the stairs in front of me, leaping two steps at a time. It doesn't matter if I stumble and get hurt. The injury will give me a sense of living.''

"The MADE IN JAPAN dream must be waiting for you at the very top of the stairs.''

"You may be right.''

Tomoko's eyes sparkled mischievously. "Let me ask you one final question. Did you lose this game?''

The fire in the electric furnace of his factory, now reduced in size, and the fire arrows shivering forlornly, floated before Fujishita's eyes, but his words came out strong, "What is it to lose?''

"You still don't know?'' Tomoko grinned, her eyelashes shining with raindrops.

A whistle split the thick air. A freighter, which had been moored in the dock, slowly turned its bow in departure.

"To lose is to become an Ippatsuya,'' Fujishita asserted to the damp wet sky.

Notes

This short story was originally published in the February 1959 issue of *All Reading* (Ōru yomimono). This is a translation of "Meido in Japan" in *Sōkaiya Kinjō*, pp. 109–56.

1. *Ippatsu* means "one shot," *ya* means a "shop" or a "dealer," the combination means something like "a one shot dealer" or "a gambler who takes chances in business activities.''

2. The "san" suffix means "Mr.," "Mrs.," or "Miss." It may follow either the first or last name. Where the "-san" suffix is used slightly differently from its English counterparts, I left it untranslated.

3. "Blanks" are unfinished products.

4. The rising sun is the design on the Japanese flag. A sleeve strap *(tasuki)* is a circular cloth strap put around both arms in a figure "8" from behind to keep Japanese sleeves from getting in the way.

Silver Sanctuary

Ikkō Shimizu

I

A strange thing happened exactly three months after Junji Tagawa was promoted to be the manager of the Nittō Bank N-Branch Office.[1] He was the youngest in the company to reach this position and was just getting into the managerial swing of things.

"There's something fishy about this," Assistant Manager Kenji Nishiyama said to Tagawa, after a business meeting, as he looked hesitantly at him. "You must know Mr. Ikuno of the fifth ward. He installs greenhouse heating systems. He called me to ask why the salesman from Daidō Bank across the street called on him."

"You mean . . . why he visited?" Tagawa parroted the question. Tagawa had once paid a courtesy visit to Ikuno's house with Nishiyama shortly after his latest promotion. In Tagawa's recollection, Ikuno's house was a weathered prefabricated hovel. A brick shed was annexed to its rusting steel frame, making it larger. It was obvious to an educated eye that the owner of this drab building with no business signboard had been cutting corners quite a bit. Yet, in the N-Branch Office alone, Ikuno had a confidential long-term savings account of 25 million yen.[2] Tagawa had trouble finding the connection between the hovel and its owner's handsome savings.

"In other words, Mr. Ikuno doesn't believe that his house was randomly picked by the salesman. He says that we are the only institution with any knowledge of his 25 million yen savings. . . . You remember his shanty, don't you? The reason he lives in that miserable thing, he says, is to get around unnecessary taxation. How does Daidō Bank know? He is panic-stricken. Now that the Daidō Bank has found out, he thinks the tax bureau will soon sniff out his actual income."

Tagawa smiled disapprovingly. He was not all that critical of Ikuno's penny-pincher mentality, but it didn't make sense to directly link the salesman's visit with the problem of taxation, and to be frightened by the possibility.

"Daidō didn't demand a transfer of his 25 million yen from our bank into theirs, did they?"

"Heaven forbid!"

"Why worry, then?"

"The only thing is—although this may only be a coincidence—Mr. Norisaka on K-Street, where I dropped in yesterday, had also been solicited by Daidō Bank."

Norisaka on K Street owned a small grocery store. Small as the store might have been, its owner was once the largest landlord in the area, and he had been a steady client at the Nittō Bank N-Branch Office. His long-term savings account contained nearly 30 million yen.

"I wonder what they are doing over at Daidō Bank—a memorial savings campaign, or something of that sort?"

"Nothing that I know of," answered Nishiyama.

Tagawa peered through the thin lace curtains at the two-story white Daidō Bank N-Branch Office kitty-corner across the narrow intersection in front of N-Station. Next door to it was a Mutual Bank.[3] In all, there were six financial institution branches in the neighborhood.

"Well then, did they decide to spirit away our good customers?"

If it were a matter of one customer, Tagawa could reasonably ignore the case as a coincidence, but his mind couldn't be kept at ease when two confidential account clients had been solicited in such a short span of time.

N-Station belonged to a private railroad company. It was only thirty minutes away from Ikebukuro Station on the heavily traveled Yamate Line. The daily flow of commuters through this station totaled about twenty thousand. The district had been enjoying a growing popularity as a newly developed residential area. New banks had appeared at a rate comparable to the speed of the regional development itself. Now that the area was completely built up, as many as six bank branch offices stood side by side. They vied bitterly with one another, each trying to pick up one more client. On top of their business competition, the new banks had another evil to combat: new homeowners were drained of the strength to make substantial savings. Enthusiastic salesmen in search of new clients had only the territories of other banks to explore.

Likewise, the bank that was managed by Junji Tagawa, a thirty-seven-year-old upstart manager, was located in one of the most competitive zones in Tokyo. Inasmuch as the bank management, by nature, demanded a steady growth of clientele, and their concerns pretty much focused on this matter, salesmen were edgy about the movements of large depositors.

"I hope nothing serious is going on. The best I can do for now is to go talk with the two clients," said Tagawa.

"That may help."

Tagawa knew that he had to defend his bank first and then counterattack. For the counterattack, he needed a clear picture of what his opponents knew and what they were after. Ikuno and Norisaka, the two clients Tagawa visited that day, gave him a piece of their mind, saying that the financial secrets of an individual should not be used as a weapon to fight the business competition. They demanded an assurance of confidentiality.

"I don't get this. The list of confidential deposits must have somehow gotten out of Nittō Bank." Ikuno kept after Tagawa, furrowing his brows nervously. His nervous fidgeting was unbecoming to his placid, chubby physique.

"I swear, Sir, there was no oversight."

"But I'm still not convinced. . . ."

"It's our responsibility to guard the confidentiality of our clients." Tagawa put a stern expression on his handsome face and spoke crisply. "May I ask the name of the Daidō Bank salesman?"

"I think it was Saeki, or something."

The name corresponded to the one on the calling card Tagawa had seen at Norisaka's house only a while ago. In Norisaka's description, the salesman was "flat and pale faced."

Tagawa made up his mind to check up on Saeki just as soon as he could. But the crisis hit him as soon as he returned to his N-Branch office. Tatsuo Aoki, another large deposit holder, was waiting for him in the manager's office.

"What the hell is going on, Manager? This fellow came to see me. Do you have a good explanation?" Bald-headed Aoki tossed a calling card on a side table. Stooping over to peer at it, Tagawa saw Saeki's name again, and almost let slip, "Oh, he went to your house, too."

Instead, he took a seat facing Aoki and asked calmly, "I see, it's

Daidō Bank. Is this the first time?''

"He asked me to put some money in his bank." Aoki's voice mirrored his disappointment in his failure to get Tagawa worked up. But his belligerence returned in no time. "First I tried to get rid of him. I told him that I had no money to save. Then, guess what? This fellow with silly-looking glasses had the nerve to say, 'I know you have some.' He said this with a big grin on his face!" Aoki's voice grew louder.

"My God, he is forward!"

"He knew what he was doing, though. Listen. The man said, 'You have 50 million yen in a confidential account at Nittō Bank alone. Since it matures next month, won't you kindly take advantage of our services and deposit just half of it with us?' Can you imagine? Can you think of anything more outrageous than this?''

Tagawa held his breath at Aoki's cutting words. Aoki's self-confidence rekindled when he caught sight of Tagawa's reaction. He became coarse and started attacking Tagawa in a sarcastic, caustic tone of voice, "I just don't see how my account with Nittō is known by people at Daidō."

"I assure you that nothing like that is going on."

"But don't you see that things are getting out of hand?"

Tagawa feared that this mix-up might turn into a fatal blow to his career. There couldn't have been a leak of the information about confidential long-term savings accounts unless there were inside sabotage.

"I don't care what you say," roared Aoki, "all I know is that I can't trust this bank; I feel stupid leaving my money with you. Let me withdraw it all." Aoki banged on the armrest of the sofa. The arteries of his boar-like neck bulged grotesquely. Tagawa feared that Aoki's 50 million yen withdrawal might cripple the achievement record of the N-office.

Tagawa felt cornered. He edged forward on the sofa and did his best to win Aoki's heart, "As you may already know, the competition among banks is horrendous. It's exactly like the saying, 'a hundred devils marching at night.' For now, it is impossible to tell what kind of trap Daidō has set up against us. But it is very unlikely that the information has leaked from within. In any event, I shall investigate the situation right away. Please be kind enough to give us time to pin down what's happening."

Suddenly, a strange anxiety welled up in Tagawa, or rather, a queer gut feeling, a suggestive brainstorm, struck him. An image momentarily loomed in the back of his brain, like a shadow floating between dark waves. It disappeared and floated back to the surface again and again and again.

"Please give me a week. One week will do. I can rectify the situation as soon as the cause is traced."

"What can you do after you manage to trace down the cause?"

"I'll see to it that you won't be inconvenienced." Tagawa bowed low.

"When the manager is young, the management is bound to be remiss." Aoki spoke spitefully, and made it clear that he would not wait more than a week.

After Aoki left, Tagawa pondered over the anxiety he had just felt, and reexamined the shadow that had wafted through the back of his mind. He felt that he had been unfair to the woman he suspected, but judging from her position in the bank, there was good reason to suspect her. Also, if her personal resentment against Tagawa was still there, she could have done this intentionally as a way of revenge.

Tagawa lifted the intercom receiver and asked two switchboard operators, "Does the name Kikuo Saeki ring a bell to you?"

"Of which company, Sir?"

"What I mean is, does either of you remember anybody from our bank calling a person named Saeki, or Saeki calling somebody here?"

The two operators whispered to each other. Holding the receiver, Tagawa tasted an acrid premonition that the girls would name the person whose image had just passed through his brain.

"If we remember correctly, Sir, Miss Yōko Takigami used to call him. She stopped calling him about two months ago."

Tagawa winced at these words. He was right . . . exactly as he had feared. He heaved an audible sigh.

II

How ironic! There was no other way to describe Tagawa's reencounter with Yōko at the N-Branch Office.

Tagawa had graduated from the Department of Economics of A-University. After entering Nittō Bank, he worked for five years as an executive-in-training. Initially, he belonged to the first section of the General Affairs Office in the main building. Subsequently, he was sent to the Ikebukuro office, which was an auxiliary branch of the bank in Jōhoku District. This time, he was an executive-in-training in branch office management. It was here that he was introduced to a co-worker,

Yōko Takigami. She was a teller at the front counter, in charge of day-to-day transactions.

Yōko had graduated from high school, been hired by the branch office, and by then had worked in the office for three years. She was twenty-one, but more experienced than Tagawa both as a teller and also with respect to the general ins and outs of life at the regional office. With the quick wit of a city woman, she covered up Tagawa's blunders. For his part, Tagawa had a difficult time adjusting to the monotony and boredom of life in a regional office, primarily because until then he had known nothing outside the colorful life of the main office.

He also learned that the frustration and chagrin harbored by the low-ranking employees in peripheral branch offices had no outlet. For instance, Tagawa's supervisor in charge of day-to-day transactions, Junichi Konno, had graduated from a provincial university and had been sent to a branch office as his first assignment. He had never been included in the high-level executive track as Tagawa had. Never in the future would Konno have an opportunity to work in the main office. It was evident that before long Tagawa and other future executives would outrank him, and he would be placed under their supervision. Because of these circumstances, Konno at times bickered with the inexperienced Tagawa as would a mother-in-law. Then he would suddenly soften up and take Tagawa to a bar to cajole him under the influence of alcohol, "Please help me out in the future."

During the interminable process of frustration and bearing up, these underdogs gradually learned to mold their personalities into firm "banker types."

Tagawa's first end-of-the-year party at the Ikebukuro Office came about shortly after he was transferred there. This party turned into an unbelievable nightmare.

"Too bad the manager is going to miss the party again," Yōko remarked after the tellers' windows were closed, giving her hands a little rest from bookkeeping.

"But isn't he sending funds for the party? We may have a better time without him."

"Only if nothing happens. . . ."

At the time, Tagawa had failed to read the delicate nuances in Yōko's conditional comment.

The party was held in a neighborhood restaurant and went on merrily. Just as the fun and games started to get out of control, the lights suddenly went off. As he heard the female employees' full-throated shrieks, Tagawa saw a number of shadows swoop toward the deputy manager sitting across from him. He took this to be a part of the frolic and had no suspicions. But then, against the noise of small tables being thrown around and dishes and bowls being broken, the deputy's pathetic cry, "Cut it out!" pierced through the darkness. Shadows swayed and muffled his yell. Startled by the heavy and bizarre atmosphere of the condensed darkness, Tagawa tried to get to his feet. Instantly, somebody grabbed his hand and pulled him down into his seat. He could not make heads or tails of the melee. He could not even tell who had pulled his hand. Then, he heard the thud of something falling down the stairs.

"Don't move. Try not to see anything. Just sit still!" It was Yōko who was ordering him in whispers.

The lights came back on and the party members cheered. But the Deputy was no longer in his seat. Only at the distraught screams of the restaurant workers did Tagawa realize that Yamazaki, the forty-five-year-old deputy manager, had been thrown down the stairs and was groaning.

The victim took nearly a week off from work to recover. It was an atrocious, incredible incident, a sinister rebellion by the underdogs against the institution which forced them into a uniformity in which one must not stand out, must not be praised or berated; one must not be in the news; one must strive in every way possible not to commit either virtue or vice.

The day after the party, the bank was again the smiling, classy workplace it had always been. No mention was made of Deputy Yamazaki's injury. Those who struck him in the darkness out of their pent-up resentment received clients as politely as they had always done. Employees threw themselves into their work diligently like a congregation of saints.

"Did you know what was cooking?" Tagawa asked Yōko a couple of days later when they ran into each other on their way home. But Yōko shook her head with a cheerless smile.

"That has nothing to do with you, Mr. Tagawa, because you don't belong here. You will return to the main office and be promoted to a section head or an executive. It's best if you forget about it quickly and finish up your service at the branch office. Please just try to avoid the mess."

Tagawa momentarily felt that Yōko had suddenly grown older than himself.

Something else happened precisely a week after the party, namely, the spotting of a forged check. Yōko, who was waiting on clients as usual, attached a small note to a check in a matter-of-fact way and sent it to Tagawa. Tagawa craned his neck to take a look at it.

"This check is forged."

He had to read it twice to convince himself.

"Please have a seat and wait." Yōko was calmly addressing a sallow-faced fellow in his forties when Tagawa cast a glance at her. The man looked like a small factory owner. Tagawa's head throbbed. He lost his composure, but Yōko, as if to divert the sallow-faced man's attention, took on another client.

Tagawa put the check and Yōko's note between other documents, and walked over to Chief Clerk Konno. His knees trembled, making it difficult to stand in front of the chief clerk.

It was a forgery all right, but a very amateurish one. The number "6" had been altered to "9" with a pen, and that was all.[4] Sixty-one thousand yen had been changed to ninety-one thousand yen. It was the kind of flaw somebody would have eventually noticed, even if a teller didn't. Seen from another angle, it showed how hard pressed the forger was. The man was arrested on the spot.

Assuming that the ideal image of a banker is not to be praised, not to be criticized, nor even to be talked about, Yōko Takigawa's difficulties, it may be said, started at this point.

Mostly because it happened to be the end of the year, when a crime-prevention campaign was at its peak, the incident attracted the attention of news reporters. Most newspapers praised the exemplary way in which Yōko had handled the situation. Newspaper captions read "An Ingenious Banker," "Skillfully Detecting a Forger," and the like. Even Tagawa appeared in the newpaper, standing next to Yōko as her fellow worker.

Tagawa learned from these articles that the criminal's name was Ichirō Hirayama. Hirayama manufactured plastic bags with a machine set up in the entrance of his small house. The minute-scale manufacturer and his wife undertook every level of work, from operating the machine to delivering the products to wholesalers. The couple labored from before dawn until deep into the night, but couldn't make ends meet at the end of the year. After many qualms, he took it upon himself to resort to forgery.

The incident precipitated an intimacy between Tagawa and Yōko. Yōko practically forced Tagawa to join a company ski trip in the Jōetsu

Highlands during the three-day New Year's vacation. They spent the entire vacation as very close friends. Yōko was in high spirits and was more buoyant than youth itself. She captivated Tagawa with her laughter and nimble movements.

It was mid-January when Yōko asked politely, "Would you like to have tea with me on our way home?"

Tagawa met her by the west exit of the station, which was on the other side of the station from his bank. The young couple walked past the unabashedly cluttered honky-tonk district in front of the station and came to a Western-style delicatessen-coffee shop near North Ikebukuro.

"There's something I'd like to ask your advice about, Mr. Tagawa," Yōko began after ordering their beverages. She told Tagawa that her father was a security officer at the Nippori Branch Office of the Nittō Bank. It was he who had arranged her employment at the Ikebukuro office. "The Deputy Manager asked me yesterday if I would be interested in moving to the General Affairs Department in the main office." Yōko announced with hardly a sign of exhilaration.

"Sounds great!"

"I have a feeling that the forgery incident has something to do with this transfer."

"Whatever the reason may be, it's an exceptional break for you. No matter how you look at it, the main office is the best. The place makes you feel that you are really working for a bank."

Apparently, the bank had been obliged to make a gesture of appreciation for Yōko's feat, now that the incident of the forged check had gotten so much publicity.

"But . . ." Yōko cast a glance downward as if she were doing some hard thinking. Then she abruptly looked up, straight into Tagawa's handsome face.

"When can you go back to the main office, Mr. Tagawa?" she asked urgently without blinking.

"I wish I knew. It's been only four months since I came to Ikebukuro. It's unlikely that I'll get to go back for another two or three years." Tagawa equivocated, flinching at Yōko's abnormally intense stare. "What does your father say? That's more important."

"He wants me to accept the offer because it's a great honor."

"I thought so. Also, the main office has a lot of good-looking men. They'll be after you as soon as you arrive," Tagawa bantered with her.

The chain of events, starting with the forged check incident, and the

New Year's ski trip which developed into three dates, had made Tagawa a bit flippant with Yōko. But his teasing instantly clouded Yōko's big eyes and made her head droop.

"That's why I'm reluctant to go. If you talk like that, I'm going to turn down the offer," she said in a trembling voice.

"What do you mean?" Tagawa didn't know what to make of the sudden change in her temperament. He was caught off guard. He didn't think he had said anything nasty to her; all he had said was that the main office was better than a branch office. That was something anyone would agree with. Yet, Yōko shook her bowed head. She shook it once again more violently after a short while, as if to brush aside Tagawa's question.

"Did I say something wrong?"

"You said that the handsome men there would come after me."

"It's true. That may really happen."

"Please. Don't talk like that. You make me feel uneasy." Yōko interrupted Tagawa, baring her virginal innocence. She had no interest in the propositions of strangers. "I like our Ikebukuro Office better."

"Oh? Even if you'd never come across another chance to go to the main office?" Tagawa suspected that if she turned down this offer, Yōko would most certainly be transferred to one office or another at the bank's next personnel rotation. Now that she had caught the forged check, had been written up in the papers, and gotten attention in the media, Yōko had ceased to be an invisible teller like all the rest. Visibility could be deadly for a career in banking.

A bank simply had to be a place where nothing unusual happened, and where people could leave their money with no hint of anxiety. Even if things were going well, the very fact that something—and this can be any smallest thing—had happened would slow down the canvassing activities. Yōko's presence at the front window of the Ikebukuro Office was undesirable in that it would keep triggering clients' memories of the unpleasant incident. A bank usually makes haste to wipe out any trace of troublesome memories. This was where personnel rotation came in handy. Tagawa meant to explain that it would be far better for her to be sent to the main office than to another dead-end place, but Yōko raised guarded eyes trying to block out his words.

"It's because, if I go to the main office, I won't be able to work with you."

"Work with me?" asked Tagawa, thrusting his face forward. Yōko gave a big nod. Tagawa looked back at her, alarmed. Yōko's eyes, ardently set on his, were filled with burning desire. He sensed her desperate affection. The sparks of her eyes were ready to ignite. He knew that this was her suicidal proposal.

"Shall we go now?"

"Please stay a little longer." Yōko shook her head wildly. And she pleaded in a yet more precipitous tone, "I would like to work with you. Please tell me point blank if it bothers you."

"So long as you don't mind, yourself." Tagawa looked slightly downward.

"I don't." Yōko spoke as if clinging to his words with her entire body.

As Tagawa raised his smiling face, rapturous jubilation spread over Yōko's blushing cheeks. Her youthful glamour captured his heart. At that very instant, he wished to satisfy his flaring passion by attaining deeper and more concrete proof.

"Let's have a drink." Tagawa took the initiative, being cautious, meanwhile, not to let her see that he had a man's desire to get down to business all at once.

Yōko nodded gently with a somewhat hesitant smile.

Outside the coffee shop, a whirling chilly wind wrapped around the two people. Yōko leaned onto the arm Tagawa casually thrust out. That night, Tagawa became engaged to Yōko, whose fair skin was stained by fresh blood.

III

It did not take long for talk of their relationship to spread among the Ikebukuro Office employees. Yōko was in constant rapture over the idea of marriage with Tagawa. When her colleagues teased her, she blushed happily and even appreciatively. Such scenes made Tagawa feel that he should conclude the marriage without delay.

"Let's talk to your father first."

No matter how quickly he wanted to proceed, he couldn't do away with certain preparations. There was a certain order in which to go about them, too. He worked at them steadily, bolstered by the euphoria of having Yōko's moral support.

Yūkichi Takigami, Yōko's father, who worked as a security officer at the Nippori Office, met Tagawa very congenially in his Takinogawa apartment.

"I've heard much about you from my daughter. Please don't worry about me. I will manage by myself after she gets married. I only have this apartment of a six-tatami-mat[5] room to keep up.''

Courteously and calmly, Yūkichi showed a sincere concern for Tagawa, who might worry about disrupting the father-daughter bond.

''I'd like to have the wedding this spring. If I wait until fall, I'll be twenty-nine years old.''

Lowering his gray-haired head, Yūkichi humbly thanked Tagawa for suggesting that the wedding be made simple so that the financial burden on Yūkichi would be minimal. Tagawa then made a plan to introduce Yōko in early February to his parents who lived by themselves in Yamanashi Prefecture.

Very early that February, Ichirō Hirayama, the check forger, committed family suicide.

Chief Clerk Konno, who had completed his work for the day and glanced at the evening paper shortly before the five o'clock closing hour, called Tagawa in a disturbed voice, ''Look! That son of a gun has committed suicide!''

Tagawa twisted his body around toward Konno and asked, ''That son of a gun?''

''Yeah, that forged check criminal.''

''What! You mean Hirayama?''

Tagawa kicked back his chair and rushed to Konno's desk. ''Small Businessman Commits Suicide.'' The large headline leaped from the paper to his eyes. Tagawa bent over the photo caption which started with a quotation from Hirayama's will, ''Once convicted of forgery, it's impossible to make a living. . . .''

''It's a suicide of a family of five,'' Konno reported to the other staff. All turned to look at him.

''A family suicide!'' someone shouted.

Two or three people rushed to look at the newspaper on Konno's desk. One of them groaned, ''With gas.''

''I never got to see the criminal closely, but I would have never guessed that he had three children so cute. What a nightmare!'' Konno desparately shook his head.

The newspaper suspected that Hirayama and his wife had waited until their children had fallen asleep, took sleeping pills, and turned on the gas.

They recalled that the so-called check forgery was only a matter of thirty thousand yen. Because there was no real loss, the bank did not even prosecute Hirayama, and he was released that day.

Having read the article, Tagawa turned away from the picture of the family of five and glanced at Yōko.

"It was only thirty thousand yen. I don't see why he had to die." Another teller voiced his comment on the newspaper article. Yōko, who had been standing pale-faced, dropped her head, put her hand over her mouth, and ran out to the locker room. Tagawa followed and found her standing by herself motionless at the end of a row of lockers. She gave herself up to tears at the sight of Tagawa, hiding her face with both hands.

"Let's not worry about it." Tagawa held Yōko's shoulders and pulled her toward him. "It wasn't our fault, was it?"

"But it's all because I found the forgery. Yes, I'm the one who drove them to family suicide." Yōko lifted her wet eyes pleadingly.

"You are too sensitive."

"But I can't forget that man's exhausted face." Yōko buried her face in Tagawa's chest and cried. "It was my fault. Yes, absolutely. I get to marry Junji-san because of that incident. Meanwhile, someone else was driven to death. . . . Does that make sense?"

"That's enough. Don't let it get you down."

No words were needed to explain how the Hirayama family must have lived after the forgery was written up in the papers. But were Yōko and Tagawa the two to bear the blame?

"Oh, I hate it. I can't stand it! He must have died cursing us. Don't you think so?"

More important than whether or not he cursed us is what kind of image Yōko and I presented to him: that of merciless prosecutors? stuck-up money mongers? In his wonderment, Tagawa's wretchedness came very close to Yōko's.

"What else could we do at the time? You see, once a forgery is noticed, a banker is not allowed to ignore it. This means that we are at least not accountable for it. Even if a family suicide followed as a consequence, that is. Who is guilty then? Money. Yes, money is the evil force."

Tagawa drew Yōko tightly against his tall body, as if to leave no room for confusion.

"I would like you to wait awhile before you take me to your parents," said Yōko the next day.

Tagawa could sympathetically agree to wait until Yōko had recovered from the trauma of the Hirayama suicide. But the wait developed into subsequent and more amplified regrets. The family suicide was but an omen for the breakup of their engagement. For exactly a week later, when Yōko was just recovering from her shock and regaining mental equilibrium, her father became embroiled in a scandal. That morning, Tagawa was awakened by his apartment manager's call, "Telephone!"

"My father is in trouble."

The call was from Yōko, sobbing helplessly. Rubbing his sleepy eyes and gathering together the collar of his robe, Takawa asked clumsily, "What's going on?"

"I was right. The man who committed suicide was cursing us." Yōko's words made little sense. Only some time later did she get a grip on herself, explaining in a choked voice, "My father is in critical condition." Patching her choppy phrases together, Tagawa figured out that there had been a carbon monoxide poisoning caused by the imperfect combustion of a gas burner at her father's Nippori office. Two young bankers who happened to be staying overnight in the Night Duty Room had died. Yūkichi alone barely survived, and had been taken to the hospital in critical condition.

"I'm calling from the hospital. My father is in the emergency room, and . . ." Upset and distraught, Yōko lost track of her thoughts.

"Where is the hospital? Do you hear me? Which hospital are you in?"

"Nippori Hospital, near Nippori Station."

"I'll be right over. Your father is holding out all right, isn't he?"

"They are giving him oxygen."

"There is no such thing as Ichirō Hirayama's curse, so calm down. Understand? Take it easy."

Tagawa rushed back to his room, changed his clothes, and ran out. It was difficult to find a taxi. The one that finally stopped for him moved cautiously at a steady speed. It was as if Tagawa were hearing Yōko's desperate voice calling from the other shore of the river Styx. *Why did that gentle Yūkichi Takigami have to . . . ?* Tagawa brooded over the nature of the accident. When he arrived at the hospital at long last, he found Yōko doubled up on a chair in a corridor. A chilly breeze blew through.

"How did it go?" he asked, running up to her.

Yōko raised her face vacantly, and directed her empty gaze at the emergency room. She was a figure drained of the energy to shed tears.

"Does it seem like he's going to make it?"

"I have no idea."

"I wonder if it's really bad."

". . . He may not make it."

"Don't be silly." Tagawa squeezed Yōko's hand firmly.

Presently, the deputy manager of the Nippori Office came running. Also, the police who had inspected the site came to check on Yūkichi's condition. The deputy manager explained what might have happened.

According to him, Yūkichi was on duty the night before. He must have allowed the two bank clerks to stay overnight. The two had gotten drunk in the Nippori area, and had missed the last train. The room looked as if the two younger men had started drinking what they had brought. Yūkichi must have joined them. In drunkenness, he must have fallen asleep on the floor without shutting off the gas burner. This was the cause of the incomplete combustion.

"Please wait," Tagawa interrupted, "Mr. Takigami can't drink."

"There's always such a thing as being obliged to drink."

The Nippori deputy manager insisted that Takigami couldn't have fallen asleep on the floor without the influence of alcohol. Tagawa asked how it could be possible that the two young men had died and the oldest, Yōko's father, had survived, if they had been drinking together. The deputy turned deaf ears to this question. Tagawa grasped that the finger of blame would be pointed at Yūkichi regardless of what he had done.

Yōko's father pulled through by the skin of his teeth and was moved to his Takinogawa apartment after nearly ten days' hospitalization. By then, muscular and brain paralysis had transformed him into a human vegetable. As if this weren't enough, the Nippori branch office fired Yūkichi Takigami on the grounds that his fingerprints were found on a teacup. The fingerprints were their proof that Takigami had been drinking on duty.

IV

Personnel rotation at Nittō Bank usually takes place in May and November. Because the bank judged that Tagawa was indirectly involved in the forgery incident as well as the gas leak accident, his name was listed as part of the May personnel rotation. He was sent back to the main office earlier than originally planned. It must have been that he and Yōko stood out too conspicuously in the Ikebukuro Office.

"We would be married by now, if nothing had happened," Tagawa spoke to Yōko pensively after reporting his transfer. This was precisely when Yōko needed him more than ever at the Ikebukuro Office, but nothing personal could countermand the periodic rotation.

"My father may get better by fall. Also, Junji-san will still be in Tokyo even after you move to the main office."

We can see each other anytime we want to. . . . Yōko wished to say, but any free moment she had needed to be spent on her father. He was no longer able to control his bowel movements. The couple had already gone three months without a date, not to mention physical contact. Yōko's financial burden also piled up. Out of a twenty-one-year-old woman's salary, she had to scrape together her father's medical expenses as well as their room and board. Yūkichi had no income. Tagawa was well aware of the magnitude of the burden, and offered to help, but Yōko would not accept.

Yōko's last shred of hope to restore the hopeless invalid was mercilessly snatched away that autumn, the very autumn she had once looked forward to. Yūkichi's condition worsened. Yōko started missing many days of work in order to look after him. As the news arrived through the staff at the Ikebukuro Office that Yōko had been absent for over ten days, Tagawa dropped by her Takinogawa apartment for the first time in a long while.

Yōko was sitting next to her father's pillow, gazing distractedly into space. A sad smile appeared on her pale, lifeless face when she saw Tagawa.

"The doctor came and gave him a shot about an hour ago."

Yūkichi was asleep, his mouth agape, like a child. Yōko voluntarily suggested taking a walk. "He just fell asleep so he will be all right until morning."

The red, round, early October moon was almost brutally bright for the couple, who found themselves walking side by side for the first time in some months. In silence, each craved for a place where they could embrace. In a narrow alley leading to Asukayama Park, Tagawa saw a poky little signboard of an inn. As he turned back, Yōko nodded, pressing her body against his.

The walls and the ceiling of the dark room were filthy. The quilt, not even enclosed in a white coverlet, looked unsympathetically cold.

"I've done something wrong to Mr. Tagawa." Yōko spoke in a formal manner, facing Tagawa, but without using her usual appellation "Junji-san."

"It's not your fault," said Tagawa comfortingly.

Tagawa held Yōko's thin, limp hand and embraced her. Yōko lay back on the quilting and sought Tagawa's lips, trembling. Not just her body, but the very marrow of her soul had been longing for gentle affection. At Tagawa's first embrace in many months, Yōko's entire body instantly flared up. She kept repeating as if in a delirium, "I've done something awful to Tagawa-san."

That night for the first time, Yōko reached climax. Engulfed by her frenzied and violent reaction, Tagawa was also drowned in intoxication.

It was shortly after this that Yōko asked to call off the wedding engagement. She proclaimed that they could not marry as long as she was taking care of her invalid father, and that there was little hope for his recovery. She pleaded desperately with Tagawa that he not let her get in his way.

"I am no longer worthy of Tagawa-san's love. I can't even offer my body when you need it." Yōko dissolved into tears, remonstrating with Tagawa—and finally shouting at him—to forget her, because there was no hope for their future.

Never after that day did Yōko telephone Tagawa. On days when he visited the Takinogawa apartment, using Yūkichi's illness as an excuse, she would receive him only with empty formality, as if he were a stranger.

A new marriage offer came Tagawa's way in early November.

On a holiday, Business Department Manager Yūzō Koyanagi invited Tagawa to his Shiba-Takanawa home and advised, "You are asking for trouble by staying a bachelor for such a long time."

The name of the woman Koyanagi brought to Tagawa's attention was Misako Oribe. She was the second daughter of the Nittō Bank's leading customer. She had a B.A. in French Literature from A-University.

"She's by no means young, but she's good-looking, as you can see from this photograph. She has the perfect background for a banker's wife." Koyanagi hammered away, "You know what kind of a place a bank is. It's different from ordinary companies. One cannot marry just anyone."

"I appreciate your concern."

Tagawa was on the verge of telling Koyanagi that he was already engaged to be married to Yōko Takigami when Koyanagi continued knowingly, "For example, one must not marry the daughter of a guard who, out of carelessness, got drunk and fell asleep and, as a result, took the lives of two young and promising men."

"But that accident was . . ."

"I know. I have talked with the manager of the Ikebukuro office. And you probably want to add that the woman is the one who spotted the forged check. But that, in itself, is a problem to us now."

"A problem?"

"Don't you see? Suppose you marry her. Every time you are reviewed for promotion, there is bound to be someone who will say that Tagawa is outstanding but his wife isn't an ideal type. Think twice about what I'm saying. I mean her father's incident and the forged check case included. Both will affect your future adversely; they make you a good conversation piece. That is, these things are detrimental to the image of an ideal banker. They add nothing to your future. This is why I transferred you out of the Ikebukuro office. Once you are tainted, it's too late. A person in charge of personnel—whoever he may be— would pick the less tainted one, if he had to choose between you and someone else."

"Tainted?"

A strange word, Tagawa mused. While it has virtually no meaning in and of itself, its connotations are boundless. In the extremely limited context of bank parlance, moreover, the word has the power to define people's characters.

"I want you to do some good thinking," continued Koyanagi, "about the expression we hear all the time—'a typical banker.'"

A banker must be trustworthy and almost impartially serious, and at the same time must not have any idiosyncrasies. Koyanagi was asking Tagawa to fit himself into the assigned mold. One could not stay in the narrowly defined orbit of an executive without agreeing to conform to this standard.

Tagawa refrained from giving a straight answer just then. He asked Koyanagi to give him some time to make up his mind. Koyanagi patiently kept after him through the end of the year, going so far as to admonish, "This is your last chance to wipe out the stain you got at the Ikebukuro office."

In January of the following year, Yōko was transferred to the Sugamo office as part of an irregular rotation. The spurious reason given by the bank was that it would be easier for her to look after her father if she worked closer to her home. But in reality, the Sugamo office took her farther away from her apartment. There was no telling where she might be sent next.

Tagawa finally made up his mind and told Yōko in a letter that he probably would be married in the near future.

His marriage to Misako Oribe took place just as he was offered a promotion to chief clerk of the Business Department, First Section. The letter of promotion was dated May 1. It was truly ironic that Tagawa heard upon returning from his honeymoon that Yūkichi had died. Yōko's father had died after a year and several months' illness. The brain damage had made him as frightened of death as a child during the last hours of his life. So the report said.

Tagawa's first son was born, and his second, two years later. In the fourth year after his marriage to Misako, Tagawa was selected to be the deputy section chief of the Business Department. This gave Tagawa a clear sense of a successful future: he was definitely on the high-level executive track. The turn of events could very well be interpreted as a reward for marrying someone recommended by Business Department Manager Koyanagi.

It was about a year before he was appointed manager of N-Office—that is, in the seventh year after he moved from the Ikebukuro office back to the main office—when Tagawa heard about Yōko, the woman he had nearly forgotten. The occasion was Kōichi Aizawa's transfer from the Sugamo Branch Office to Tagawa's section. Tagawa sponsored a small welcome party for him.

"Sir, have you heard of a woman named Yōko Takigami?" asked Aizawa as an afterthought, when the conversation drifted to the topic of personnel.

"Yōko Takigami!" repeated Tagawa, taken aback. It was a name he had put out of his mind quite a while ago.

"I've heard that she has worked with you before, in the Ikebukuro office." Aizawa went on, with the easy smile of an ignorant bystander.

"We used to sit next to each other at the customer window. But that was when I was twenty-eight years old; seven years ago, I guess. How do you know her?"

"Because she's in the Sugamo office."

"In Sugamo? Is she still single?"

"Of course. Didn't you know?"

Oh, she hasn't married yet. Tagawa recalled his affectionate relationship with Yōko which never came to bear fruit.

"And how is she doing these days?"

"They say that she will be transferred to another office. It's because there's a problem."

"A problem?"

"Nothing serious, but we call her Miss Nymphomania in the Sugamo office."

At Tagawa's question, "Miss Nymphomania?" Aizawa nodded with an eloquent smile.

"To make a long story short, I think she wants to get married."

"That's understandable. She must be getting on in years. But what exactly do you mean by Miss Nymphomania?" The expression was new to Tagawa.

Two or three young clerks looked at each other and giggled.

"Haven't you heard, Sir? It's a type you often see among old maids. She'll be the first one to have a date with a newcomer to the office. Nobody who's been in the office for a while pays attention to her. From what I hear, women like her will even date men who talk to them at the teller's window, or call sight unseen over the phone. At least so they say."

Yōko!

Every year around April or May, Tagawa would notice couples comprised of what appeared to be experienced office women and newly employed company men. They were seen in such popular dating places as Chidorigafuchi and Yoyogi Olympic Park. The thought that Yōko— now twenty-eight years old—had become an expert in this role, worrying one minute over her peeling face powder and acting quite sophisticated the next, was disturbing. Worse yet, it was a scene of moral depravity, as Tagawa saw it.

"I wonder why she can't get married. She's a smart, polished woman."

"I don't know. She does strike you as a nice person when you talk with her. She is kind and thoroughly considerate to men. It's just that she occasionally acts licentious. Maybe people are turned off by something soiled about her."

"Soiled?"

"Betrayed and trampled on by many men, that kind of impression. . . ."

Tagawa found the word distasteful, but apparently this was the very word to describe the history of Yōko's relationships with men for the entire period following her separation from him. He felt guilty.

Of all places, Tagawa found Yōko in the N-Office to which he had moved with so much ambition. It was to the N-Office that she had been transferred from Sugamo.

"How are your children?" Yōko would ask casually when they

passed each other in hallways. But that was all. Tagawa invited her out once, but she smiled lightly and turned away.

V

It was Yōko Takigami who had disclosed the confidential information that could determine the fate of the bank . . . ! Tagawa fought the idea. But Yōko had been in charge of the long-term savings accounts and was familiar with the confidential large-account holders. Now that it was evident that she had had contact with Kikuo Saeki from the Daidō Bank, there was no room for further debate.

First, Tagawa thought of calling Yōko to his office, but in the end he couldn't bring himself to make the interrogation quite so official. So, he told Yōko over the telephone, "I have something to ask you about Kikuo Saeki. I think you know him."

Yōko's reaction was difficult to ascertain over the telephone, but after a moment's hesitation, she returned a short reply, "I see." Tagawa told her that he wanted to meet her in front of the department store by the west exit of Ikebukuro Station.

At 7 P.M., the appointed time, Yōko was standing in front of the iron grille of the closed department store. She wore bright lipstick.

"Shall we take a walk?" asked Tagawa.

Yōko nodded in agreement. Her face, which used to be round and chubby, had become angular, and her cheek bones protruded. Her skin looked strikingly rough in the neon light at dusk.

"It's been eight years since we walked like this the last time." Tagawa spoke warmly, turning back toward her.

"Mr. Tagawa, won't you be in trouble if someone sees you walking with a woman like me?" Yōko cast her glance slightly downward.

"Let's not talk that way. How about some food?"

". . . I'd rather drink."

"You drink?" Tagawa could only throw back the question. That evening eight years ago, when she so passionately proposed to him, Yōko had turned crimson after a glass of gin.

"Yes, that's the only way to . . ." Yōko gave a short petulant answer.

The honky-tonk shacks had been cleared away from the area in front of the west exit of the station, and there sprawled a wide street. Tagawa went to the bar district near north Ikebukuro and walked down one flight to a basement Suntory Bar. Yōko ordered whiskey on the rocks.

Watching her movements, Tagawa knew that he would have to keep cool about the problem. Yōko impatiently reached for the first glass that was brought to the table. In a way, this was the only thing she could do to avoid Tagawa's eyes.

"Do you hate me?" Tagawa started slowly. This, in fact, was the worst thing imaginable. Suppose it was proven that Yōko had leaked the confidential information out of her personal animosity against him; if she had intended to deprive him of his professional title, there was nothing he could report to the main office.

"If you are disgusted with me, I won't ask any more."

As Tagawa repeated the same sentence, Yōko burst into wild laughter.

"What's the matter?"

"Don't worry. I neither hate nor have a grudge against you. I was the one to ask you to break off the engagement."

"Then, am I right in saying that this is not revenge against me?" asked Tagawa cautiously.

Yōko took a king-size cigarette out of her pocketbook, held it in the corner of her mouth, and lit it with a lighter.

Tagawa's life had changed greatly in many respects after he married Misako, thereby getting on the executive track. But he realized that Yōko had changed even more, much more than he could imagine.

"Mr. Saeki . . . " Yōko began to talk, but smiled, and shrugged her shoulders slightly, "looks like Mr. Tagawa."

"Me?"

"Especially his physique. He is tall and thin and slightly hunchbacked."

"Are you going to marry him?"

"Why?"

"Aren't you?"

"He has a wife. I can't marry him." Yōko blew a puff of cigarette smoke at the blue lights overhead as she spoke.

Why does she wear such heavy makeup? Tagawa's eyes were fastened on Yōko.

Yōko lifted her eyes, challenging Tagawa's sympathetic gaze.

"You'll never understand why a woman goes out with a married man. But please stop looking at me as if you feel sorry for me."

Whatever may have come to her mind, Yōko abruptly placed her pocketbook on the table. "I'll show you the things I always carry with me." She opened the metal clasp with a dull click.

"Four handkerchieves. Do you know what I do with them? Men often forget to bring their handkerchieves, so I let them borrow mine. I tell them just to bring them back unwashed. Here are needles and thread. See? Not just black and white, I have navy blue, brown. . . . I have every kind from cotton thread to nylon thread. Three kinds of spare buttons. I mend all men's lost buttons and ripped clothes. I even keep an iron in my desk drawer at the office."

Poking around in her pocketbook, as a child searches in her toy box, Yōko started lining up all sorts of paraphernalia on the table. Then she took about ten one thousand yen notes out of her red leather wallet.

"Since young men spend a lot, their salaries don't tide them over till the next payday. I can at least help out with a little. But I never lend more than two thousand to one person. Because they'd stop coming to me as soon as the debt gets higher than they can pay back."

It was a strange scene: Yōko would put down her cigarette, pick up the glass, put the cigarette back in her mouth, and ransack her pocketbook.

"Say, shall I tell you something else? You know Mr. Kaneko who is getting married this fall? I introduced his fiancée to him. I used to go out with him until quite recently. Can you guess why I did that?"

"You've told me enough. Don't torture yourself any more."

"I'm used to it. It doesn't bother me. It was like this when I worked in Sugamo. While I'm going out with a young man, I'm always afraid that he may refuse to go out again, or may ask to call off the date that day. You won't understand what I mean. I feel desperate. So, just before I'm thrown out, I introduce the man to a young girl who is a good match for him. This way, I'm never totally thrown out. I can do without the pain of being abandoned. And later on, too, they may even go on seeing me once in a while."

Yōko's words were strangely dry. After a while, she carefully put back the thread, the needles, the handkerchieves, and the wallet which had been lying on the table.

"Laugh at me if you want to. But so much has happened. And I'm already twenty-nine years old. Nothing can change that. Mr. Saeki has been really nice to me. But, you see, there was nothing I could do for him. I was just wondering what I could do for him when he asked me for the list of confidential clients."

Tagawa felt a turbulent anger churning upward in his chest, a feeling diametrically opposed to the nonchalance with which Yōko told her tale. Did she have to go that far? Just because Saeki was nice to her, did she have to ruin herself by being taken advantage of, like a toy or a tool, by a middle-aged married man? Bastard! Our enemy has taken advantage of Yōko, a woman coveting men, starving for a chance to get married, full of weaknesses, and defenseless as a naked person. Tagawa could not tolerate even the idea that Saeki resembled him.

"Are you going to keep on seeing Saeki?" asked Tagawa, barely suppressing his boiling anger. He made up his mind to march into the Daidō Bank early tomorrow; he would uncover Saeki's cowardice, and bring back Yōko's list. Saeki would have to suffer the consequences as a banker as soon as it became known that he had used a woman—even if it had been done for the benefit of his bank. Banks try to stay out of trouble. This case smelled scandalous.

Yōko called a nearby waiter and ordered another drink without answering Tagawa. Simultaneously, the two people let out a sigh of despair.

". . . I suppose it won't work," said Yōko in a low voice. "A man's career ends when people start talking about him. It's the same in any bank, isn't it? No matter how hard I try to keep him, Mr. Saeki, in his turn, will start running away from me."

My situation was different; I didn't run away from her. Tagawa controlled his desire to speak. He realized that a man who had chosen to project the image of a model banker had no right to defend himself in front of a woman like Yōko. He lacked even the confidence to help Yōko, who had no prospects for the future. He even wondered if Kikuo Saeki, who had taken advantage of Yōko, was far more humane than he was.

"I'll get the list back. Please don't make an issue of it. I'm sure Mr. Saeki will understand that a scandal would be disadvantageous to him." Yōko talked with her head gradually dropping down.

Yōko was absent from work for two days. On the third day, a special delivery envelope from her arrived in Tagawa's office. The contents were a letter of resignation and the list of the confidential long-term savings account clients. In one corner, a single line had been scribbled, "Mr. Saeki went along with my request."

"What shall we do, Sir? Shall we mail Miss Takigami her retirement benefits?" Deputy Manager Nishiyama came to ask for Tagawa's advice. Yōko was probably still living in the Takinogawa apartment.

"Yes, please do."

"The electric iron in her drawer—we will send that back, too."

"An iron?"

"Yes, she used to press young men's shirts and things like that."

"We'd better not. That would be too heartless."

"Oh?"

"I'll keep it."

At Nishiyama's direction, one of the office girls brought Tagawa a rusty iron. Tagawa's hands responded to the feel of the cold iron and the peculiar weight of the lead inside. He carefully buried it deep in his bottom desk drawer.

Notes

This story was first published in a Japanese monthly magazine, *All Reading* (Ōru yomimono), January 1969. My translation of this story has been published in *Bulletin of Concerned Asian Scholars* 17, no. 3 (1985): 17–27; *Harper's Magazine* (June 1986): 27–28; and in *The Other Japan*, ed. E. Patricia Tsurumi (Armonk, N.Y.: M.E. Sharpe, 1988), 119–129. This is a translation of "Gin no seiiki" in *Nine Consecutive Hits* (Chūren pōton) (Tokyo: Kadokawa Bunko, 1984), 5–46.

1. Some recent Japanese novels use only initials for people's names and place names.

2. The exact year of the story time is not mentioned, but judging by the housing condition and the geographical setting in the story, the period is likely to be several years before the international exchange rate of $1 = ¥ 360 was altered in 1973.

3. Traditionally, a Japanese Mutual Bank used the system of mutual financing, wherein the members of the "bank" would pool funds, and some of them who were selected by drawing, for example, would have the privilege of borrowing from it. Nowadays, Mutual Banks are more like short-term financers.

4. Number "6" is written in Japanese as 六 ; number "9" as 九 .

5. The size of a tatami mat in the Tokyo area nowadays is 5.6 by 2.0 feet (1.7 by 0.88 meters) according to *Kodansha Encyclopedia of Japan*.

Kinjō the Corporate Bouncer

Saburō Shiroyama

I

"Aye!"

"Approved!"

"It's been decided unanimously that this bill . . . " shouted President Ohmura, tousling his gray hair. His voice was wiped out by the waves of yelling and did not reach Kinjō and Mamiya, two men sitting by the rear exit of the conference room. Kinjō always chose this spot in shareholders' meetings because it commanded a full view of the participants' backs. There were only a few empty seats.

The older man had jet black hair. No loose skin hung from his oval face, which was as firm as a wood carving. He looked perfectly handsome at a glance, but on closer look, his developed jaw revealed his inner strength. An old sword scar on the upper lid of his right eye glistened pink every time he blinked. The man had his arms folded. Newcomers to stock meetings felt uneasy sitting in front of this peculiar man.

The old man looked well advanced in years, yet full of vitality. While waiting for the meeting to start, the newcomers glanced at this man, being cautious at the same time not to look offensive. They became particularly curious when a stockholder or an acquaintance went close and whispered in his ear. Taking advantage of these occasions, they turned back to take a closer look.

That's Kinjō Naitō, doyen of sōkaiyas. He used to be called Killer Kinjō. He actually killed a man in a meeting. He cut the man with a Japanese sword. The blood splashed to the ceiling. . . .

Professional stockbrokers and sōkaiyas, who used the rear door, would bow slightly, or cast a friendly glance at Kinjō each time they walked by him. These professionals were receptive to Kinjō's request that greetings be made inconspicuously. Kinjō returned a nod in his usual posture of eyes slightly open and arms folded. He maintained this position from the time he sat down until he got up to leave. The proceedings were not worth staying awake. Agreements with forty, fifty, sometimes one hundred sōkaiyas were made prior to stockholders' meetings. Kinjō had even rehearsed scenarios with those sōkaiyas who had the potential to disrupt his plans by way of asking impertinent questions. Kinjō had sixty years' experience in this field. He was faultless in distributing alms and honorariums. No sōkaiya would venture to confront Kinjō even if unfairly treated. An actual shareholders' meeting, then, was no more than a ritual at which Kinjō monitored the flawlessness of his prearrangements. With his help, shareholders' meetings held by mammoth corporations—a several hundred million yen venture, a multi-billion yen venture, or one with forty or fifty thousand shareholders—were concluded in no time. The length of the session, the loudness of the applause, or the fluency of the chairman made some difference, but most meetings ended in several minutes or ten minutes at the most. The gains and losses of the company in the past half year were approved, amendments were passed, and the new board of directors of large corporations for the next several years was elected in that brief period of time. It was the continuous heckling by the sōkaiya, "No objections!" "Point of order!" and their imposing applause that forced the ritual ahead. There was no chance for timid stockholders to speak. Sōkaiyas were there to seal off questions, to say nothing of objections.

"The meeting is adjourned," the wavering voice of Ohmura, chairman of the assembly and president of the bank, echoed in the hall. A final burst of applause roared out. Mamiya impulsively looked at his watch: four minutes from the opening remarks. The brevity of this meeting hardly justified the anxiety felt by the attendants. The sōkaiyas got up. Some still clapped as they walked out of the hall. The acoustic vortex moved toward Kinjō.

"The meeting is over, Sir," Mamiya told Kinjō in a businesslike tone.

Kinjō, however, made no move to stand up. He opened his eyes slightly wider and watched the ebbing tide of people.

"It's over with no problem," whispered Mamiya once again. He meant to brighten Kinjō's spirit by adding, "with no problem," but Kinjō did not answer. His eyelids drooped under the weight of fatigue. Seen at close range, nearly eighty years of life were marked in the old sōkaiya's face. Mamiya stared at Kinjō to examine if the meeting had ravaged his old body, still convalescing from illness.

"With problems," a low but distinct voice came back. "Ohgiyama's men didn't show up," added Kinjō while Mamiya searched for the next word to say.

". . . But Izumi was here."

"By himself. He came just to check on us."

"Only to check on us?"

"Ohgiyama and his group played it easy this time, but they are scheming at something elsewhere." Kinjō's voice was calm but firm.

"What can it be?" asked Mamiya impatiently.

Kinjō smiled for the first time as he said, "You are a sōkaiya, too. Figure it out for yourself."

A wave of people breaking off from the crowd now surrounded Kinjō.

"I'm glad that things worked out well."

"It was worth making all your effort to be here, wasn't it?"

"The Ohgiyama camp seems to have chickened out."

Most of those who spoke with ease were the affiliates of securities companies. They seldom attended these meetings. Had the meeting lasted any longer, this cohort would have been the first to exclaim, "The Taiyō Bank is in trouble!" and to undermine its share prices.

Kinjō wanted to be left alone, but responded to these greeters with a show of pride that he deserved their compliments. Some sōkaiyas bowed wordlessly as they walked past. Amateur shareholders strolled out, disappointed by the unexpected brevity of the meeting. They had the look of having left something behind by mistake.

"Ladies and gentlemen, those who have not picked up a souvenir box, please stop at the reception table. . . ." The announcement came from a man to whom the chairman had turned over the microphone. Now, a fresh and pithy male voice compelled the lazily shuffling guests to move outside.

Attendants had anticipated that major shareholder Tomiaki Ohgiya-

ma's family would stir up a commotion at today's 59th regular shareholders' meeting.

Ohgiyama was the manager of a chain of recreation facilities including cabarets and skating arenas. No one knew his background before
World War II. All that was known was that he had made a mint during
the war by trucking blackmarket goods. After the war, he turned this
profit into Taiyō Bank shares. This being done, the big shareholder had
only to pressure the bank to finance his amusement industry.

Banks cower at shareholders' swashbuckling. Ohgiyama aimed for
this soft spot when he raised funds from the Taigin.[1] He was shrewd.
He took out 3.5 million yen[2] to start, 6 million yen next, and 8.5
million yen the third time around; the total of the three loans was 18
million yen. He made no gesture of paying back his loans after the first
or even the second due date. Instead, he went on to demand an additional loan of 10 million yen. Rumors started to flow: "Ohgiyama thinks
that money belongs to him once it is put in his pocket." The Taiyō Bank
was stirred into action. It demanded that Ohgiyama pay his debt and, at
the same time, tried to confiscate his deposit.

Ohgiyama maneuvered to reverse the charges. Claiming that the
bank gave out "reckless loans," he sued the delinquent board of directors. In this, he used his own "irresponsible loan" as an example of
sloppy management. Ohgiyama already held over three percent of the
bank's shares. These shares entitled him to appeal, in the name of
Commercial Law Article 237, to convene an emergency stockholders'
meeting. Upon the bank's refusal to convene a shareholders' special
meeting, he charged the bank with "managerial flaws," and brought
the case to a local court. It took clever maneuvering by the bank
lawyers to stamp out the suit. This was a matter of only a month ago.
Ohgiyama was outdone by the bank, but it was not beside the mark to
suspect that he would look for another chance. It was because of this
fear that Kinjō accepted Taigin President Ohmura's request to direct
the shareholders' meeting and dragged his aged and convalescing body
to the meeting.

Mamiya surveyed the people still dawdling in the hall. The majority
had gone out. Ohgiyama had not come to begin with. Mamiya had met
Ohgiyama only once, but his striking appearance was seared indelibly
on his mind. His physique was a contrast to Kinjō's. He was stubby,
slightly bent forward, and sallow faced. Loose folds of skin, drooping
from his cheeks to his jaws, were wrinkled in vertical lines around his
mouth. His broad face directly joined his torso. His small eyes were as

immobile as if welded in. Mamiya had heard that Ohgiyama had weak eyesight and was nearly blind. Partly because of this, the old man walked leaning on a young woman. The woman was in her twenties; she was perhaps the select beauty out of all the bars Ohgiyama patronized. The old man, in his grubby black kimono, only reached the woman's shoulders, as she wore high heels. Together, the pair resembled a wilted leaf clinging to a large white flower. Yet one glance was enough to tell that the flower was no heavier than a dewdrop, up against Ohgiyama's stubby body and heavy spirit.

One couldn't possibly miss Ohgiyama if he had come. His sons, hot tempered Tomio and Tomijirō, were also absent. Only sōkaiya Izumi, who was then employed by the Ohgiyama faction, had attended, but this gigantic sumō wrestler had already slipped out. What was the Ohgiyama family plotting to do? Pacing behind Kinjō, who finally got onto his feet, Mamiya kept looking back toward the conference hall, as if trying to sniff out the scent of Ohgiyama's cigarettes.

II

Kinjō broke out in a cold shiver after coming home from the general assembly and went straight to bed. He only poked twice at his dinner with his chopsticks. At seven o'clock, he said to his wife, Moto, who was sitting by his pillow, "Ohmura-san[3] is here; help me put on my half coat." A car had just come to a screeching halt in the darkness of the neighborhood, and it seemed that Kinjō had taken the sound to be President Ohmura's visit. Moto tilted her head quizzically, but got up without a word. By the time his lattice door was pushed open with a gentle sound, Kinjō had sat up on his bed and had put on his half coat with Moto's help. Mamiya had only to go to the entrance hall to find that Kinjō had guessed right. Probably because Ohmura was on his way home from the party to celebrate the successful stockholders' meeting, his cheeks were rosy and shiny.

"I'm truly grateful to you for today's success," said Ohmura jovially as he opened the sliding door to Kinjō's room. But he halted as if he had tripped over Kinjō's miserable condition.

"Gotten worse again?" asked Ohmura.

"He seems to have the chills," enjoined Moto.

"You should lie down. Mrs. Naitō, please have him lie down."

Kinjō brushed off Moto's hands, saying, "I'll suit myself after our business talk is over." He protested against his guest, who kept insisting that he lie down, and started talking in a slightly husky baritone voice about what he had mentioned to Mamiya after the assembly. The bank president's silver hair and the bright glow on his red cheeks gradually lost luster as he listened to Kinjō.

"What do you think Ohgiyama is doing?" said the president with a deep sigh.

"As I've told my research assistant," Kinjō continued without looking at Mamiya, "Ohgiyama will call for an emergency meeting."

"An emergency meeting?" "Another special meeting?" Mamiya and the president exclaimed in unison.

"But Ohgiyama has just missed the chance to convene a special meeting," protested Ohmura.

"That's over. That motion was based on Commercial Law Article 237. There's another way to summon a special assembly, right, Mamiya?"

Mamiya shook his head ambiguously.

"Commercial Law, Article 294." Prefacing his narration, Kinjō closed his eyes. "In cases where there is any cause to supect that there is a dishonest act or a grave fact in contravention of a law or ordinance or of the Articles of Incorporation in relation to the administration of the company's affairs, shareholders who hold shares representing not less than one-tenth of the total number of issued shares may apply to the Court for the appointment of an inspector whose duty shall be to examine the affairs of the company and the state of its property."[4]

"More than ten percent?" The president let out a gasp.

"Ohgiyama will open a frontal assault on the 'untrustworthy staff' in the coming special assembly." Kinjō put force into his voice. "The mere rumor that Ohgiyama would fight today has depressed the price of your stock. That's all they wanted. They must have frantically bought the devalued shares until the bitter end of the meeting."

The president put his chubby, womanlike hand on his forehead. He looked as if he were trying to find a weakness in Kinjō's foresight, which had never before proven faulty.

"We must closely watch the movement of the share prices." So saying, Mamiya found himself frightened by the vision of the old, semi-blind Ohgiyama walking toward him, surrounded by a dark gray mist.

Presently, the president looked up at Kinjō, as if devouring the other's face with his eyes.

"Even if he stores up shares, the court verdict must stay the same."

"There's no telling. You will do well to give your lawyer, Ishida, about one million yen."

Ishida was Taigin's company lawyer who had protected the bank from Ohgiyama in the previous meeting.

"I've already given Ishida-kun[5] half a million yen," replied the president immediately.

"I'm not talking about the payment for what he has done. This is a separate issue."

"Why give so much, then?"

"Don't temporize. Just give it to him," snapped Kinjō.

The president turned his eyes away from Kinjō. "We pay him eighty thousand yen monthly. Why more?"

"It's a giveaway, but a remunerative one."

The two men's eyes met again in silence.

"Maybe you need to rest," Moto intervened timidly. Mamiya seconded her suggestion.

Kinjō and the president would not stop staring at each other, but both soon burst into laughter. Outside, the nipping winter wind, which had blasted all day long, calmed down. The laughter of the two old men pierced through the strangely silent air.

Their laughter took a load off Mamiya's mind. While revelling in it, nevertheless, Mamiya thought that he heard another laugh reverberating in the distant air of the night. This laughter was too cracked to be a voice. It sounded like Ohgiyama's. In an effort to rid himself of the auditory hallucination, Mamiya glared at Kinjō. Kinjō was now shaking, not from the laughter, but from chills. Alarmed, Mamiya asked for Moto's helping hand and lay Kinjō down on his bed.

The two old men reentered their camaraderie of sixty years ago. Their first encounter had been in a dark accounting room of a bank, which had once been a drug store. They had argued over interest terms. Ohmura as a bank clerk, and Kinjō as a cloth shop clerk; both wore aprons. Soon afterward, Kinjō quarreled with an older clerk in his shop. He then started hanging around with a reporter from a communist newspaper, who had covered the dispute. And before long he drifted into the thorny paths of the racketeer news reporter, a social ruffian, and so-called untaxed, jobless, modern yakuza.[6] He was also imprisoned numerous times.

"You may decide to go back to your dungeon, but for heaven's sake, please stay away from the illness," joked the president.

"Even the dungeon would not take this body. If anywhere, it would be to the ultimate dark place that I'll be going."

"Enough pranks, friend. Just look after yourself. I still need your vigilance. This is the age for a man like Ohgiyama. I want you to watch over our stockholders' meetings for a long while more."

"I've run out of gas. I want you to call today's meeting my last."

Having made sure that the conversation was running smoothly, Moto stood up to prepare tea.

Silently watching Moto leave the room, the president kept Mamiya in his seat with his stare, and put his lips next to Kinjō's ear.

"I hear that your daughter, Miwako-san, came to our Fukuoka office."

"Miwako?" Kinjō lifted his head from the pillow momentarily. "I wonder what she is . . ." He noticed Mamiya, and held back his words. Mamiya and Miwako had been fond of each other some time ago. Kinjō had planned for them to marry. But Miwako fell in love with a married man with children while she studied at a women's college in Tokyo. She made the man divorce his wife so that she could marry him. Kinjō disowned Miwako at that time.

"Apparently she remarried in Fukuoka."

Miwako had recently left the man she had loved so profoundly, and moved in with a medical practitioner in Fukuoka. The president had tried to touch on this lightly, but the mention of Miwako opened Kinjō's old wound.

"I'm sorry. . . ." Kinjō kowtowed to no one in particular. Then, as though he had trouble expelling the black clouds from his mind, he said, "I hope she didn't make an unreasonable request?"

"No, not at all. On the contrary, she came to put money in our bank. I hear that she asked after you. She is your only daughter, after all."

Miwako was born of a geisha named Miwa, past Kinjō's middle years. She was raised as his only child after Kinjō's son with Moto died in the war.

"Bloody beast!" Kinjō grumbled, burying his face in his pillow.

"A bloody beast is one like Ohgiyama. Miwako-san is far from one. She is just practical-minded. She gets rid of the man she is tired of, and joins the one she likes. No fooling around. She has your temper, I might say," continued the president, trying to smooth out the rough edges.

"I'm not talking about her personality. I'm worried about her innocent child who is made to suffer." Kinjō opened his eyes, and opened them wider still, as if he had spotted something wrong in the ceiling.

The president's face had regained its color while he talked about

Miwako. Idle talk made him increasingly eloquent, and Kinjō turned taciturn, partly because of his condition. Yet, when the president got up to leave, Kinjō raised himself on his elbows and repeated in a business-like tone, "Let me remind you once more, just to make sure."

The president gave a wry smile, and pulled out a leather-covered notebook to hide his expression. A sense of reprieve brought by the safely ended stockholders' meeting revisited him in the form of luke-warm contentment. His eyes, still drifting with intoxication, gleamed as if he were teasing a child.

"Pay attention to the ups and downs of share prices, so that you won't be cornered," ordered Kinjō, carefully choosing his words. His eyes were fixed on the president's.

"Give Lawyer Ishida one million yen. All right?" Kinjō under-scored this to the president, who had opened his notebook but wrote nothing. "A resident lawyer has all sorts of information about a com-pany. He can easily turn the information into cash and reverse judicial verdicts. He is a dangerous friend. You know that, don't you?"

The president nodded lordly. Kinjō's sharp stare did not waver as he added, "And please spare me another meeting."

III

Kinjō had undergone a pylorostenosis operation several years before. Since then, his atrophied body hadn't kept up with his mental vivacity. Dapper by nature, he used to change clothes as many as three times a day, keep a small bottle of perfume in his pocket, and dye his hair every morning. He had defied old age by refraining from smoking or drink-ing. At parties, which he was obliged to attend, he had drunk tea in a sake cup. In spite of all these precautions, Kinjō had paid a heavy toll for the operation undertaken at his advanced age. The dammed up senility burst out to destroy him. The stockholders' meeting he attend-ed after a long absence did additional harm to his health. The heavy sound in his chest lingered after the chills went away. Varieties of breathing problems attacked him. When he was in his mid-thirties, Kinjō had been imprisoned in the serious offense prison in Abashiri, Hokkaidō, for nearly ten years and had contracted tuberculosis there. The symptoms had returned.

Kinjō's doctor forbade outings. On days when he felt good, Kinjō walked back and forth, swinging his arms in the house, which was a small 320 square feet. The house was located halfway up a hill, and from the guest room window adjacent to the entrance hall, Kinjō could see the sacred dome of the Shinmei Shrine atop the hill and over the defoliated treetops. On rainy days, beggars crouched together at the shrine. Every time Kinjō spotted a certain beggar with a child, he had sent Moto with a one hundred yen note. "Tell her to go home right away."

The beggar woman got the taste of this, and made a habit of coming there, but Kinjō didn't mind. He kept on giving money, each time saying, "This is for that poor kid." Kinjō watched from his window, even after Moto had given the money, until the beggar had walked out of sight. If the woman was not seen for some days, he kept peeking out the window, mumbling, "I wonder if the kid has gotten sick." As Kinjō had developed a habit of getting up in the middle of a conversation to walk up to the window, Mamiya came to see another side of the veteran sōkaiya.

Mamiya was Kinjō's direct disciple. When healthy, Kinjō was seen in the sōkaiyas' hangouts in company boardrooms and hotel lobbies. There, the senior sōkaiya struck Mamiya as stiflingly severe and heartless. Kinjō had a chic appearance—apart from the sword scar on his eyelid—but there was no telling when he might just whip out a sword to slash a person in one blow. Such a menacing air came both from his sixty years' experience, including crimes of various kinds—like the offense of "contempt of government officials"—and from his verve and disposition which intensified by the year.

Fresh in Mamiya's memory was the scene of the N-Electric Company special meeting. There, Kinjō challenged Kiyoemon Ienaga, chairman of the N-Electric Company and a man of influence in Japan's financial circles. He demanded that Ienaga convene a special meeting to explain his company's management. Kinjō's point was that the company's staff bonus amounted to a hundredth of its gross income, while the rule book specified it to be a hundredth of its net profit. The company agreed to hold the special meeting, confident that it would suffer no harm beyond minor embarrassment; even at the worst, the volume of voices raised by its widely sought after and patronized sōkaiyas would take care of Kinjō. But Kinjō did not give in. On the day of the meeting, Kinjō spoke for over thirty minutes. He paid no attention to the sōkaiyas jeering "Obstruction of proceedings!" In the end, the floor, including the amateur stockholders, boiled over with applause for Kinjō. The company's last resort was to use its prerogative as the majority stockholder. But Kinjō walked straight up to the chairman's seat and put in front of Ienaga a bundle of half a million blank letters of proxy. The company representatives shrank back. Excited shareholders took over the chairman's seat. Kinjō won the case, but the payoff for the victory was imprisonment. He was indicted as a black-mailer and was put in Hamamatsu Old People's Prison for fourteen months. This was the last imprisonment of a man who did not know how to compromise. Since then, a strange friendship had developed between Kinjō and Ienaga. It was the bond of two nonconformists who didn't even know what compromise meant. The incident was the foun-dation for Kinjō's unshakable reputation.

Kinjō wasn't tightfisted when it came to financial matters. He was unlike some sōkaiyas at his age who had saved up over one hundred million yen, or who sent their sons to schools in France. He never tried to buy shares of more than a few companies which were familiar to him, although it was very easy for sōkaiyas to earn an honorarium simply by paying courtesy visits to the patron companies. To Mamiya, Kinjō's world was enclosed in darkness, impossible for him to enter. Only once did the interior of Kinjō's world come into Mamiya's view—when Mamiya and Miwako became very close to each other. At that time, Kinjō became uncomfortably tender towards Mamiya. But Miwako's flight brought the tenderness to an abrupt standstill.

Kinjō cleared his throat and walked away from the window. He took some steps behind the sofa, but returned to the window, as if something had come back to his mind. He had a difficult time getting away from the beggar child. Mamiya lit his second cigarette and stared at the old man's angular back. Kinjō's history, which had been unfolded by Moto, now engulfed Kinjō. Moto's favorite saying was, "I know nothing about my husband before he was thirty." This was true. Kinjō was born to a branch house of the Mitsui family in Osaka, but he had no recollection of his father. By adolescence, he had been separated from his mother also, and was raised by his grandparents. He was a short-tempered child and had a speech impairment until he was nearly six years old. This was all Moto and Mamiya knew about Kinjō's child-hood. This forlorn past added another page to Kinjō's legendry. Sepa-rated from the present by a long span of time, the legend sparked like phosphorescent lights. But Kinjō's childhood was, really, a bygone past. It merely rumbled in the distance. In front of Mamiya, Kinjō was quite another person, nothing more than an old man frantically trying to breathe life back into his desiccated past. A mixed sympathy welled up in Mamiya's mind: weren't "Kinjō the killer" and "the patriarch of sōkaiyas'' only cursory masks, and hadn't Kinjō truly been born starving for familial affection?

"Is the bank's share price moving?" asked Kinjō, returning to the couch, his eyes still narrowed.

"Not in the slightest. No fresh buying or selling."

"That's odd." Kinjō tilted his head. His beard was closely shaved. His hair, dyed black as usual, was neatly combed. Nothing hinted that he was ill, apart from his swollen eyelids and dry voice.

"It's true that bank shares never move fast, but . . . ," said Mamiya glumly, recalling the convulsive change of share prices during the last shareholders' meeting and the subsequent doldrums caused by Ohgiyama's bulk purchase.

"I wonder if Ohgiyama has given up the idea of buying more; or has he gotten the ten percent shares already?" asked Mamiya.

"I bet he hasn't. He may have 900,000 or one million shares at the most."

"Four hundred thousand more will make it ten percent. Do you think Ohgiyama can find enough sellers?"

"Corporations won't release theirs. If anyone, it will be small shareholders who will sell, but the problem is that there are too many small shareholders. Only one person in Tokyo has disposable shares in a block of 100,000. It's Ienaga-san."

"Ienaga-san?" The dramatic scene of the N-Electric Company special meeting flickered before Mamiya's eyes.

"But Ienaga-san won't sell," added Kinjō resolutely.

Mamiya was aware that Ienaga was one of the largest shareholders of the Taiyō Bank, but Kinjō's optimism made him worry.

"Shall I feel him out?" asked Mamiya tentatively.

"You don't have to," answered Kinjō in a deep voice.

Mamiya didn't say another word. There was the sound of Moto preparing supper for the old man and herself. Icy rain began to fall again. Blackened leaves that were stuck onto the windowpane fell off. In their place, white trickles of rain streamed down. Kinjō noticed the change of weather, and got ready to stand up.

"This cold weather must be getting the share prices, too." This was a hard-to-come-by joke of Kinjō's. But Mamiya could not laugh because he knew that Kinjō was really concerned about the beggar child. He dropped his gaze to his cigarette fire. Violet-colored smoke split the old sōkaiya's face in two and rose straight up.

"By God!" Kinjō suddenly slapped his thigh. Mamiya's cigarette smoke wavered and the ashes fell. "The bank employees must be selling their shares!"

Mamiya telephoned the bank immediately, only to find that President Ohmura, regular executives, and the chief of secretaries had all gone home.

"Taigin sells its shares to employees. The bank subsidizes them. So, the employee shares are transferable below the officially quoted price, and also inconspicuously. I bet Ohgiyama is sponging those shares," Kinjō said, resting at each breath. He abruptly reviewed his own words and questioned, "But who gave him the idea?"

"Izumi, perhaps?" Izumi, who is patronized by Ohgiyama, used to be a sōkaiya subordinate to Kinjō.

"He's big only in body. He doesn't have a brain to match."

"Who would it be, then?"

"I can guess."

"Who is it?"

Without answering, Kinjō folded his arms and uttered, "It's going to be a mess. A special meeting can't be avoided."

IV

Kinjō's ominous foresight hit the mark. The Ohgiyama faction had bought 400,000 employee shares and secured ten percent of the bank's total stock. For the second time, the entrepreneur appealed to the local court to convene a special session on the ground that the bank's management was fraudulent.

The bank was flustered. But while being frustrated, it nurtured the optimistic conviction that the case would never develop into an actual stockholders' meeting. The bank's recent victory in the shareholders' meeting had given it self-confidence. When the chief secretary of the bank visited Kinjō with such optimism, Kinjō made a point of reminding him that the bank must pay Lawyer Ishida a competitive bribe, and if possible, also pay Ohgiyama's lawyer Minami. The chief secretary retorted that the bank had already given Ishida one million yen, but Kinjō saw him off with searching eyes and asked, "Honestly?"

"No way out for us. A special meeting will be called," Kinjō told Mamiya.

"Why, sir? " asked Mamiya in surprise. So far, he was going along with the bank's optimism.

"The man who instructed Ohgiyama to load up on the employees' shares has an insider's knowledge about the bank. He can point out any number of weaknesses the bank has, if he wants to." Kinjō's vulture-like eyes, with flabby bags hanging below, expressed resignation.

Mamiya did not have to ask the name of the man. He moaned, "Lawyer Ishida, of all people . . ."

"My suspicion is that the bank hasn't paid Ishida the million yen. That's why the chief secretary, instead of the president himself, came to see me. Ohmura and I have been friends for over sixty years by now, but he must feel that there's no need for a bank president to do everything a sōkaiya tells him to do," said Kinjō. "Another stockholders' meeting . . . I suppose I will have to attend. I owe Ohmura for looking after Miwako," he mused.

For four years after World War II, Miwako had commuted to a woman's college from President Ohmura's Tokyo house.

"I suppose a sōkaiya can never forgo a stockholders' meeting," smiled Kinjō, screwing up his deathly pale mouth. A series of dry, cold days promised no improvement in his condition.

Inspectors were sent to the bank from the court, and the verdict was given ten days later. Ohgiyama won the court case against the bank, just as Kinjō had feared. The court summoned a shareholders' special meeting at Ohgiyama's request.

"To tell you the truth, we haven't paid Ishida-kun one million yen," said President Ohmura when he visited Kinjō shortly after the court verdict was issued. He combed his well-groomed silver hair with his fingers. "I gave him only 300,000 yen in cash, in addition to the cancellation of the 650,000 yen loan he made when he built his law office."

"I thought even one million was on the stingy side. . . ," said Kinjō, disappointed. "Ohgiyama must have given him at least two million."

"Two million?" uttered Mamiya in a surprised voice. It occurred to him that a lawyer was a grotesque mite.

But then he realized that a sōkaiya is a mite, too, himself included. Kinjō is one as well. There may be differences in expertise and potency, but they all suck on the dark blood of society. Every large company has several or scores of mites nestling in it. Their sole mission is to bluster threateningly at the biannual shareholders' meetings. These leisurely bodies, who have no registered jobs or tax responsibilities, mill around the secretarial zones of companies. They live on unrecorded funds. Bigger mites than the sōkaiyas are the companies' lawyers and certified accountants. Unsatiated with clear blood, they go after a quantity of dark blood. Industries and the mites fatten each other. Banks, department stores, and manufacturers are ravaged below their white outfits by mites of all sizes sucking away their dark blood. The carapaces of those mites glittered golden green in Mamiya's vision. They were swollen and round with human blood.

Kinjō and the president started making plans for the stockholders' meeting, and Mamiya took notes.

First, the list of stockholders had to be examined. Properly speaking, Ohgiyama's group hardly had the resources to defy corporations as majority shareholders. But proxy votes and the mood of the session could very well change the wind. The temperament of a shareholders' meeting is fickle. This fickleness is the breeding ground for sōkaiyas' work. One way to avoid a perilous turn of affairs was to deny Ohgiyama a chance to speak, refuse to allow him to take the lead.

President Ohmura began paying frequent visits to Kinjō again. Board executives and the chief secretary tirelessly commuted for thoroughgoing preparations. Now that the critical battlefield had moved to the shareholders' meeting, the bank had no alternative but to entrust the entire matter to Kinjō.

Mamiya summoned leading sōkaiyas by Kinjō's order. They were the familiar four, known as "Kinjō's Four Devas,"[7] full-fledged authorities. Various others also came one after another to Kinjō's bedroom—faultfinders, influentials, a failed reporter, failed politician, dropout policeman, former boxer, former monk, and part-time sōkaiyas. As he faced them, Kinjō's smooth scar suddenly glowed. A network to flush out practically all the so-called sōkaiyas was gradually knit together at this stage of the game. The only one left out was Izumi, Ohgiyama's sōkaiya.

"The only way to get back a man who's been bought for money is to buy him back."

After Kinjō talked the Taigin into giving Izumi 200,000 yen, Mamiya went to see Izumi with the ex-boxer. Izumi was caught as he came out of a cabaret. He accepted the bribe, his large body oscillating in embarrassment. He lacked the courage to stand up against the battalion of Kinjō's colleagues. It also looked as though he had not received a good sum from Ohgiyama lately.

Catching a chance to speak in a shareholders' meeting is not an easy game to play. Timing and courage are critical. Supposing that Ohgiyama was importunate and his sons untempered, how well could they make use of their chances? Kinjō engineered a plan to debilitate the Ohgiyama camp in the meeting summoned by Ohgiyama himself. But it would be better yet if he could destroy the Ohgiyama family altogether. He took it to be a stroke of luck that the single agendum of the meeting was pointed at the Ohgiyama group. Kinjō would turn the tables on them. He would make a motion to reclaim instantly Ohgiyama's shares and let the bank seize his security deposit as part of the bank shareholders' resolution.

"This is what they call bringing good out of evil." Kinjō looked up at the president and laughed silently. Had he been healthy, he would have patted the president on the back. But for now, only his eyes glinted mischievously above his sunken cheeks.

The Taigin lent a hand this time. It did not skimp on its budget for bribing Lawyer Minami of the Ohgiyama camp. The one million yen bribe and Minami's help shaped up a detailed list of Ohgiyama's security deposit. Part of the deposit was traced from an "off-the-record" document, which had been drawn up earlier by the bank under pressure from Ohgiyama. All worked covertly towards the goal of ultimately confiscating all of the deposit the instant the mood of the floor shifted.

The New Year arrived with a heavy traffic of visitors bustling in and out of Kinjō's bedroom. Kinjō turned seventy-eight years old. Visitors were many, but the only relative to share Kinjō's New Year was his old wife. It was a lonely New Year. The date of the special assembly was set for February fifth. Kinjō's preparation was at its final stage of polishing. As might be expected, fatigue caught up with him. He hardly got out of bed. Still, every so often, he asked his wife and Mamiya about the beggar's child.

From mid-January, after the first snow, piercing cold weather persisted, as if to make up for the earlier warm days. The ground and the cement floor of the sanctuary at the Shinmei Shrine froze. The beggars did not return. Even Mamiya missed them. Mamiya was another person who had fallen into the habit of giving some money to the beggar child every time he passed him. He could not quite afford to give a hundred yen as Kinjō did, but because ten yen was too little, he compromised with fifty.

One day, he was descending the Shinmei Shrine slope, toying with the silver coins in his pocket, when he heard a smothered shriek and the crash of breaking glass. It was as if he had lost his balance, not so much because of the two sounds' volume as by their impact. While running down the slope toward Kinjō's house, his eyes still kept checking the shrine precinct. He was appalled for the second time when he looked ahead at the house. There in the entrance hall, with its glass doors wide open, stood a white and stern-faced Kinjō. He held onto a walking stick. A shadow leaped out of the house and ran up the hill toward Mamiya. Mamiya's body impulsively turned toward the shadow. He had already decided that the shadow was Ohgiyama's man, or Ohgiyama's swashbuckling son, but there was no time to take a second look. As he pulled his chin down and tried to bump into it, the shadow cried out, "Oh, it's you, Mamiya-san."

Mamiya stopped, stumbling on his own feet. Because of its height and dark coat, Mamiya had thought the figure was a man.

"How are you?" The woman passed before his eyes, and then halted with a stiff smile. Mamiya's eyes lost focus, stupefied by the shock. They could not capture the image. Mamiya wondered if the woman was Ohgiyama's mistress. Only her brazen smile filled his eyes.

"How are you?" It was Miwako's voice. Her friendly smile tempered the severe expression she had inherited from Kinjō. Mamiya's mind was dragged back to many years ago, and was drawn toward Miwako's image standing almost contemptuously before him.

"I came all the way. . . but my father . . ." She looked away from Mamiya, and her expression became strained again. Mamiya also sensed behind him an oppressive cloud surging from the direction of Kinjō's house.

"Well, see you." Miwako cracked another smile, and walked off in long strides, nearly running. She moved with agility, as if not minding in the least the long trip from the southern end of Japan or the futility of her first visit in several years. Mamiya was left behind without having returned a single word to Miwako.

Miwako had accompanied her husband on a business trip from Kyūshū. She parted with him in Osaka, and continued on her way to see Kinjō. She did this in response to Moto's secret letter about Kinjō's condition. This was the sixth year since she had upset Kinjō by marrying a man with a wife and children. All she had sent home in those years were printed New Year's cards and a wedding announcement.

Kinjō had been lying in bed. The moment he heard that Miwako had come, he kicked back his quilts, got up, and stood at the threshold of the entrance hall. Moto was shocked to learn that this explosive force came out of anger, not from joy. But before she could mediate, a storming voice came booming down.

"You've gone with another man!"

"Yes, I did," answered Miwako, looking defiantly at Kinjō.

"What did you do with your child?"

"I left the older two with their father, and my Kenzō, too."

"Left him there?" Kinjō stepped forward. The older two children belonged to the woman who was chased away by Miwako. Kenzō was Miwako's son and Kinjō's single grandchild whom he hadn't seen.

"He won't let me have him. He thinks I'll come back if he keeps Kenzō."

"Haven't you got any feelings for Kenzō?" Blue arteries popped up on Kinjō's face and on his clenched fists.

"Also, my new husband doesn't want a child because of his job. I can't help it. It doesn't make sense to let a mere child spoil my life."

"Fool!" Kinjō's voice ended abruptly. Only his jawbones clattered. "Think of the boy!"

"Children grow strong on their own when they don't have parents. You are a good example."

"You don't even know what I had to put up with." Kinjō's sharp voice cut in.

"Please, dear, and Miwako, too! You can talk about that later." Moto finally joined in, but the man and his daughter ignored her.

"I don't care how you go wrong, but you've got to take care of your child," continued Kinjō, and softened the tone of his voice. "Miwako, go back, go back to Kenzō and the other children."

"Go to bed, Father. Aren't you sick?" Miwako's voice was cold and repulsive. "I came all the way from Fukuoka. It's four already. I was on the train for sixteen hours straight. You don't even. . . ."

"What did you come here for? Who wants to see a woman who has no feeling for her own child?"

"I don't care. I'm just being my own boss."

Kinjō stepped down from the elevated floor.[8] His bony hand reached for a walking stick.

"Get out of here! You!"

"I'm going! Who do you think you are? All you talk about is the child. Why don't you start a nursery school? A sōkaiya nursery school! I'm sure you'd get tons of active devils there."

Kinjō's cane split the air, and lunged at Miwako. Miwako barely dodged it. Kinjō lifted it again. This was new to Moto. Things were happening in another world, as if they were somebody else's problems. She saw "Killer Kinjō" with her own eyes for the first time.

The second blow smashed the latticework glass into pieces.

Mamiya heard all about this from Moto after the fact. Her lips still quivering, Moto stiffened her large body as she reported, "I thought I'd be killed if I tried to protect Miwako."

Kinjō was back in bed. His face was colorless, and the arteries stood out around his temples. His shoulders lurched with each breath. Mamiya wondered what would be the best thing to say.

"Ienaga-san sent me a letter of attorney with regard to Taigin's shares." Kinjō's voice was even and tranquil, and his eyes were fixed on the space above him. "He must still remember the time when I gave him a hard time with proxy ballots. He shows friendship in a sarcastic way. But we probably will not need letters of attorney. We'll crush Ohgiyama right from the beginning. By the way . . ."

Kinjō slowly turned his face toward Mamiya. He meant to ask how far along the preparations had come.

Just then, tumultuous footsteps resonated outside. Mamiya impulsively leaped to his feet, believing that Miwako had come back. But the noise was wilder. Several people were stamping their feet. Some seemed to wear wooden clogs. A shoe kicked the outside wall with a humbling thump while a low male voice shouted, "Back down, Kinjō!"

"Back down!" "Don't meddle in Taigin's business!" The voices piled on top of one another. Together with the stamping noise, they shook the air of the room.

Kinjō called Mamiya back, "Let them be. They are no better than school children." The old man had a smile on his face.

"But . . ." Mamiya was afraid that the vibrations from the uproar might widen the cracks of the already smashed glass door of the entrance hall. Moto must be cowering; there was no sound from her kitchen.

"They must be really desperate," Kinjō said.

"They must not have collected enough proxy letters." Mamiya restored his smile. The major shareholders' letters of attorney had already gone to Taigin. "And, because they can't depend on Izumi alone, they are trying to bribe other sōkaiyas just as fast as they can. Of course, nobody pays attention to them." Mamiya expressed more confidence than he actually had.

There was no guarantee that a handsome bribe from Ohgiyama would not buy the minds of some sōkaiyas. The "Killer Kinjō" reputation still existed, but that very Kinjō was hopelessly ill.

"Everyone has promised not to sell himself, as long as Kinjō-san is alive," added Mamiya, with a wish to buck himself up, but he was taken aback by his own words. He blamed himself for having said the ominous word. It was true that Kinjō's life was draining away like water disappearing in the sand. These days, the doctor would not allow Kinjō to walk in the house, let alone outdoors. The doctor's interdiction did not discourage Kinjō from attending the upcoming shareholders' meeting, however. The reason was his friendship with President Ohmura and his sense of indebtedness to him with respect to Miwako. Besides, Kinjō seemed to have a kind of obsession with this case. His conviction that a sōkaiya must not give up a case once he had taken it up gnawed at his fatally beaten body.

"This is my last shareholders' meeting. I shall not let them betray me," said Kinjō in a firm low voice. His eyes had been shut for some time. Behind his eyelids, he must have been greeting each and every face of the more than one hundred sōkaiyas.

The noise outside went away, as if it had been absorbed by the sky. Mamiya went to the living room window. Three shadows of different sizes were climbing up the Shinmei Shrine hill. The middle one, as heavy-set as Ohgiyama himself, looked like one of Ohgiyama's sons. On either side of him walked genuine yakuza-like tall men with angular shoulders. The yakuza nature showed in the way they walked, stooping their shoulders forward.

V

The night before the special assembly, Kinjō took a bath for the first time in a long while. He had Moto help him wash his hair. Preparations for the meeting were complete. Sōkaiyas had stopped visiting him. It was a peaceful night for the old couple. There was no wind. It was so calm that one could almost hear the sound of the snow freezing. Kinjō sat on his bed, bundled up in a quilted jacket, and drank the tea Moto had prepared. Moto could hear the tea pass through his dried throat. Luster came back to his cheeks for a change, and his spirits were high.

Moto examined Kinjō's expression from the bottom of his face to the top, and started talking.

"Are you still determined to go to the meeting tomorrow?" Her palms pressed hard on her lap. She was well prepared to be yelled at. There was no answer from Kinjō. Moto went on, almost closing her eyes, "The doctor says that he will not take responsibility for your health if you go."

What are you saying, at this stage of the game? Moto's own voice scolded her. Defeated by this voice, she added, "Maybe I should go with you."

"Don't talk nonsense. Only shareholders can go there." Kinjō spoke for the first time. His voice was gentle.

"But maybe I can, as a sick person's attendant. . . ." Moto tried to cling to Kinjō with these words. "This is an emergency. Everyone is concerned about your health."

"I'm not going as a sick man, you know," retorted Kinjō without looking at Moto. His words were gentle but weighty for her.

There was a sound of clogs from behind the Shinmei Shrine. The faint, distant sound, gently splitting the night-fallen air, spoke of the firmness of the frozen snow. Moto added charcoal to the brazier. Red fire sputtered and sparkled on the ashes. The couple's eyes met while following the path of the little fire. Without budging, Moto spoke a bit louder.

"You are just directing others, aren't you? Please don't say anything in the meeting." An uproar was expected at the meeting. One big speech, she was afraid, might wear him out.

"Give me more tea." Kinjō did not answer her.

Moto hadn't noticed that Kinjō's cup was empty. She got up, replying happily that this was the first time since he took to bed that Kinjō had had a second cup of the tea he used to drink so much of.

"I wonder how that beggar child is doing," Kinjō said, looking up at Moto.

"Yes, indeed. It's awfully cold."

Behind his languid eyelids, Kinjō's eyes stared at distant space. They were not focused on anything.

Whenever my husband talks about the beggar child, his mind seems to join his own grandson Kenzō, a child as unfortunate as he. Moto then decided to speak out about something she had kept in her mind for some time. "Shall we adopt Miwako's child?"

"Kenzō?" Kinjō looked surprised, but Moto could tell that this was just a put on expression.

"Now that Miwako has gotten married, the idea of keeping Kenzō as a hostage has no meaning. I'm sure Miwako's ex-husband will let him go, if we insist. I'll be his mother in Miwako's stead."

"Yes, but . . ." Kinjō hesitated.

Moto interpreted the equivocation to be Kinjō's consideration for her, for Moto was not Miwako's biological mother.

"A grandchild will cheer me up, and you, too," she said merrily. She hoped to free her husband's single-track mind from shareholders' meetings by having Miwako, or at least Kenzō, in the house.

"Don't mention Kenzō." Having said this much, Kinjō folded his arms and closed his eyes.

"No, never again." Moto responded submissively, sympathizing with Kinjō. Her biggest concern was for Kinjō's health, not for her grandson. "Please take it easy tomorrow. And please take care of yourself."

Kinjō remained silent.

"Spring is coming soon. Let's go see cherry blossoms in Hamamatsu in the spring."

"In Hamamatsu?" Kinjō looked back at Moto, puzzled.

"Yes, in Hamamatsu. When I went to see you at the old people's jail for the first time, I saw cherry blossoms on the banks of the small stream there. The embankment was in the middle of a black paddy field. It wasn't a place for people to come for flower viewing. I walked along the bank and watched each cherry tree very closely." Moto spoke as if she missed the empty feeling she had harbored then. That was shortly after Miwako started living with the married man and had given birth to Kinjō's first grandson, Kenzō. Although Kinjō was upset about Miwako's decision, he had Moto send toys and other things in her name. The first thing Kinjō would inquire about from the other side of the metal fence of the jail was his grandson. Miwako did not write to her parents, other than telegram-like post cards which acknowledged receipt of the toys. Moto used to make up stories about Kenzō, recalling the infancy of her own child who was killed in World War II. Because she worried about Kinjō's health at the advanced age of over seventy, a year and two months' imprisonment felt like several years. She prepared a new story about Kenzō every three months when the permission to see Kinjō arrived.

The river in which naked children had once swum soon froze over, and now the next round of cherry flowers blossomed. Walking along the bank, she pondered over how ill-fated her husband was. His prosecutor was Mr. Ienaga. There were numerous opportunities for compromise, but Kinjō had chosen a head-on collision with the big gun.

Moto looked at the sliding closet door behind Kinjō, as if to review the nightmare. Handouts were hidden there just before the arrest. They were waiting to be distributed. Moto and her husband had burned them in a hurry to erase all the material evidence of the blackmail of Ienaga, but a single piece remained crumpled up in the corner of the closet. Certainly, the handout discovered by the police was not the only determinant of Kinjō's imprisonment, but Moto could not help feeling that the particular sheet of paper carried a curse. Heaven only knew whose curse it was, other than that of the man who was knifed by Kinjō.[9]

Moto was used to raids while young, but she never dreamed that she would have to go through one past the age of seventy. She couldn't believe that Kinjō had the boisterousness to fight at the risk of imprisonment after he had established himself as a member in good standing among the old-timers. She felt that she had been betrayed by Kinjō's countenance which had grown progressively dignified.

Kinjō took a long time emptying his second cup of tea, and spoke as if he had read her mind, "I've given you a hard time. But I can't picture myself staying in the old man's prison ever again."

Kinjō's smile filled Moto's eyes and became blurred. Moto tried to make her hot eyes smile.

"I wish I could get in there once more." Kinjō spoke to her smiling face. His words did not sound altogether playful.

"Oh, come on!"

"Too bad, I don't know how to live other than as a sōkaiya. It was my fate to be one." Kinjō kept smiling at Moto who acted very upset.

Moto was wordless.

"I don't want my grandchild to be the like of me. But Miwako . . . " Kinjō bit his bloodless lip.

The violent sound of his cane resounded in Moto's ears.

VI

February the fifth. The number of attendants at this day's shareholders' meeting was nearly five hundred. This was the largest number of participants Mamiya had seen in a shareholders' meeting. Anticipating a high turnout, the bank had reserved a hall in the M-Hotel, but still the staff had to bring in extra chairs. The hall was already filled with cigarette smoke before the meeting started. The attendants were tense with excitement about the coming event, and they smoked like chimneys.

The two front rows of the hall were occupied by Kinjō's henchmen who had arrived early. Ohgiyama and his sons sat in the third row, right behind them. Ohgiyama's shoulders in a charcoal-black garment were as wide as usual. His boar-like neck sunk down between them. His head would not turn even in response to those near him who whispered into his ears. Next to Ohgiyama, there was a gently sloping shoulder in a pure white coat. He must have given some thousands or tens of thousands of Taigin shares to this woman to gain her entrance into the hall. Ohgiyama's two sons, seated on either side of the couple, took turns glancing around the hall, as if they were having trouble tempering their animosity.

The nervous movements of the silhouettes in the next several rows behind them revealed that these people had little experience in shareholders' meetings. They seemed to have been recruited by Ohgiyama, or to have been given new shares. Their roving eyes were fierce and yet somewhat awkward.

Izumi's large body was at the center of the swaying human waves. Like a rock in the middle of autumn weeds, it wouldn't move. Its stillness had nothing in common with that of Ohgiyama. Izumi was paralyzed by the weight of the stares from behind. His shoulders and neck twitched periodically. This sizable body, which had once enjoyed the rank of a third-class junior in sumō wrestling, now bore some resemblance to a pinned cicada.

The one hundred sōkaiyas led by Kinjō formed a thin line along both wings of the Ohgiyama camp. They also occupied some rows of seats behind the Ohgiyama group, surrounding Kinjō. In other words, Kinjō's camp, including the two front lines, perfectly sealed in the Ohgiyama camp. But Ohgiyama had no way of knowing this layout on account of the differences in the sōkaiyas' clothing and ages.

Inquisitive amateur shareholders, as well as those who were sent by securities companies to reconnoiter the session, packed the back half of the hall. This group of people was uncommitted and could change sides in dangerous ways. One of the reasons why Kinjō always took a seat in the last row was to keep an eye on this group. Rings of babble and cigarette smoke circled around this section in a most confused manner.

An examination of the entire hall through the violet curtain of smoke revealed that the central location surrounding Kinjō was unnervingly quiet. The tranquility was due to the sōkaiyas' consideration for Kinjō's health, as well as their professional sophistication. Kinjō's hair was freshly dyed black. His tall body, with its back stretched upright, was shrouded in a dark gray suit. He gave no hint of illness to those who saw him from a distance. By the time he was wrapped in a blanket and carried sideways into a car, however, he had once again become a sick old man.

On the dot of ten o'clock, President and Chairman Ohmura appeared, as might be expected, with a stiff expression. He reported in a businesslike manner the process by which the special meeting was convened.

"In accordance with the law, we ask the shareholder who summoned this meeting to make an overture," he concluded.

The hall fell silent. All the attendants held their breath with anxiety. A sound of rustling clothes echoed as if to peel off the silence. The rustling came from Ohgiyama's woman, in her pure white coat, raising her torso toward Ohgiyama to prop up the semi-blind man. At this very instant, a hacking, sharp voice split the hall in half.

"Chairman," rang out Kinjō, standing erect and glaring at the Chairman, "I move that you tell us whether or not the party directly involved in the economic interest of this matter can vote."

Ohmura momentarily lowered his eyes, a gesture of giving the issue serious thought, but soon lifted his face and declared cautiously, but clearly, "I understand that it has no vote."

"This means that Mr. Ohgiyama, who convened this meeting, has no right to vote. Am I correct?" It was a question, and yet an imposing one.

The president nodded. Murmurs rose from Ohgiyama's surroundings. But prior to this, an outburst of catcalls rose from the back seats.

"No ballot to Ohgiyama!" "Ohgiyama is the culprit." The voices were harmonious.

The Ohgiyama camp had no voice to yell back at these surprise calls. Several individuals stood up impetuously and directed their bloodshot eyes at the rooters.

"This means," the hubbub quieted down when Kinjō started speaking, "that there is not much sense in asking Mr. Ohgiyama, who cannot vote, to explain his appeal."

"Nonsense!" "We have proxy letters, too!" Two sharp voices hollered back from the Ohgiyama camp.

Kinjō turned in that direction for the first time. His manner also changed. His eyes were now tender and inquisitive.

"Obviously, Mr. Ohgiyama did not come with too many proxy letters," said Kinjō, forcing his dry lips to grin.

The Ohgiyama camp fell silent. Everyone seemed to know that they could not compete on the basis of the number of proxy letters. Then Izumi broke the brief silence. He lifted his large body, making his chair squeak.

"Protect minority shareholders! Don't you know the law to protect minority shareholders?" As large as his body, his voice traveled to all corners of the hall. Clapping started around him. Izumi turned his body around, in the middle of the intermittent applause, and confronted Kinjō with his stare. Sporadic applause continued. The truth of the matter was that this was only a gesture made by Izumi. Izumi's speech had been contrived to usher in Kinjō's next speech. But Ohgiyama and his people did not catch on. They relaxed a little. Then Kinjō's voice reverberated through the vacuum of tension.

"You talk about protection, but it is the bank that needs to be protected. For the sake of the depositors who have business with the bank, as well as its shareholders, the bank needs to be protected first." Each word carried force. Kinjō's voice had grown firm enough to weld steel by the time he said, "What's endangering the bank?"

"Bad debts!" "Irrevocable loans!" Battle cries bounced in the hall, from the back to the front rows.

The former policeman sōkaiya rose to his feet. He glanced around the hall slowly and started to speak. "Chairman, this is a voice of a shareholder. Please make public the list of outstanding loans."

Then from his left side, an ex-monk picked up the speech, "Right now!"

The business division chief and executive staff had stood up before these voices ended. Perfect timing and the volume of voices kicked the meeting forward.

"Ohgiyama, 18 million yen; Chūbu Business 5.5 million yen; Tōkai Fabric . . . "

"Ohgiyama is hurting our bank!" The former policeman's high-pitched voice echoed into the chairman's microphone.

"Garbage!" An angry voice contended from behind.

Sōkaiyas in the front two rows seized this moment to turn around. They faced the Ohgiyama group, ready to grab hold of them. The numbers of people in the two groups were about the same, but the layout of the staff and its spiritual climate put the Ohgiyama camp at a disadvantage.

"Let's beat up Ohgiyama!" Someone howled from the right wing.

"Go home, Ohgiyama!" Another shouted from the left rear.

Each voice shook the Ohgiyama camp.

Kinjō stole a short interval of silence in the hullabaloo and shouted: "Chairman! A motion! I move to confiscate the security deposit of the bad debtor!"

"Yes!" "Confiscate!" Jeers echoed.

People applauded. The vortex of clapping spread through the hall from the front, the right, the left, and the back, as it grew thicker and louder.

"Bank, be brave!" "Be brave!"

Mixed with this heckling, the clapping continued for two to three minutes. Several angry men from the Ohgiyama side ran up to the stage, jumping over some seats. Izumi's gigantic body started to move as though it were pulled by these men.

Mamiya became worried. Practically everything up to this point was Kinjō's victory, exactly in line with his scenario. Would the drama end in violence? Mamiya found himself looking at Kinjō.

"Kinjō the Killer!" A voice rang from somewhere.

Kinjō's face was white. The breast of his suit heaved up and down in large waves. His throat whistled at each breath. He was falling victim to his illness.

What came out of the microphone was Chairman Ohmura's voice. It was shaky but clear enough. "The proceedings are complete. The meeting is adjourned." The switch was turned off there.

Clapping resumed. Mamiya, too, applauded zealously for the president's extemporaneous and quick decision. He thought that the president had been emboldened by Kinjō's ardor.

The voices of Ohgiyama's men, now shouting from the platform, were inaudible, overwhelmed by thumping noises from the back seats of those who were getting up to leave. All of Ohgiyama's one hundred men rose up.

"That's not today's agenda!" "Thievery!"

They yelled aimlessly. They could not figure out what had happened. Only the old man, Ohgiyama, remained seated. His woman was crouched down, showing only her impressively fair profile.

"What time is it?"

Mamiya was brought back to himself by Kinjō's hoarse voice. It was Kinjō's habit to ask the time whenever a meeting lasted long. The success or failure of a meeting could be measured in terms of time.

"It's eighteen past ten. It took eighteen minutes."

"That's not bad for having turned the tables on them." Kinjō took a deep breath. His throat whistled.

Late that night, Mamiya braced himself at the sound of the entrance hall door being quietly pulled open. The door had a piece of new glass. Izumi walked in.

"Didn't they come?" Izumi's eyes were terror-stricken. "They were badly beaten. They never dreamed of such a complete loss above and beyond the purpose of the meeting. Things were taken away one after another in a matter of a day. Ohgiyama's sons are having a fit. They ran out with firemen's hooks. They went with young men. I was sure they came this way," said Izumi, still searching other rooms with his eyes.

"They haven't made it up here. They must have gone to Lawyer Minami's."

"Oh, the lawyer. Yes, he sold them out. Otherwise, their properties couldn't have been taken away this fast."

"Money can buy anybody. You, too."

Izumi scratched his head. It cost the bank more than one million yen in total to buy back Izumi and to sponsor over one hundred sōkaiyas. Besides this, one or two million yen had been paid to Ishida and Minami, in addition to their forty to fifty thousand yen monthly stipend, by both the bank and Ohgiyama. There was no telling just how much money had moved for one shareholders' meeting. It was all dark money, off the record.

"Kinjō-san must have gotten a fat check," murmured Izumi, archly narrowing his eyes.

"What gall you have! Not a bloody yen." Mamiya raised his voice.

Kinjō had told Ohmura with a smile that he would accept only medical expenses so long as the meeting had cost him his health. He never requested payment for profit.

"Old people are beyond me," lamented Izumi. "I can never figure out Kinjō-san or old Ohgiyama. What do you think Ohgiyama said to me after the meeting? 'I wasn't beaten,' that's all. He talked as if he knew I duped him. He made my legs shaky that time. . . . He's still thinking of going after the bank, after all that horrible loss."

"What for?"

"I don't know. First, he thought of getting a loan from the bank. But then, he started thinking of suing the bank. Doesn't he understand that he has no way of winning, and he can't make money that way?"

Sliding doors rattled, perhaps in the wind. The new pane of glass reflected the electric light brighter than other pieces. This was the memento of Kinjō's impulse to strike Miwako with his walking stick. The situation was complex, true, but Kinjō no longer had to worry about what other people thought of him. Why didn't he share a few moments with his only child who came a long way to see him? Why the old man threw his daughter out quite so murderously was something beyond Mamiya's power to resolve. Reasons for Kinjō's single-mindedness were inferable but not comprehensible.

"Old people are hard to understand." Mamiya sighed this time.

A doctor hadn't left Kinjō's side ever since the old sōkaiya returned from the meeting. Why Kinjō went about the sōkaiya business at so much risk was a puzzle that made Mamiya sigh.

VII

Kinjō's condition deteriorated as if he were rolling down a flight of stairs. The malfunctioning of the respiratory system affected his heart. His pulse leaped occasionally. As if to declare that things were beyond a doctor's responsibility, now that Kinjō had attended the meeting against his advice, his doctor announced without hesitation that Kinjō's life was a matter of several days, and that whoever should pay him a final visit should be notified. Moto sent Miwako a telegram and a special delivery letter to explain the situation. She asked Miwako, with an apology for the earlier incident, to come at once.

There were three trains coming directly from Fukuoka: two early in the morning, and the other in the evening. At these hours, Moto listened carefully for the sound of shoes outside.

On the eve of the third day after Moto sent the telegraph, soft footsteps came to a halt outside, and a woman called out, "I beg your pardon."

Kinjō was feeling slightly better, and was having Moto sponge his body as he lay on his bed. The only etiquette Kinjō could still observe, after his hair had gone back to white, was to have his body sponge-bathed. He demanded this petulantly. Moto and Mamiya got up simultaneously at the woman's call in the entrance hall. Although the footsteps did not sound like those made by Western shoes, the two were sure that Miwako had come.

"I beg your pardon." After another soft call, the door opened.

Mamiya saw the small entrance hall overflowing with bright colors. A short young woman in a flamboyant golden red gala kimono stood with an elderly woman in a crested kimono with bright designs. The young woman's face was painted white. Only her flushed cheeks looked pink. Both women had silky skin.

"It's been a long time, Madam." A beaming smile filled the older woman's face. She was greeting Moto, who now stood behind Mamiya. "I came to introduce . . . Her name is Sayo." The young woman bowed in unison with her senior's voice. Her flower-shaped hair ornament trembled as she said, "I beg your courtesy."

"Is Kinjō-sensei home?"[10]

At the older woman's question, Moto let out a high-pitched voice, "Ah, yes," and turned back to Kinjō's room.

"This is the young geisha's initiation. Don't mention my illness. It will give her bad luck." Kinjō spoke curtly and urged Moto, with his eyes narrowed, to go back to the women.

Moto returned to the entrance hall with a celebration gift and said, "He has company right now, so . . ."

The women went away, leaving a coquettish aroma in the hall.

"You too couldn't believe your own eyes, could you?" said Kinjō in a low voice.

"No, because I thought it was Miwako."

"Miwako?"

"This is the time she might get here, if she took a train from Kyūshū. There are only three train services, at four in the evening, and five and seven-thirty in the morning."

"Oh, it's four o'clock." Kinjō nodded to himself. He faced Moto as if he had just remembered something. He added, "Don't call Miwako," and turned away.

Moto resumed sponging him in silence. Some moxa cautery[11] scars stood out on Kinjō's colorless back. There were two circles as big as rubber bands at the tip of his shoulders. Others scattered around them like constellations. Kinjō used to be so mettlesome that he had had a speech impairment until he was six years old. Punishment for his quick temper was always a moxa cautery. Kinjō's back spoke for this sad biography that Mamiya had once heard from Moto.

Kinjō was sound asleep by the time his body was thoroughly cleaned, and his quilts were put back on. Now that the piles of magazines, *Jurist and Law Reports,* had been put away, Kinjō's bed lay in a sad emptiness.

Moto put her face close to Mamiya's, as soon as she returned to the living room, and started questioning him. "Don't you think she was pretty?" She went on without waiting for Mamiya's reply. "That young girl had her bangs down and looked cute, like a teenage boy actor, but Sawayo-san, the older one, was pretty, too. Don't you agree?"

Because Mamiya was fascinated by the young girl, he couldn't recall the older woman's face.

"She was my husband's woman. They had relations. My husband only went after good-looking women," spoke Moto in the manner of humming a song, with blazing eyes. This surprised Mamiya even more.

"Miwa-san, who gave birth to Miwako, was a striking geisha. She was called Gunjō Komachi." [12]

Mamiya did not know how to respond. He simply stared at Moto's tanned face. Her eyes sparkled in excitement.

"But I am his only registered wife. It's because I had his child first." Moto smiled sheepishly. Her smile suggested her modest guilt that a plain woman like herself had sneaked into Kinjō's life from a side road. She was not boasting about putting other women to shame.

"My husband had lots of women, and exclusively geishas. He never liked bar hostesses. He says that women who scrounge for customers' food and drinks are base." Moto spoke emphatically, as if she and her husband agreed on this point.

Mamiya looked back at Moto. She was more than twenty-four years younger than Kinjō, only a little over fifty. She wore no makeup, but he could guess that she took good care of her face. There were neither spots nor flaccidity in her suntanned skin. Mamiya likened it to a freshly washed, and not starched, cotton kimono. He appreciated Kinjō's choice of her as a spouse. Moto's explanation made sense, but Kinjō must have had reasons to marry her other than the child's birth.

Kinjō coughed lightly. Moto got up in a hurry to look after him. On her way over to Kinjō's room, she changed the topic as if to atone for the excited manner in which she had talked. "Well, Miwako didn't come today, after all."

Mamiya lit a cigarette to blow away the settling chill of the night. Then he tried to glean words Moto had innocently dropped.

He had relations only with good-looking women; attractive geishas; he doesn't like bar hostesses. . . .

In the dark, there came a vision of Ohgiyama's woman all wrapped up in her white coat. Dwarfish Ohgiyama surrendered his half-blind body to her. Mamiya saw a deep-rooted difference between Ohgiyama and Kinjō, like water and oil. Old Ohgiyama's sliminess in asserting that he had not lost the case yet, after his properties had been completely confiscated, traveled in the dark, assailing his nostrils.

Every day, at five, seven-thirty, and four, Moto and others held their breath, waiting for Miwako's call, but to no avail. They could do nothing other than read the total absence of her response as her one-sided refusal. By the same token, Kinjō refused to talk about Miwako, and detested hearing even her name.

Late in the afternoon of February 14th, nine days after the stockholders' special session, Kinjō's condition became critical. His consciousness, which had been alert until that morning, faded away every now and then. He would move his mouth sideways, but no distinct words came out.

Taigin telephoned often to ask after his condition. This irritated Mamiya, for he interpreted it to be the bank's way of saving its time to visit Kinjō until the old man was on the brink of death. The confiscation of Ohgiyama's estates was supposed to have been completed. The bank, however, had not reported its result. Besides, President Ohmura had paid only a single visit after the special assembly.

After nine in the evening, Kinjō opened his misty eyes, and kept on trying to speak. His ashen lips trembled. Moto guessed at what he wanted and vocalized for him, but Kinjō only shook his head feebly. He looked frustrated that no one understood him. The nurse in attendance suggested, "Why don't we let him write?" They made Kinjō hold a soft lead pencil, and they put a sheet of paper with a board behind it in front of him. Moto and Mamiya supported Kinjō's arm and hand. Kinjō's pencil moved.

"What," dancing letters were drawn. The attendants moved the paper to give more room to write the next word, "time."

Kinjō's attendants shouted together, "Twelve past nine!" Someone moved a clock to where Kinjō could see. But Kinjō's eyes closed, never to see it. Kinjō had breathed his last while they were busy moving the clock.

"He was anxious about Miwako. He wanted to know if it was time for the train to arrive," Moto cried openly.

But "What time is it?" was something Kinjō always asked when a shareholders' meeting lasted long. Nothing concerned a sōkaiya more than the length of a shareholders' meeting. There was no telling which time Kinjō's last consciousness had been attached to.

While people were deep in their own thoughts, the nurse carried out her duties mechanically. She rubbed his slightly parted right eyelid to shut it. From the shade of her tender fingers, a salmon colored sword scar appeared, shining smoothly as if this part of Kinjō still lived. Kinjō's eyes were closed forever.

Notes

The word *sōkaiya* is translated as "corporate bouncer" by *Newsweek* (August 11, 1986). *Newsweek* cites Tokyo Electric Power Co., Meiji Confectionery, and Mitsubishi Bank as examples of companies that used corporate bouncers in their shareholders' general meetings. It reports that open payments to corporate bouncers ended in 1982, but there are still 1,400 active corporate bouncers by police count. By *Newsweek's* definition, these people "have managed to feed off Japan's largest corporations by playing one or both sides of a narrow street. Either they've threatened to dig up company scandals and irregularities by asking embarrassing questions at stockholders' meetings or they've taken the company side, offering to shout down—or even beat up— anyone who might try to challenge management." This is a translation of "Sōkaiya Kinjō" from Saburō Shiroyama's *Sōkaiya Kinjō* (Tokyo: Shinchō Bunko, 1963). Although *sōkaiya* is a Japanese word and denotes both singular and plural forms, I added the English plural suffix "s" to this word when it is to be construed as plural.

1. Taigin is a shortened name for Taiyō Ginkō, meaning the Taiyō Bank.

2. About 100 thousand dollars.

3. In some business contexts the "*-san*" suffix shows intimacy between the speaker and the addressee (or the referent), or recognition by the speaker of his own higher status than that of the addressee (or the referent). If the addressee's (or the referent's) status is higher, the speaker is likely to suffix the addressee's (or the referent's) name with his professional title or "sensei."

4. The entirety of this quotation comes from: Japan Commercial Law Service, *Commercial Laws of Japan* (Florida: Foreign Tax Law Association, Inc., 1987), 58–6.

5. "*-kun*" is suffixed to either the first or the last name, and most commonly means "Mr." Most often, the addressee (or the referent) is a male who is younger or lower ranked than the speaker.

6. *Yakuza* are members of Mafia-like brotherhood organizations.

7. *Devas* are the four warrior gods who protect the entrances of temples.

8. Usually, a Japanese house has a cement area called *genkan* to take shoes off; the living area beyond it is slightly elevated.

9. This refers to the episode gossiped over by the sōkaiya attendants on page 59.

10. *Sensei* usually means "teacher," and is also used as a title for teachers, in such a way as Suzuki-sensei (Mr. Suzuki). However, politicians, writers, and other professionals are also addressed or referred to by this honorific title.

11. Moxa cautery or *okyū* is a relative of acupuncture. Small piles of moxa herb are laid on medically designated spots on the body and burned by incense.

12. The geisha's name relates to Ono no Komachi, a ninth-century poetess, known for her good looks.

In Los Angeles

Saburō Shiroyama

I

Yukimura thought he had prepared himself for the worst, but the trip to the Los Angeles International Airport proved otherwise. Morito, the new branch manager, just in from Japan, berated Yukimura right there in the terminal. The Yukimura couple were quick to catch sight of the tall Morito stepping out of a customs gate in the JAL lobby and also very fast to duck their heads and bow. Morito, on his part, generously raised a hand and strode up to them. So far so good. But as soon as Morito had staged his formalistic handshake, he glanced all around the lobby and let the couple know of his dissatisfaction.

"Nobody here to meet me?"

"We . . ."

"I'm talking about others."

Because the tone of Morito's voice meant *You two don't count,* the Yukimuras were at a loss for words. They felt insulted, but even more, disheartened to find their new manager so unpleasant.

Most Americans, of course, do not have ceremonious greetings and farewells at airports as the Japanese do. It didn't seem possible that this "legend" who had studied in the United States shortly after World War II and who still spoke in English in his sleep was that ignorant about American ways. Besides, he should have known that the Los Angeles branch office of Yukimura's Q-Trading Company had only five staff members, including the local employees. Wasn't it good enough that the deputy manager and his wife had come to pick him up?

"Katō-kun is in Phoenix, and Nakano-kun is in San Diego at the moment," Yukimura spoke apologetically as he looked up at Morito's sparkling glasses.

"And our clients?"

Yukimura caught himself from saying *This isn't Japan, you know* only with some effort.

"Some asked for your arrival time, but I didn't give a definite answer."

"Why? Why didn't you have them come?"

"Because they are Aron Orchards, Halifax Limited, and other nettlesome companies." Yukimura listed the names of the companies that his former manager Ohkubo had tried to avoid and about which the new manager Morito was expected to do something. "They might have given you a hard time right at the first sight of you."

"You don't have to worry about me. I can take care of them. It's not your place to fix things for me," Morito chided unsparingly.

Yukimura's wife, Sayoko, tensed up as she stood next to him.

"I'm not built as delicately as Ohkubo-kun. Nervous breakdowns and ulcers are foreign to me. I'm going to forge ahead without worrying about little things. Please keep that in mind," Morito went on.

Yukimura and Sayoko nodded together in a chain reaction. Actually, they felt that they had to.

This wasn't the end of Morito's carping. When Yukimura drove his Ford Capri from the parking lot to the terminal building exit, Morito looked down at it from where he stood.

"Are you driving it yourself?"

"Yes."

"Don't you have a driver?"

Yukimura's nerves seethed. In the United States, only corporate executives, millionaires, and the like could afford a private chauffeur. Morito should know that by now. What kind of nonsense was he spewing?

"If you don't have a driver, why don't you let your junior staff drive for you?"

This made no more sense than anything else Morito had said. All the Japanese staff were out of town, and no American employees would consider being treated like a chauffeur.

Morito finally settled into the back seat, plopping his gigantic rear onto it.

"You make me feel as if I'm here to depend on you." Morito's abusive talk was another way of scolding, *This isn't the way to receive your business manager. Don't take me for your friend visiting here for a vacation.*

Yukimura started the car wordlessly just as soon as Sayoko slid into the seat next to him. Silently, he retorted, *Coming to the airport with my wife was the best welcome a deputy manager of a small trading company could give to its new manager.*

"It would have worked better if you had brought me a car. I could have driven it back myself," added Morito with annoyance.

This was even more nonsensical. Even assuming that the company would buy a car for the manager, he would have wanted to select it for himself. Renting a car wouldn't have pleased him either.

Having run out of complaints, Morito cut the tip of a cigar and lit it. A powerful smell filled the car. Sayoko usually got a headache from cigar smoke but she was too frightened to roll down the window.

What a nuisance of a manager I've gotten, Yukimura commiserated with himself once again. He had heard of Morito's nickname and reputation, but this was the very first time he had to work directly under him. In a firm the size of his Q-Trading Company, a person with a degree from a top-notch national university and from an American college as well was treasured as the company's "prince" from the beginning of his career. To Yukimura's knowledge, Morito was very demanding at work, yet he would also do a friendly thing like inviting his juniors to a house party. The "prince" used a whip and candy very generously, so to speak. He was thoroughly Draconian in business transactions but had been a big hit in his departments thus far. One could guess that Morito would join the board of directors just as soon as he turned forty if he straightened out the problems of the Los Angeles office during his tenure there. Morito was a big shot and he knew it—or rather, he was a bundle of self-importance. And he made sure that Yukimura felt it under his skin.

Yukimura drove on in silence. Off in the distance, the Santa Monica Bay glistened blue in the twilight. The wind seemed to have blown off the infamous smog. The sky of Los Angeles, with a hue of emerald green, was deep and high.

Suddenly, Morito started showering questions onto Sayoko's back.

"Mrs. Yukimura, how are your children? There's a girl in the sixth grade and a boy in the second grade, isn't there?"

"Yes!" Sayoko nodded in such amazement that her head almost knocked against the windshield.

"I hear that your daughter is good at drawing pictures." Morito had more surprises up his sleeve.

"Oh, no, not at all. . . ." Sayoko blushed like a girl whose hand had been asked for in marriage, and her body stiffened. Earlier, she had been frozen from trepidation; this time she sat in a rapturous trance.

It flashed across Yukimura's mind that this was Morito's trick. He must have checked up on the family situations of his subordinates at the personnel office or somewhere. But how did he uncover a detail like his daughter's drawings? This was the art of winning over people's hearts. It was something Yukimura begrudgingly had to take his hat off to.

"Art transcends nationalities. Things are more colorful, and sceneries have a larger scale over here. It will be good to take her for landscape painting and such," Morito continued as he blew out the cigar smoke. Sayoko nodded, drugged by the thick curtain of smoke.

The traffic on the freeway became more congested as Yukimura approached the downtown area. This time, Morito's voice took aim at Yukimura.

"Talking about pictures . . . , isn't Fumihiko-kun, President Hori's son, living with hippies and trying to paint somewhere near here?"

"I think he's taking it seriously these days."

"How hopeless! He has a degree in economics, and is supposed to be continuing his studies here in the United States. The president is very disappointed in him. How is it that a shiftless son like that comes from such an outstanding father?"

Yukimura knew that the question didn't ask for an answer, but he put forth his opinion just the same, "Maybe it's because his father is too outstanding."

"What do you mean?"

"He's compared to his successful father in whatever he does. It's hard for the son. In fact, I've heard Fumihiko-san[1] swear that he would give up his success so that his son wouldn't feel pressured. I think I can understand how he feels."

"Humph." Morito wheezed in a nasal tone. "No matter how you look at it, though, hippies and delinquents are human garbage. He has no right to lecture us as long as he is mixed up with that sort of gang."

"But Fumihiko-san doesn't use drugs; nor does he go for free love. He's just looking to be a free spirit. He just wants to indulge in art."

"If he's that serious, why doesn't he go to Paris or New York?"

"He says he'd be overwhelmed by too many recognized artists in

Paris and New York. He feels that there's no spot left for him to sketch.''

''Doesn't professionalism mean overcoming that sort of competition?''

Yukimura nodded lightly and continued, ''But he's not sure if he really wants to be a professional artist.''

''That's precisely where the problem lies. That's why he's a bungler. No wonder the president is disgusted with him.''

Yukimura sidestepped Morito's comment and went on. ''As you may be aware, the United States is a country of professionals. It's believed that survival depends on professionalism.''

''It sure is.''

''But more and more laid back young people are choosing to do only what they believe in. You may call them anti-professionals. Success isn't part of their vocabulary.''

''The Vietnam war has blighted their minds; that's it.''

''Maybe so, but it seems to me that the United States has turned a corner in history. I feel that the whole country is drifting on a lake of lethargy, trying to survive on the borderline between professionalism and amateurism.''

''Come on, you softboiled egg! This is why you can't make clear-cut decisions. If you had taken a firmer stance, you could have solved the problems with Aron and Halifax more forcefully.''

Yukimura took it in stride. It was possible to insist on Q-Trading Company's way of doing business, but unfortunately the problems weren't the kind that could be solved in a hardheaded business manner. For example, Q-Trading Company was the only Japanese trading company that bought lemons, grapefruit, oranges, and other fruits from Aron Orchards in Riverside City. The original contract called for Q-Trading Company to purchase exclusively all the fruit products of Aron on the condition that Aron discontinue their business with large fruit retailers in the United States. But lately the Japanese market for lemons and grapefruit had become sluggish. And a chronic glut was projected for the future. As a result, Q-Trading Company decided to discontinue purchasing lemons and to begin selectively purchasing grapefruit and oranges. This change was advantageous to the Q-Trading Company only—and there was a ruthless calculation behind it: Aron Orchards wouldn't survive long; the bankruptcy would solve Q's problems.

Aron Orchards was outraged. Intimidated by Aron's violent reaction, Ohkubo, the former manager, stopped going to the Riverside region altogether. There was also a time when armed Aron-affiliated farmers barged in on Q-Trading Company. The branch office found it impossible to force the main office's decision onto the American producers and requested that the main office reconsider the new order.

A similar tension existed with the Halifax Distributor. Two years ago, Q-Trading Company nominated Halifax as a distributor of a Japanese spray system. Halifax Headquarters in Ontario City, some fifty kilometers east of Los Angeles, had a good reputation in the farming communities in southern California and the spray system sold better than expected. Q-Trading Company attributed its success to the high quality of the machinery, while Halifax assumed that it was due to its sales efforts. In either case, commissions bulged significantly along with the sales figures. The Q-Trading Company, now chary of the sales commission, decided to terminate the distributor contract at the time of its renewal. But the contract was supposed to be renewed every two years, unless a breach of confidence intervened. As a pretext, Q-Trading Company accused Halifax of negotiating with an American maker of spray systems. This was another source of headaches at the branch office.

Rather than lose its temper, Halifax went on pleading its case. Because Halifax had entrusted the sales to about twenty salesmen, the contract negotiations directly affected the employment of these people. Naturally, the salesmen came to the Q-office in relays. Some threatened to appeal to the court; others menaced the staff by showing their tatoos and guns. They implied, "If you go about it illegally, we will do the same." Ohkubo requested the contract be renewed once more, but the Tokyo office responded by replacing him with Morito.

Morito suddenly cried out, "Oh, the good old City Hall! It hasn't changed!"

The twenty-eight story, uniquely white City Hall loomed in front of the car.

"You must have lived in the Los Angeles area before." Sayoko turned around to keep Morito company.

"It was over fifteen years ago. I didn't actually live here. I used to live in San Bernardino. I came here from the country now and then. Every time I saw this building I was excited to be in Los Angeles. I felt much closer to Japan."

"It must have been difficult for you."

"Well, there still was a shortage of foreign exchange. I had to make my living at dishwashing, lawn-mowing, orange-picking, and other odd jobs while going to school.''

''San Bernardino is on the other side of Ontario and Riverside, isn't it?''

''Right.''

Isn't this ironic? Yukimura was tempted to remark, *That's near Aron and Halifax!* But he said, ''Do you have acquaintances around there?''

''There may still be some, but they were all my enemies. I was pushed into cheap labor everywhere. There was only one old man, the owner of an orchard, who was very nice to me. He was a 'half-breed' with American Indian blood. He told me to marry his granddaughter, get permanent residency, and manage his orchard with her.''

''But you didn't.''

''Of course not. Who wants to live an empty life at the end of the world? Also, how could I marry an Indian and have kids that holler 'wa wa' all the time?'' Morito imitated the voice of American Indians in Western movies and made Sayoko laugh.

Yukimura drew a mental picture of Morito in a Native American village. Somewhere in a corner of that endless orchard, sunburned Morito would be working with his half-breed wife. Vigorous, copper-toned children of mixed blood would be circling around barefoot or on horseback. Not bad at all. Morito fit in the scene neatly. On the other hand, Morito now looked more like himself. One thing Yukimura knew for sure was that if Morito had taken the other path, he could have done without this nincompoop for now.

''The old man passed away last year. It seems that nobody was there with him. I think I will go to San Bernardino one day and build a grave for him.''[2]

Sayoko nodded approvingly. Yukimura felt as if his wife's gaze had disparaged him in the light of Morito. He could almost hear her thinking, *My husband is so different. . . .* Yukimura was only one year younger than Morito, but there was nothing noteworthy in his schooling and degrees. A lack of business enthusiasm had already removed him from the success ladder. He had by now served as the deputy manager in Los Angeles for three years. If he didn't watch his step, he might very well be buried alive in this town.

Back in the apartment later that day, Sayoko let out a sigh, ''He notices small things. Morito-san deserves his reputation.'' She looked at her husband with a fresh glance and continued, ''Come to think of it, this is a rare opportunity. . . .''

"Opportunity for what?" Yukimura wanted to ask, *An opportunity to be flattened out?*

"You know, a chance to get on in the world," Sayoko smiled gently. "He is the future leader of our company. What if you followed him closely?"

"No way!"

"Not just to get ahead, but this may be a way to return to Japan a bit sooner."

Yukimura didn't bother to answer.

"Living like this, our children go funny. And you and me, too."

Again, Yukimura didn't reply.

"Or else, would you rather live with the Indians somewhere around San Bernardino, like mud dolls?"

"Why don't you shut up?"

Sayoko became quiet for awhile; she checked Yukimura's face and repeated loudly, "It's a chance; believe me."

II

The Q-Trading Company was on the third floor of a small building on Flower Street near the University of Southern California. The first thing the new manager did was to remodel the small office. He enclosed a corner of the manager's section with a decorative glass partition, put in a new desk, and brought in a new set of waiting room furniture. He also put up an American flag and a Japanese flag beside his desk as some presidents of large American companies do. These modifications added dignity to his office, but they made the rest of the floor space that much smaller. The sad thing was that, after all that renovation, Morito hardly ever stayed in his office.

He took off in his new Cougar XR7, always saying, "A trading company should be in motion." He visited customer companies, stopped by financial organizations, and met with banks and Japanese authorities. In between, he went to play golf for "socialization," as he put it. He was truly energetic. Yet, he left the negotiations with Aron and Halifax—the pending problems—to Yukimura. He didn't pay a single visit to these companies. If somebody from either company came charging in, he made Yukimura deal with them. The partitioned manager's room was a cozy den for Morito. One could even suspect that his frequent outings were a way of avoiding these unwanted visitors. The problem was that Morito, while taking no part himself, commanded

Yukimura to bring the two contracts to a complete closure exactly as dictated by the Tokyo office.

"There's nothing to negotiate about. Just spurn their requests. Don't give in to Americans. No, not an inch. Don't even give a hint of giving in," Morito tried to fire up Yukimura.

If Yukimura proposed, "But we need some kind of concession," Morito would raise his voice, "What the heck!" and yell, "We're not one of those large trading companies; we have to be grabby in order to survive; we must earn every penny we can."

"If you're that resolved, would you please talk to them directly?" Yukimura ran out of patience.

"My job is to march forward, to expand our business. This mess you are in is like a postwar cleanup job, a retrenchment, something you staff are entitled to." Morito pounded on the table, and repelled Yukimura with some insults.

Days went by. Yelled at by Morito and beleaguered by Aron and others, Yukimura was lonely. Local employees became standoffish towards him in deference to Morito and Aron. It was more like working in a one-man office rather than a branch office staffed by five. Before, the previous manager had been there to discuss problems and had tried to talk the Tokyo office into reconsidering the contract. But Morito was heartless and couldn't be caught off guard. He had trapped Yukimura behind an iron wall so there was no way out. Yukimura felt crucified. When he was threatened with murder, he felt like casually retorting, *Yeah, go right ahead!* He wasn't all that ready to die, but the apprehension that he might in fact be killed one of these days was always there. Q-Trading Company's business policies were so slipshod that such vengeance almost seemed fitting. But whenever Yukimura threw his life at his opponents, the aggressors backed down. In the end, Q-Trading Company scored a victory, and Morito as its manager got the credit. Yukimura vacantly brooded that the art of using subordinates to personal advantage was another of Morito's talents.

The only salvation for Yukimura was that both Aron and Halifax seemed to understand that their true enemy was not Yukimura but Morito. As their visits became more frequent, they gave up on Yukimura and became proportionately more inquisitive about Morito's whereabouts. The antagonistic clouds hovering over Morito became so thick that his enemies' hostility became palpable.

One day, the president's son Fumihiko showed up, dangling a large necklace of chained nuts and dragging a robe stained by oil paints.

Morito abhored hippies. He wanted to throw a bucket of water over the youngster, but had to politely receive the president's son into his office.

"I should have gone to inquire after you, but because Yukimura-kun told me that your residence changed constantly and it is rather difficult to find you . . . ," began Morito.

"My place isn't something you can call a residence. It's just a den, a temporal inn where a bunch of us sleep, so you'll never find me." After answering Morito, Fumihiko surreptitiously winked to Yukimura.

Actually, Yukimura knew where Fumihiko had his nest. Fumihiko had contacted him at home every time he moved. Not merely because Yukimura had been long in the area, but also because there was something about Yukimura that Fumihiko trusted. Yukimura knew he may have been thought of as easy to win over, but he didn't mind. It would have made him feel good to be depended upon by a young man, even if he weren't the president's son. Because Fumihiko had made it perfectly clear that he didn't want the new manager to know his address, Yukimura had kept it confidential as a token of his sincerity.

"The real purpose of my trip here is to borrow about three thousand dollars," said Fumihiko, brushing his long hair back with his fingers. He explained that his favorite avant-garde artist was holding a private exhibition in New York, he didn't want to miss it, and that, if possible, he wanted to purchase copies of his sketches and other works.

"Do you have your father's permission?"

"Of course not. My father is dead set against my getting into art."

"That's a problem." Morito put a hand on his forehead.

President Hori had a personal savings account with the Bank of America and his bank book was kept in the Los Angeles office. This was an emergency fund to be utilized at the manager's discretion. The exhibition had already started. Fumihiko said urgently, "I may miss the show if I don't get going soon."

Could this be called an emergency case? wondered Morito. If the president was against his son's art fad, drawing on the fund for this purpose would generate his resentment. Morito couldn't make up his mind.

"Would you let me think about it? I'll get back to you. Please leave your address or telephone number."

"That's O.K.. I'll come back tomorrow."

"In that case, how about dinner tomorrow?"

Fumihiko shook his head, "The kind of restaurants you go to don't like sloppy-looking people like me. I don't feel comfortable in those places, either."

Morito didn't reply.

"Do you know that some of us collect scrap cabbage and meat from the trash cans of those restaurants?"

"Like beggars."

"Not really. We do so for another reason. It's an effort to stay out of money-bound society. We don't spend money on luxury; we don't work for money. It's not the easiest thing in the world to do because we are living in a society where a bit of work can quickly earn a meal, as you must know. It takes a good determination to go against the current."

Morito listened to Fumihiko open-mouthed. Fumihiko was talking about a world outside the imagination of a single-minded businessman like himself. The businessman didn't know how to respond other than saying, "It doesn't mean you have to follow their example. . . ."

"I'm not a thoroughbred. I still know the value of money. My visit here proves that."

"That sets my mind at ease a little."

"Also, I'm not about to deny the value of the older generation completely. It's awkward for a son to say this, but I think that my father is a fine man. At least he was good enough to build a company of this size in one generation." As Morito nodded deeply for the first time, Fumihiko added mischievously, "Although his contribution to the financial world may be cancelled out by me."

Having said all he wanted, Fumihiko left, the tail end of his long robe sailing in the air.

"What a scrap of human garbage that is!" Morito spit out. He was truly angry.

Yukimura felt like giving him a bit of a twit. "Isn't that an easy life, though? And, as Fumihiko-san always says, his son will have it made, won't he?"

"He has no qualification to be a father; no qualification even to live."

"But he is harmless."

Perhaps because this sarcasm was a bit too strong, Morito was offended. "What of it?"

Yukimura didn't confront Morito directly. He said, "There wouldn't be wars if the world were inhabited only by his type of people."

Morito lit his cigar and sighed deeply.

"So, what am I going to do about the three thousand dollars?"

Yukimura didn't answer. This truly was none of his business, and it boosted his ego to watch Morito suffer. The easiest solution would be to telephone Tokyo, and ask the president. But the upshot would be at best a presidential scolding, "Can't you make up your mind about a small thing like that?" Morito probably would have to make his own decision and then report the result afterward. It was impossible to guess whether the president would be grateful or resentful for having spent the money. Morito appeared to be tearing his hair out over the problem. It was a very minor affair for the company, but it was a life-or-death problem to him.

Morito's cigar smoke rose higher and higher. In the end, he asked for Yukimura's help, "What do you think?"

"It's up to you."

"I know that, but what would you do in my place?"

"I would help him."

"Why? The president would rather get him out of art, you know."

"I just thought of Fumihiko-san. I didn't think of the president."

"Why not?"

"Well, the money isn't going to be spent for destructive purposes. On the contrary, it may serve as a springboard for Fumihiko-san's growth. Whatever profession he may eventually choose, there's no reason to deprive him of something that enriches his cultural background and spiritual life."

Morito remained silent.

"Furthermore, Fumihiko-san is not the type to ask for something so ardently. He is usually very nihilistic. He sounded unusually enthusiastic today. I could tell how earnest he was about the exhibition."

"Do you mean to say that a hippie may reform?"

"It's not a matter of reforming. I just think that we should give him the thing he truly craves, and beautiful things, too."

"All right, I get it. I'll handle the rest." Morito shut off Yukimura's advice with the whisk of a hand. His expression said that he had suddenly become exasperated at having consulted Yukimura.

"You seem to have lived here long enough to turn yourself into a hippie supporter. Just watch out for yourself so that you can still be useful in Japan," Morito snarled. "Are you ready to prove your worth with the Aron and Halifax cases? Go at it and teach them a lesson!"

In the end, Manager Morito handed Fumihiko the three thousand dollars. This pleased Fumihiko, but his father's response was different. When Morito reported to the Tokyo office with some fear and trepidation, the executive secretary conveyed the president's message that he was outraged by the manager's "putting his hand on uncalled-for business." Since the president was planning a trip to the United States in the near future, he would inquire about the details of the matter when he stopped in Los Angeles, so "Morito had better be prepared for the worst." The message was unexpectedly harsh.

Morito was out of sorts. He wreaked his frustration on Yukimura. "It wasn't my idea to give him the money. It's you who made the decision."

"But you said to leave the rest up to you."

"I just got here, and didn't know anything. That's why I respected your opinion."

"Even then . . ."

"I had nothing to base my judgment on. As a matter of fact, that was the first time I met Fumihiko-kun. How could a stranger to a place make the right decision? All I could do was to be guided by your information and suggestion." Morito got heated up by his own argument as he talked. "The original sin was that you let that hippie have the run of our office just because he's the president's son. You and Ohkubo-kun spoiled him. No, the general easy-handed way you go about managing welcomes this sort of disaster." Morito had completely forgotten how civilly he had welcomed Fumihiko into the manager's office. "Listen, this problem was handled by you, not by me. Let's make it clear that you took the responsiblity; you made the decision. It's your job to vindicate everything to the president. Don't drag me into it because I have no idea what's going on." After this bout of excited proclamation, Morito swung his gaze behind his shiny glasses in another direction.

Yukimura couldn't believe it. He was dumbfounded. Not only was he irritated by Morito, but he had also become disgusted with the shallowness of his wife, who was infatuated by this man's personality. What did she know about big shots and great chances? Following this man would only make one rotten to the core.

How could a deputy manager venture to explain his position to the president? All Yukimura could do was to own up to the truth, to describe the situation plainly. After that, he would just have to sit through a flurry of presidential abuses and wait for the verdict, which would probably be a demotion.

"Enough. You may go back to your work." Morito was all authoritarian.

Yukimura was glad to leave; not seeing Morito was as much his wish as Morito's. He was beginning to fear that if he stayed there much longer he might throw Morito out the window.

III

Morito built a grave for the orchard owner who took care of him during his student days. He replaced the simple wooden marker, which had been put up by those who were not related to the orchard owner by blood, with an ostentatious black marble tombstone. The graveyard was in the suburbs of San Bernardino.

It was decided that the branch office staff would attend the renovation ceremony. Morito drove his Cougar XR7, and Yukimura and his junior staff member Nakano were instructed to follow in the Ford Capri. Morito assumed the role of an authoritarian leader, making them go in two separate cars when one would have done the job just as well.

Morito's tombstone renovation plan was picked up by a local paper, the *San Bernardino Times*, which didn't overlook even the smallest local event. Neighboring small-town newspapers like *The Ontario Chronicle* and *The Riverside Evening* joined the chorus and printed flashy illustrated articles about the "beautiful Japanese spirit."

It was the "beautiful Japanese spirit" all right. Morito's feeling for the half-Indian orchard owner was genuine, the gravestone was of fine quality, and it was built with great care. Yukimura could appreciate this generosity. But Morito was embarrassed to have Yukimura and others see things in that light.

"I'm doing this out of sheer self-interest. No growing bud comes out of everyday business transactions. But this sort of publicity expands our business network. You people should quit digging small holes for yourselves and start looking for new ways," he said.

The newspaper articles struck some people quite differently. Many threatening letters and protesting telephone calls flew in from the Aron-related people around Riverside, and from Halifax salesmen based in Ontario. They threatened, "Don't try to make yourselves look noble at our cost," "Remember you're going to pay for this when you come this way," and many more maledictions. The "beautiful spirit" grated on them. Their abuse was not in their words alone; a true threat of violence resonated between the lines. Any mention of this, however, only made Morito bellow with laughter.

"It's just the American way of doing things. The United States prides itself on toughness. Haven't you learned that yet?" After saying this, Morito suddenly frowned and added, "Businessmen in trading companies are no different from the foot soldiers on the battlefront. Nobody says so, but we all came prepared to find a watery grave, and death in an open field. We don't get anywhere if we let these screwballs get on our nerves."

The sky was clear and there was no wind on the day of the renovation ceremony. This meant that a thin gray smog hung in the Los Angeles sky.

Morito, Yukimura, and Nakano left work early. The two cars, one following the other, sped straight east on Interstate 10. Up until halfway through the two-hour drive, the scenery was like an extension of Los Angeles, sprinkled with factories and clusters of houses. After that, farmlands and orchards sprawled over the vista. Farmhouses played hide and seek every so often from behind avenues of palm trees and forests of eucalyptus. There were people driving tractors and spraying chemicals.

This part of the scenery was something Yukimura couldn't watch so innocently. The spray equipment might have been sold by the Halifax salesmen, and some of the orchard workers might be members of Aron-affiliated farms. He feared that his car as well as Morito's might be identified by these people and ambushed. Maybe Morito shared the same anxiety. When they passed through the suburbs of Ontario City, where the Halifax headquarters was located, Yukimura sensed that Morito's car speeded up.

Before long, the San Bernardino National Forest and the Box Springs Mountains started to loom in the mist to the north and south of the highway respectively. San Bernardino was situated in the middle of a basin.

Morito had said that the orchard at which he previously worked was sold and the old man's house was torn down after his death. He had shown no interest in visiting the remainder of the orchard, but headed directly to the graveyard on a small hill slightly east of the town. It was surrounded by an ocean of orchards. In the orange orchard just before the graveyard, Mexican immigrants silently trimmed the lower branches. They wore rags and squirmed like mud dolls. Everyone had the gloomy face of a serf. Yukimura felt that calling them serfs was not too wide of the mark. Mexicans surge into the United States to escape poverty, but the immigration regulations are strict. The situation helps create a number of illegal immigrants who will put up with any adverse working condition. Their "bosses," who use their influence to find employment for them, exploit them and may go so far as to cut their lives short. Only recently, for example, a "boss" who had murdered nearly ten Mexicans was arrested at an orchard in a border region.

Below their feet, ever so many oranges formed a carpet of golden yellow. Nature shakes off the bad oranges at an early stage; only the ripened, good quality fruit is harvested in the end. As the result of this highly expensive procedure, the oranges harvested in the end had the richness and luxury of having absorbed the life force of countless premature relatives.

Mulling these things over in his mind, Yukimura was suddenly awakened from his drifting thoughts. His Q-Trading Company had promised to buy all of these oranges but had suddenly switched to selective purchasing. They had reneged on the original contract and chosen a way that was much more costly to the producers. The angry oranges and the orange workers assaulted him in lifelike vividness.

The gigantic sun gradually reclined westward. A breeze had started to pick up. At the graveyard, the priest gave a short prayer. Three men and women chosen from the church choir sang several hymns. Finally, Morito offered a bouquet of flowers and knelt in front of the tombstone. As directed, Nakano took some snapshots from different angles.

Morito remained motionless long after many pictures were taken. He would not get up. His large body froze into a statue, and a larger shadow drawn by the setting sun stretched along the ground. *Apricot flowers?* Petals of cherry-blossom-like flowers alighted on his shoulders. Morito's glasses glistened in the twilight. Facing the sun, Yukimura couldn't tell for certain, but it seemed that Morito's tears made his glasses shine. The graveyard fell into total silence. The only sound was the movement of the Mexicans some distance away drifting up like waves. Morito did not raise his head. It looked as if he would stay there for many more hours.

The priest cleared his throat. Morito's large sunbeam-laden shoulders finally rose. Dark clay clung to his pants knees. Morito briefly thanked the priest and the choir, and took care of the business matters by himself, hardly looking at Yukimura or Nakano. He only said, "All right, let's go," and got into his Cougar XR7.

Yukimura and Nakano rushed to their Ford Capri and chased after him.

"The manager is acting strange today," said Nakano, who had joined the company only three years ago.

"He may have been crying."

"The old man must have taken really good care of him."

"I guess."

Their cars raced by the Mexican laborers. In the evening sun, the workers looked worn out. They turned vacant and apathetic eyes towards the cars.

"The manager must have been made to work like them."

"I doubt it." Yukimura answered dryly, but remembered that there were some places around there called "Chino," which was Spanish for "Chinese." There was a time when Chinese and Japanese were dirt-crawling laborers. It wouldn't be surprising if Morito had been included in the penurious labor force of Chinese and Japanese students during the postwar period. The shame and regret of having fallen slave to the pitiless drudgery . . . The difference in treatment must have made the old orchard owner seem like a saint. Was it an outburst of dammed up sentiment that had made Morito a praying clay statue?

Come to think of it, Morito had shown no interest in visiting the places of his memorable past other than this graveyard, after coming this close to them. Could it be that all the other places would only open old wounds with painful freshness? He had once said, "They all mistreated me." Stretching his imagination one step farther, Yukimura recalled that Morito had two false front teeth. Morito had casually explained that he fell and broke them while he was in the United States, but did they have a hidden connection with the hard labor? Yukimura also wondered if Morito's avoidance of Aron and Halifax might not have been rooted in his resentment of the white people of the region, and not a matter of business strategy.

The basin opened up toward the west as if beckoning to the open pasture. A huge red sun was about to set on the horizon. The Cougar XR7 sprinted past the vast scenery, like a white leopard, aiming at Los Angeles. Morito's silhouette looked much smaller than life-size.

And every now and then, the gold of the setting sun bleached out the white Cougar and Morito's silhouette. They looked lonely and neglected.

"That car has been following us for a long time," said Nakano when they approached Ontario.

Yukimura looked in the rearview mirror. Two old cars were trailing behind them. Lanes were open on their right and left. The two cars had plenty of time and space to pass, but they stayed very close behind. Each had three or four passengers. Strange! Should he honk at Morito and let him know? What would Morito do about it? It was a straight highway in the middle of empty land. There was no service area; exits and junctions were some distance away. Oncoming cars floated up and down into their vision on the other side of the highway, but the lanes on this side had nothing other than the taillights that had just disappeared in the horizon. The highway was already darkened by the violet dusk.

"It's weird. What shall we do?" asked Nakano.

At that moment, the two cars suddenly sped up and pulled into the passing lane. They passed Yukimura's car. One of them raced its engine and flew in front of the Cougar. The other stayed right next to the Cougar to cage it in. The Cougar, now sandwiched between the two, reduced speed and stopped in the breakdown lane. Yukimura's Ford passed them before it came to an abrupt halt. Many shadows rolled out of the black cars and ran toward the Cougar. Then came the ring of swearing voices. The blasting of a bullet cut through the wind. With their doors open, Yukimura and Nakano hung back. Another bullet. The Cougar honked. It kept on honking. Morito's torso seemed to have fallen across the steering wheel. The men floored their accelerators, and the two cars that had swallowed those shadows sped off.

Yukimura and Nakano ran up to the Cougar. A front tire was shot out, tilting the car body. Morito's bloodless face hung over the steering wheel. It rose slowly and the honking stopped. Blood soaked his left thigh. Apparently the men didn't intend to kill him. But Morito's body was stuck to the steering wheel. When the two men tried to lift him, a horrible stench stung their noses.

"Oh, I . . ." Morito tried to say something with unfocused eyes.

Yukimura and Nakano looked at each other. They detected the cause of the stench. Morito had excreted in terror. It wasn't anything to laugh about; it was pathetic.

IV

President Hori arrived in Los Angeles. Because Morito was hospital-ized, Yukimura had to explain the three thousand dollar incident. The thought that he was saving Morito's skin rather than being in-criminated by the manager made it easier to surrender himself to whatever fate awaited him. He prepared himself for the severest scold-ing, but the president started talking before Yukimura had finished, with a friendly smile on his face, "Fumihiko wrote to me from New York. He said that he gave up the idea of becoming an artist. He realized that he wasn't gifted enough. The show must have had some true masterpieces. He was crushed. He even hinted at coming back to Japan. He said that he couldn't keep on goofing off with the assumption that we are always there to wait on him."[3] The president then broke into a genuine smile and changed the subject, "I'm going to ask you to manage this office from now on. I don't mean temporarily; I mean officially."

"But Morito-san is . . ."

"I'll send him back to Japan as soon as he comes out of the hospital. I'll have him take it easy in our research division or somewhere. I misunderstood him. I used to think that his type made good business-men, but I think perhaps not any more."

"His type?"

"You know what I mean. Those who have worked under him can explain better than I."

Does "his type" mean a practical and bluffing kind? Yukimura wanted to ask. Had the president seen Morito praying stone-still on a hill aglow with the setting sun? And what did the president know about Yukimura himself? Did he know that Yukimura wanted to go back to Japan? Rather than taking the managerial post, he wanted to go back now, even if he had to miss a promotion, and maybe catch another chance sometime later.

The president took Yukimura's silence as his expression of gratitude and carried on, "It's about time you made it to a manager's post. Besides, we need someone like you from now on who is familiar with the local circumstances. We are stepping into a world where many more conflicts, graver than those of Aron and Halifax, are likely to turn up."

The exhausted faces of the Mexican workers flashed in Yukimura's mind, and so did the golden carpet of oranges lying around their feet. He felt an unexplained load fall on his shoulders. Looking up with his inner eyes, he saw the white tower of the City Hall rise in the navy-blue sky of southern California, like an insensitive giant.

Notes

This work was originally published as ''Rakujitsu no oka ni: Rosanzerusu'' in Saburō Shiroyama's collection of short stories entitled *A One-Man Office in Broad Daylight* (Mahiru no wan-man ofis) (Tokyo: Shinchō Bunko, 1974). This is a translation of the original edition, pp. 7–42.

1. Note how Morito calls the president's son with the *-kun* suffix to show superiority to Yukimura. Yukimura refers to the same person with the *-san* suffix to show respect to both the president and Morito.

2. Building and attending the ancestral grave is highly regarded in Japan.

3. *Amae*, translated as ''passive dependency'' by psychiatrist Takeo Doi, is a strong component of the Japanese mentality, generated by the original mother-baby bond, developing into a master-disciple bond and other socio-psychological tendencies of Japanese life. It is an unspoken deep-seated trust and dependency on another.

From Paris

Ryō Takasugi

I

Matsuoka sat relaxed, with his feet propped up on his desk and the soles of his shoes facing Komiya. "I just got a telex from our Tokyo Main Office. It says that the Queen is coming to Paris later next week. Luckily she'll only be here for three days this time. It won't be too bad. I hope you can handle it. She's supposed to go to London from here. She has two others with her."

"No problem. Three days will be manageable. Last time was rough; she stayed for a week and a half!" Komiya's Westerner-like face cracked into a smile from relief rather than joy.

"She's fond of you. The crank may be coming to Europe mostly to see you." Matsuoka looked up at Komiya, flashing a grin.

"Please! You don't have to rub it in!"

"Settle down. You can't be all that unhappy having a VIP chase you. I guess women fall apart at the sight of a good-looking man no matter how old they are. Or is it your *Français* that's gotten her hooked?"

"That's enough! This is no spring chicken we're talking about.[1] The woman must be sixty, a granny. She makes me sick." Komiya scowled in disgust. In fact, the memory of the overperfumed, heavily made-up woman could make him cry. Komiya was embarassed to be seen in her company, although there was no denying that someone else might call her adorable. Everything was a matter of preference. It wasn't as if she didn't have her cute side. She even had something rather childish about her.

"Say what you want, she's very important to us. Be sure to do everything you can. Her company buys half its raw material from us. As far as I know we're their number one trader."

"I know, I know. Why else am I breaking my back without a word of complaint?" Komiya laughed, remembering that he had just finished complaining.

"Good! That's the spirit," said Matsuoka, pulling his feet off his desk. "The Queen is a superwoman and ruler of her husband, the company president. There's a saying in Tōa Chemicals that you're a goner if she ever turns on you. Just be sure to get on her good side. Here's her three-day itinerary." Matsuoka handed over a piece of paper. The "itinerary" was very simple, just her flight schedule and a timetable of her visit to a chemical company.

"Other than the afternoon of the second day when she goes to P-Company, her schedule is wide open. Think up something good for her. And reserve rooms at the Ritz as soon as possible. She seems to like that hotel."

"All right, I'll get on it."

Komiya left the manager's office, stopped at the restroom, and then went back to his desk. One of the major tasks of the trading company employees living abroad was to escort the company's business customers and their relations, as well as any officials from the main office. This was particularly true of Komiya, who practically made a full-time job of the practice. He knew painfully well how critically his relationship to his clients affected business negotiations with his company.

Three levels of hospitality were offered by the company. The levels were set by the main office or branch offices overseas. Rank C, the lowest, generally meant just treating a casual visitor to a meal. Rank B included meals and trips to the airport. Rank A was further divided into A–1, A–2, and A–3. In the A–3 rank, the company paid expenses in full for the entire period of the guests' stay, and a staff with a good command of the country's language accompanied them night and day.

Noriko Hasegawa naturally rated A–3. Plus, being as she was, everything had to be first-rate. The cost to the company was enormous. But on the other hand, Noriko's extravagance was insignificant compared to the several billion yen business that T-Trading Company did with her company.

Ryōhei Komiya was the manager's attaché at the Paris branch office of T-Trading Company, a trading conglomerate. He worked in the General Business Department. Thirteen years after graduating from a university, his rank was only one step short of section chief, but this was already his tenth year in Paris. During the first three years with the T-Trading Company, he had worked at the Chemical Product Division in the main office in Tokyo. During his first two years in Paris, he was in charge of the three-nation trade of chemical products. What got him started as the manager's attaché was a tour through Europe by President and Mrs. Hasegawa of Tōa Chemicals. The couple was very pleased with Komiya's services.

Komiya was a public relations specialist of sorts. Although he jokingly referred to himself as "Mr. Tour-Guide," the rest of the office never trifled his role. Everyone knew that his fluent English and French had tempted Mr. and Mrs. Hasegawa to ask the president of T-Trading Company to make him a tour-guide.

Because Paris is a popular sightseeing spot for the Japanese, visitors streamed in incessantly throughout the year. Komiya was completely tied up. Others envied his opportunities to drink, eat, and have fun, yet still get paid for it by the company, but to Komiya, there was nothing fun about it. He had already lost his taste for fancy food. He wished he could make a clean break with the same old business and get into real work. But the company would not consider letting go of this handyman, the attaché to the manager. His wife's pleading to go back to Japan and his parents' pressing for his return via telephone and letters from Tokyo had been getting on his nerves. He had come to the point where he sincerely wished for a new posting. He was genuinely homesick.

Ten years was too long, no matter how he tried to justify it. The managers had changed three times since he'd been there. Ordinarily, promising staff were promoted to other offices every three years or so. Only so-called local employees stayed at a single post longer. Cases like Komiya's were unheard of in the reputable T-Trading Company, which employed nearly ten thousand people.

A longing to return to Japan had grown within him. He had pressed the manager on this point numerous times. He had once written a long petition to the Personnel Office and the Chemical Product Headquarters in Tokyo, but to no avail. He felt more desperate after reading Marco Polo's *Record of the East,* spending three months with the help of a dictionary.

II

Back at his desk, Komiya's next-door neighbor, deputy department chief of the General Business Office, a homely-faced Satomi, talked to him in a low voice. Satomi was two years Komiya's senior.

"Is it a VIP visit this time?"

"It's Mrs. Hasegawa."

"Oh no! Her again! Wasn't she here just last month?"

"Amen. Don't you know it. I guess these big shots have to travel a lot."

"It's great that you got picked out. She sure knows who can best show her around and introduce her to the bigwigs of Paris. I've got to respect you for that."

"I just got harassed about it by the manager. The nerve of him. I wish you could take my place. My job is a bigger strain than you think."

"I don't know, you may be right. But it's all yours since nobody else can do it. I guess that's how it goes. When it comes to speaking French fashionably, my kind just can't cut it, even if we stand on our heads." Satomi shrugged his shoulders, his palms facing upward.

Komiya was chafed by Satomi's manner, but said nothing.

"Well, permit me to go back to checking through vouchers, something my kind can do." Satomi spoke in a theatrically slovenly way, and went back to his desk.

The chain of events this morning led Komiya to decide that he would definitely have to go back to Tokyo this year. The decision jelled his frustration and took him straight back to the manager's office.

"Now what?" asked Matsuoka, looking up at Komiya who stood in front of his desk glaring at him. Matsuoka lit a cigarette.

"Manager, would you see to it that I go back to the main office at the June personnel rotation? I don't remember how many times I've asked you this before, but I mean it this time. In the first place, do you realize that I've worked here for ten years? And I've been doing the same work all that time."

"Ah, is it ten years already?" said Matsuoka as if it had nothing to do with him, and blew out some cigarette smoke. "If I were you, I would be delighted to stay in Paris."

"But I'm not. I have to think about my child's education. My wife is going out of her mind these days. If you keep me here much longer, it'll become a morale problem for you."

"Goodness! You seem determined. You know that you're vitally important here, and even the personnel department in Tokyo can't move you as it wishes. It's really not my decision."

"Seriously. I might have to leave the company if you don't act on this."

"So, now you're threatening me, huh?" Matsuoka finally scowled.

"Well, I'm not asking for anything so outrageous, am I?"

"Why all of a sudden, though?"

"This isn't sudden at all. This is my second request since you came here."

"I never thought you'd come down on me quite so hard." Matsuoka had been smoking languidly, but abruptly crushed the butt in an ashtray, got up, and told Komiya to have a seat. "Komiya-kun, haven't you heard anything from the Queen?"

"What am I supposed to hear?"

"When my predecessor tried to take you out of our Paris office, the personnel office in Tokyo called it off. It was because Mrs. Hasegawa didn't want that to happen. She wanted you here. You see, it's very convenient for her to have you here. I hear that she calls you Ryōhei and treats you like her own son. Apparently, she has threatened either our president or manager that she would drop her business with us if we transferred you." Matsuoka narrated in a stern expression. "What I'm trying to get at is that you have to get the Queen's permission if you really want to move out of this office. Why don't you make use of her visit this time, and talk to her when you catch her in a good mood?"

"Are you kidding me? Do you really mean this crap?" Komiya stared at Matsuoka, flabbergasted.

"What do you mean? Of course I'm serious."

"This is the most ridiculous story I've ever heard. I know how important Tōa is to us, but it's beyond me that our company lets her step into our personnel problems. If you mean that our company is dancing to Mrs. Hasegawa's tune, it doesn't make sense." Komiya almost laughed.

But Matsuoka shook his head, still keeping a hard expression, "That's what you think. You think it's a joke. But think about this: Mrs. Hasegawa comes to Europe a dozen times every year. Especially these days, she's all over Paris, for opera, ballet, Japanese dance, you name it. She's drowning in art. She's deep into cultural exchanges, too. She needs you here. You're too valuable and useful. Her talk about cancelling orders may be an exaggeration, but she has plenty of reason to keep you here."

Komiya didn't know what to say.

"Why else would our company keep you in Paris for more than ten years?"

Komiya's face tensed and his heart sank.

"I should say that the best thing for you to do is to talk to the Queen directly. You are better acquainted with her than anyone else."

"I will, but what a mess! How unbelievable! This is really bizarre."

"Let's face it: life is full of strange things. But, personally, I would appreciate it if you kept still for a while. You are the Ace of our Paris office, and indispensable. I don't want to lose you. I've been here for less than a year. I need your help, and in fact, I wouldn't know what to do without you."

"You are kind to put it that way, but I can't end my life in Paris. And I'm dying to get out of the escort business—it's been ten years."

"Believe me, I feel for you." Matsuoka took a cigarette out of a case with a sulky expression on his face, and kept tapping the table with the filtered end.

III

Noriko Hasegawa arrived at the Charles de Gaulle Airport with her two secretaries in late April. Trees in Paris were just beginning to bud. Although Noriko had traveled for about seventeen hours via the North Pole, she showed no sign of fatigue. Komiya couldn't help but be impressed by her energy. In contrast, her companions, an elderly man and a secretary-like man, were bleary-eyed and obviously exhausted.

As soon as she saw him, Noriko walked briskly over to Komiya and gave him a hug and kiss. Komiya was ready for this, but because of what Matsuoka had said, he couldn't respond to her as easily as usual.

"This time, I came only for business. I'm taking the place of my husband."

"I'm glad to see you looking so well. And how is your husband?"

"He's going strong. Too much so in fact. He's got so many meetings he can't manage to leave Tokyo."

"Well, I'll get the full report later. You probably want to go to the hotel first. I reserved you a suite at the Ritz."

"Thank you. I'm lucky to have my Ryōhei in Paris."

"Glad to be of service."

"My husband appreciates you, too. He keeps telling me that nobody in Tōa compares to you when it comes to the ways of the world. He wants you to quit the T-Trading Company and come to ours, but we want you in Paris too, so . . ."

"I'm flattered." Komiya bowed lightly, but the memories of Matsuoka's earlier comments made him very uneasy.

Komiya took the three guests by Mercedes Benz to their hotel, went back to his office, and returned to the Ritz at six o'clock to pick them up. The Mercedes was the manager's vehicle. There was a chauffeur, a local employee, but Komiya had decided to drive himself, making more room for the three guests. He had chartered a taxi for the evening trip, however, because Matsuoka was with him this time.

Matsuoka and Komiya found Noriko in her luxurious hotel suite, all prepared to go out with them in a dark evening dress. She summoned her two companions by telephone and introduced them to Matsuoka and Komiya for the first time. The elderly man's name was Okiyama, the director and head of the president's office. The younger introduced himself as Arai, a member of the secretarial office.

They had a duck dish at the Restaurant Tour D'Argent in Bandome Square, as they viewed the Notre Dame Cathedral on the other side of the river. Afterward, Komiya accompanied Noriko to a nightclub until midnight, and then went home with a promise to meet for lunch the next day in the Ritz dining room. Matsuoka had left after the dinner, making apologies, ''Maybe it's best if a hybrid like me gave the floor over to you.'' Komiya couldn't tell if Matsuoka was trying to please Noriko or to keep a respectful distance from her by leaving her with Komiya.

Komiya found an opportunity to appeal to Noriko on the evening of her second day in Paris. Okiyama and Arai had gone off on their own somewhere. He sat face to face with Noriko in a room of the Japanese restaurant Miki on the Champs Elysées. Nicely waited on by a Japanese waitress in a navy-blue kimono, they exchanged sake cups. Noriko was petite, but when it came to drinking, she was a giant. She had had an incredible number of drinks. She was chirpy, but her bloodshot eyes were already halfway closed.

''My husband will be jealous to hear that you and I drank sake all by ourselves.''

Komiya decided that this was the once-and-for-all chance.

''Mrs. Hasegawa, I've been in Paris for ten years now. Would you please consider releasing me from my Paris assignment?'' What he was trying to say sounded odd to him, but at least he spoke earnestly. He felt the effect of the sake instantly wear off, and realized that he had just thrown a wet blanket over the little private party. ''The manager told me that he couldn't transfer me without your permission.'' Komiya scratched his head to indicate embarrassment. At the same time, he felt bad about posing a sorry figure in front of Noriko. He simply couldn't bite at her the way he did with Matsuoka.

"What are you talking about, Ryōhei? What do I have to do with it?"

"You must know how much influence you and your husband have on our company. I need your help. My wife is going crazy and I feel powerless." This time Komiya managed to make it sound humorous.

"I know your wife. She seems like the type to like it here. Talking about your wife, why didn't you bring her with you tonight?"

"Oh, I'm sorry. I forgot to give you her best regards. She has a slight cold, and couldn't come."

"Oh, poor Ryōhei! It must be hard for you if your wife has a cold and is going crazy at the same time." Noriko's tone was ambivalent. She gulped another cupful.

"Our child will be in school next year. My wife is an only child, and her parents are very anxious to have her back. It worries me."

"For Heaven's sake, I thought you were more of a male chauvinist."

"I'm sorry."

"Don't worry. I'll have my husband talk to Okamoto. But really, we aren't the ones to decide your future, you know." Perhaps out of sorts to some degree, Noriko arched her eyebrows sharply. The deepened wrinkles on the corners of her eyes exposed her age. The man she called "Okamoto" happened to be the president of the T-Trading Company. Her appellation without a title made plain her power over the T-Trading Company. Komiya felt insulted, but said nothing.

"Don't trading company employees enjoy working abroad? I had imagined that London and Paris are the best of all possibilities. What's so great about going back to Tokyo?"

Komiya didn't answer.

"An alternative is that you leave your T-Trading company and come to ours." Noriko made her vocal cords ring high, and banged the table with her palms. "That's it! What a great idea! A trading company isn't a place to stay forever. Nothing is waiting for you at the end of it all. On the other hand, you'll be a smashing success in Tōa. I'm sure my husband will extend a hearty welcome. I'll talk with him as soon as I get back. That's it. That's what you should do!" Noriko was excited about her own idea.

As her nickname Amazon indicated, Noriko had an insider's wisdom about the nature of trading companies. Komiya was impressed.

The development of the Japanese economy was impossible without trading companies. No small number of "trading company men"[2] go so far as to embrace an evangelic passion to serve their country. As a result, a new expression "civildom"[3] was created to pair up with the existing "officialdom." It referred mostly to the "topflight trading company men,"[4] and suggested that the private sectors abroad contributed to Japan in the same capacity as the diplomatic corps. Actually, only a very limited number of internationally minded, globe-trotting and able trading company men remained in civildom. A majority dropped out or were casually thrown out of the competitive arena like a used dishcloth.

Even among leading industries, the attrition rate of trading company men was high. Many young people had glowing ideas of trading companies, but the reality was dismal. In fact, international commerce was one of the most hazardous of enterprises. It was a world of clear meritocracy. Getting along without committing a major offense was not enough. Komiya shuddered when he tried to estimate how many of his peers would survive to retirement age. The whole process was like tightrope walking. How many trading company men in their thirties and forties had resigned and gone into manufacturing and other foreign investment enterprises?

Komiya was one of those who had once entertained some of the civildom consciousness. But the escort business had cremated such idealism. His memory was littered with tragic examples, like the person who killed himself after incurring a great deficit in the Chicago wheat trade, or the one who passed away from an endemic disease in Africa. Noriko's words, "it isn't a place to stay forever," weighed heavily on him. Nevertheless, he couldn't imagine himself leaving the T-Trading Company just yet. It was also upsetting to realize that he hadn't done any work of significance as yet. He had put a great store on future possibilities.

Not knowing how resolute Noriko was, Komiya could only simper. He would modestly judge her remarks to be a drunkard's mischief, but couldn't get it out of his head when Noriko cast an excited glance at him and kept on saying, "Ryōhei, let's do that. My company needs someone like you so badly we can taste it."

"I'm flattered. But I should at least go back to Tokyo, do some work, and recover from culture shock before trying to work for a first-rate company like yours," Komiya pussyfooted with a noncommittal answer.

"What culture shock? How can a henpecked husband like you feel it?"

Noriko was starting to slur her words. But her final clear words—

which were delivered with her back pulled up straight—truly showed her size. "I'll take care of your transfer to Tokyo. But make sure that you follow proper procedure. You write a request to your personnel office. And don't mention my husband and me. We aren't supposed to be more than bystanders."

"Thank you very much." Komiya bowed deeply, and happily mused that it might not be a bad idea to move to Tōa Chemicals sometime in the future.

IV

It was after the long holidays in May that Makiguchi, personnel department chief of the T-Trading Company, was summoned by President Okamoto through the latter's secretary. Makiguchi tightened his necktie, braced himself, and knocked on the president's door.

"Have a seat." Okamoto lifted his eyes from the paper he was reading, removed his gold-framed glasses, and strolled over to the sofa Makiguchi was on.

"I met President Hasegawa of Tōa Chemicals at a party yesterday, and heard something funny. He wants us to bring Komiya back from our Paris office. I thought that Komiya was Mrs. Hasegawa's pet. Has he done something wrong? He guided me around Paris more than once. He did a great job."

"Now that you've mentioned him, it comes back to my mind that Komiya has sent me a transfer request. Do you suppose it's a coincidence that the president's request and Komiya's letter arrived at the same time?"

"Hmm, that's interesting. The president's exact words were, 'I hear that Komiya has been in Paris for ten years now. Why don't you let him go somewhere else?' You know that it was President Hasegawa himself who had stopped our former president from replacing Komiya. I don't know whether to believe him or not."

"Mrs. Hasegawa just returned from Paris. I'm sure Komiya showed her around. Have you heard anything about it?"

"No, nothing beyond what President Hasegawa has told me. He said that Komiya had helped him and his wife a great deal, so he wants to give him a big welcoming party when he comes back. It didn't seem like he held anything against Komiya-kun, and he hopes that we find someone at least halfway as good. I told him not to worry because our company has plenty of qualified people."

"Does that mean that we should bring Komiya back?"

"I suppose so. I don't know what happened in Paris, but it couldn't be too bad. I'll let you pick his post over here. For the one in Paris, try someone more fluent in English and French than Komiya. I want Tōa to see how resourceful we are."

"I'll try." Makiguchi nodded and left. Back in his office, he asked the section chief to compile a fast list of several good-looking men in their thirties who were fluent in English and French.

One week later, Komiya received the order to return to the Tokyo office. He was impressed with Noriko's influence in Tōa Chemicals. Invited to lunch by Makiguchi immediately on his return to Tokyo, he was unknowingly interviewed about the details of his conversation with Noriko in Paris.

"If it's the Hasegawa couple's wish, it would be difficult to say 'No' wouldn't it?" Makiguchi glanced at Komiya as he lackadaisically fished for information.

"I don't think so. I didn't make any promises. Personally, I would like to work here for another ten or twenty years, that is, if I'm allowed to."

"But her request to free you from your Paris job is based on her plan to scout you for her company. If she thinks that you're going with them, you can't refuse. In other words, you've got to say 'Yes' to her."

"You aren't talking sense, Manager." Komiya raised his voice, coloring.

"As you know," said Makiguchi, picking his teeth with a toothpick, "the relationship between the T-Trading Company and Tōa Chemicals is very close. I don't think our president can refuse if President Hasegawa asked for you. Especially if this transfer is prefaced by Mrs. Hasegawa's talk with you in Paris, I'm sure the Hasegawas assume that you're coming."

"What about my plans, though?"

"You don't think this offer is exactly bad for you, do you?" Makiguchi went on smiling loosely. "One way or the other, you make out."

"Not necessarily. I know I'm only a two-bit salary man but I still don't like Tōa's way of doing things. I'm going to turn them down."

"Aren't you brave. Take it easy."

"I suppose I should take their offer, but I've always seen myself as a trading company man. Please don't give up on me yet. Besides, even if Tōa makes an official offer, don't I get a choice?" Komiya smiled bitterly. He felt that there was something wrong about the whole situation.

"The world we live in is not logical."

"Mrs. Hasegawa could have been leading me on in Paris. It seems unlikely that they would actually ask for me. You may find out that you've misread the situation."

"As far as I'm concerned, it's just too bad to lose a talent like you. Our company is just beginning to get a payoff for your training. But if Tōa asks, we'll just have to smile and let you go. That would probably be best for everyone."

"Sentiment has lost its popularity. It's a cutthroat world. No point in worrying until it happens," Komiya laughed, wondering who was advising whom.

V

Makiguchi outlined the essentials of his talk for President Okamoto and the Managing Director of Personnel, Yokouchi, and appended his own view that Komiya would most certainly move to Tōa. The two seniors did no more than make halfhearted "Hmm, hmm" sounds, but they appeared to have resigned themselves to the possible outcome.

Komiya was the only one from his age group to be promoted to the section chief level at the time of the June 1 personnel rotation. And Makiguchi's decision to give Komiya the post of the head of the Chemical Product Synthetic Resins First Section was based on a deal he had made with Miyagawa, chief of the Chemical Product Division.

The former section chief of the Chemical Product Division, Kihara, Komiya's senior by three years, was an upstart star among his age group, and had sped quickly up the "elitist highway." While he did high caliber work, his connection to the company as a distant relative of the president had helped pave a rosy way for him. Komiya couldn't help but be excited about taking over Kihara's post. What Komiya didn't realize, unfortunately, was that he had been chosen for a devious reason. Komiya did notice at the time of his transfer that his predecessor looked beaten. It bothered him at first, but he was too taken up by his new assignments to be concerned. Kihara left for the New York Branch Office too soon. There was no time for Komiya to learn that he was to be Kihara's scapegoat, set up to cover his predecessor's errors and to save face.

The story went like this: At the end of the year before, the oil-producing countries raised the price of crude. As a result, the cost of raw materials for a great variety of commodities rose. Fears of a price hike resulted in an early placement of purchase orders and a subsequent shortage of vinyl chloride resins. Precisely when the shortage was at its peak, R-Country in Eastern Europe made soundings through the Japanese embassy to see if Japanese trading companies might be interested in purchasing its surplus vinyl chloride resins. The products of this country were inferior to Japan's, but this happened to be the time when companies could not afford to argue over quality. Various trading companies jumped into the purchasing competition. It was a seller's market even for a low-quality product.

Nevertheless, the manufacturers identified the low-quality products as substandard. They would not buy them. Some trading companies quickly caught on to this new development and discontinued importing, but the T-Trading Company missed the chance to pull out. It accumulated a 5,000-ton stockpile. This was entirely Kihara's fault.

Just then, the price of vinyl chloride resins started to drop precipitously, as a repercussion of the surplus stocks and a general recession. From the peak price 190 yen per kilogram, the price was down to 150 yen in March, and the future market looked weaker yet. Because the import price from R-Country was 170 yen per kilogram upon unloading, there was a loss of 20 yen per kilogram and 100 million yen for 5,000 tons. A 100 or 200 million yen loss was nothing to be startled by; it occurred every now and then. But the problem was that the 5,000-ton stock had no buyers. The loss for the 5,000 tons was 850 million yen, not counting storage costs and interest. Kihara had struggled to recapitalize but nothing worked. Adding up the costs of storage, interest, and others, the loss easily exceeded one billion yen. Komiya returned from Paris just when his company was struggling with this problem.

Komiya's face had flashed across Makiguchi's mind when he was informed about Kihara by the Synthetic Resins Division head, Yoshioka. He saw no harm in putting the blame onto someone who would be leaving the company soon. In the highly competitive trading company, a one billion yen loss would be blamed on the staff in charge, the supervisor division head, and in some serious cases, even the department head. But in Makiguchi's plan, Komiya would shoulder the burden alone. And by freeing up the Chemical Products Division head and the Synthetic Resins Division head, Makiguchi could make them feel indebted to him. He could even gain the gratitude of the president. And most important, he could save the company's

"Prince" Kihara. Were Komiya not under the spell of culture shock, and had he familiarized himself earlier with the everyday transactions, he would have questioned the abnormal quantity of vinyl chloride resins imported from R-Country. But his mind was not quite all there.

VI

It was a hot late July day. Makiguchi invited Komiya out to lunch at a neighborhood restaurant.

"Haven't you heard from President Hasegawa, yet?"

"No. It must have been a joke after all. It had to be a joke."

"No news to our president, either. What if you reminded Mrs. Hasegawa?"

Komiya looked at Makiguchi terror-stricken. First he thought that Makiguchi was teasing him, but it didn't take long to figure out that he was dead serious.

"To be frank, you'll have a better future there. Our executives think so, too," Makiguchi continued.

"What do you mean? Does T-Trading Company want me out?" Komiya stared at Makiguchi.

"It's not that we don't need you. It's just that we have planned things on the premise that you would be recruited by Tōa. I want you to understand that it was a special arrangement that got you appointed section chief."

"Aren't you basically telling me to quit the T-Trading Company? Did I slip up? Is there some reason why I should be leaving?"

"Nothing like that." Makiguchi hastened to wave his hand across his face in response to Komiya's impassioned voice. "You haven't done anything wrong. But I think you should talk to the Hasegawa couple. How shall I say it . . . a man of your capacity will do well no matter where you go. If you are going there anyway, I think that the higher echelons of our company would rather have you move right now and make Tōa feel indebted to us."

"Please don't make excuses. It's hard for me to resign until I'm convinced that the T-Trading Company doesn't want me. Do you understand my point? It's been less than two months since I got my new post."

"You don't have to raise your voice; I'm right here. Just finish your meal."

"I can't. How can I?" Komiya put down his silverware and took a long look at Makiguchi.

Knowing the Hasegawas' strong personalities, and particularly of Mrs. Hasegawa, Makiguchi had thought that they would be coming for Komiya posthaste. The realization that they hadn't done so nearly three months after Komiya's return started grating on him. If Komiya had no place to go, Makiguchi had to come up with a way to get rid of him. He may have miscalculated.

Makiguchi contracted a business newswriter and obtained a report on the inside affairs of Tōa. The report said that Tōa's bullish facility investment had backfired, and that the company was presently in a financial crisis. In panic, it had cut back production, but this alone was not enough to make up for the slow growth. The interest payment for the new sodium hydroxide production facility, which had been installed on misadvice from the government, magnified the crisis. Tōa's economy floundered so badly that its main banks were compelled to suggest a major layoff.

"I'm afraid I didn't find out anything beyond what everyone at the T-Trading Company already knows." The financial reporter hung up the telephone after this sarcastic remark.

Makiguchi was totally unprepared to learn about Tōa's disaster. He absentmindedly stared into space for a while. *So, this was why the Hasegawa couple didn't send for Komiya. Tōa must be in a poor way if it is laying people off.*

If the Chemical Products Headquarters was to get rid of the bad quality vinyl stock by the mid-September account-closing day, not much time was left. After some serious thinking, Makiguchi called in the head of the Synthetic Resins Division, Yoshioka.

"I think that Taiwanese factories will be buying up the chloride resins. The price is going to be less than half of what we paid, but it's better than nothing," said Yoshioka. "Komiya worked hard for this. Our actual loss will be around 600 million yen, but you know, we should consider ourselves lucky if we can make up for even a small portion of our loss. Since the overall synthetic resins trade is in the black, we really didn't have to send Kihara to New York in such a hurry, in a way." Yoshioka spoke unconcernedly as he picked his nose. His greasy and shiny face was well suntanned from playing golf, and he had about him the air of an active and able trading company man.

"But we can't let this slide. Somebody has to take responsibility for the loss sooner or later," Makiguchi answered.

"If you are thinking of Komiya, you can't send him to Tōa. They're having problems right now."

"Yes, apparently. But a group of people including our president have made an arrangement about Komiya. I'm stuck. Or, perhaps I can slip him in Yamada's slot. Yamada will be finishing up his three-year term in Tanzania soon."

"Oh brother! From 'gay Paris' to Tanzania is a big step down! I'm not sure I can put him through that."

"I'm with you, but what else can we do? Our excuse will be that we want to see whether Komiya will sink or swim."

"When can you send him out there?"

"On September first, I hope."

"You should at least wait until October first. That will give him just about four months in Tokyo."

"All the same, he'll wonder what this is all about. I wonder if he will connect this transfer to the chloride resin problem." Makiguchi felt a pang of conscience and grimaced.

"Of course he's going to wonder, but I doubt he'll figure it out. I hear he didn't even suspect the problem when he picked up the new assignment. It was Kihara who bought the chloride resins from R-Country. There's no changing that. But we can say that Komiya miscalculated the time for selling the stock. That way, it figures that I as his senior would receive an official reprimand," Yoshioka said.

"We've made poor Komiya pay to keep Kihara clean. But we did it because of Mrs. Hasegawa's offer."

"Ha, you're turning everything on Mrs. Hasegawa." Yoshioka lowered his voice and stuck out the tip of his tongue.

VII

Komiya interpreted the transfer order as Makiguchi's expression of annoyance about how he had behaved. Perhaps Makiguchi thought he was too uppity with the senior staff in general and particularly with Makiguchi. The best he could do now was to leave his wife and child in Tokyo and go to Tanzania by himself. At the same time, the possibility of leaving the company also piqued his curiosity. Really, he couldn't help being rankled by the way things were going. Why did the aspiring star of his age group have to be exiled to Africa after a mere four months' service in Tokyo? The worst was that people had begun to wonder. They suspected that Komiya had gotten into an unidentified scandal and was not allowed to stay in Tokyo. This transfer simply did not make sense.

Komiya visited President Hasegawa of Tōa one afternoon towards the end of September, shortly before his trip to Tanzania. The purpose was to say goodbye. He had made an appointment through a secretary, but when he walked in to the president's office, Mrs. Hasegawa was there.

"I hear that you are being sent to a very distant country. Did they find the skeletons in your closet?" Noriko wagged her slanderous tongue at Komiya, giving him quite a turn.

"Not at all. I'm all square. I can't figure this out myself, but as the saying goes, 'the life of a government official is not an enviable one.' There's nothing I can do about it."

"Paris is where you belong. You would look out of place in Tanzania. What if you went back to Paris?"

"Things aren't that simple."

"Your successor, what's his name . . . ?"

"You mean Orihara?"

"Yes, I suppose his name was Orihara. His French is good, but he's a little dense. If you want, I can push for your return."

"Come on, that's enough. You're ruining my reputation. How can I ask them to send Komiya back to Paris?" interjected President Hasegawa, pulling a cigar out of his mouth.

"I'll ask Okamoto." Noriko was not daunted.

"Thank you for your concern, but I've had enough of Paris. Tanzania is more interesting." Komiya put on a bold front, doing his best to appear satisfied. In the end, Mrs. Hasegawa made no mention of his moving to Tōa. Komiya couldn't lie to himself; he would have liked a job offer. He wasn't sure if he would have accepted it, but he wished that she had at least offered.

Had Noriko forgotten everything she had said in Paris? Or was she just keeping it to herself? Perhaps the labor union wouldn't let the president hire someone new when the company was about to practice a mass layoff.

After two months in Tanzania, Komiya received a letter from his colleague, Ohta. The letter explained in full about the vinyl chloride incident. It said that Ohta heard it from an old colleague who now worked in the Synthetic Resins Department. Komiya got cold shudders at this discovery, but there was nothing he could do.

Notes

This short story was originally published as ''A Civildom Who Tripped'' (Minryō no zasetsu) in *A Rebellion of an Elitist* (Erīto no hanran) (Tokyo: Kōdansha, 1984). The word ''civildom'' means a civilian employed for patriotic goals. This is a translation of ''Minryō no zasetsu'' in Takasugi's *Bank Personnel Office* (Ginkō Jinjibu) (Tokyo: Shūei-sha Bunko, 1984), pp. 73–105.

   1. The original phrase used here is *''hana no kanbase''* (a face as fair as the May rose). The sound of the word *''kanbase''* rhymes with the word ''conversation'' (written in katakanaized English) which is used by Matsuoka and translated here as ''language skill.''

   2. The original Japanese for this word is *''shōsha man.''*

   3. In Japanese, *''minryō''* as opposed to *''kanryō''* (government employed official-dom).

   4. This is written in katakana *''bijines erīto.''*

The Baby Boom Generation

Taichi Sakaiya

PART 1

I

"Hmm, a convenience store chain . . ." Seizō Ohkura tilted back his bald head, gazing at the ceiling. He had already listened to the briefing about the new project. Advancing age and the problems of his company had darkened the thick fat on his face. Ohkura had been running the A-Electric Company for twenty years, from the late 1950s. He ran it as if he owned it.

"Yes, they are popular these days in the United States. . . ." Shigeki Tomita started to answer, but stopped himself when he saw Junji Yoshifuji put his finger to his lips.

Yoshifuji had served Ohkura for eight years, first as his executive secretary, and later as the head of the presidential secretariat. He knew all of the old president's habits and idiosyncrasies. One of the things he knew was that the president, who lived by the logo "mature thinking and resolute decision," didn't care for "noise" of any sort during his deliberations. Tomita, who had worked under Yoshifuji as an assistant executive secretary, had a lot to learn from him.

Ohkura pulled his obese body forward and began clumsily packing tobacco into his pipe. The deep vertical furrows on his fat forehead showed that the old man was still thinking. His eyes were still directed toward the paper on his desk. The several-page document had been written by Tomita, and was titled "Convenience Store Chain Plan."

Tomita sat facing President Ohkura, on a leather sofa in the middle of the large office. The sofa was surrounded by unmatched furniture—a wood-grain print steel desk, dark mahogany ornamental shelves—and light-colored walls with geometric designs. Time seemed to move slowly in this room. The mixed tension of expectation and anxiety was something any employee would feel when he sat face to face with this autocratic president.

Ohkura seemed to be reviewing the document leisurely, indifferent to the young man's discomfort. Yoshifuji sat next to Tomita, as motionless as Tomita, poised on the edge of the sofa. The glazed window glass of the president's office shut out the July sun, and the room was comfortably air conditioned. Nonetheless, Tomita felt the perspiration oozing on his forehead and in his armpits.

Tomita, who had been chosen to be the section supervisor of the presidential Corporate Planning Office at the age of thirty-eight, understood that President Ohkura's evaluation of his "Convenience Store Chain Plan" would determine his future. He dropped his eyes to the paper piled on his lap. There was no need to review the paper; he could almost recite it by heart, line by line. But he had to do something to overcome the tension of the moment. The first page outlined in seven subcategories the company's "Current Situation and Problems." The next page had graphs showing various incomes and expenses of the company for the last ten years. On the left, there were three diagrams shaped like sake bottles.[1] These were the "Demographic Diagrams of Our Company Employees." Tomita had seen enough of these. There was an "Evaluation of Various Policies" on the third page. The fourth page defined the nature of the so-called convenience store: "It is a small but all-purpose retail store that maximally answers the needs of the general consumer. It operates from about eight in the morning till about eight at night. It sells preservable products for basic daily needs and general groceries; it takes catalog orders; it arranges for the repair of home electrical appliances; it is a small, friendly store."

After this definition, Tomita had listed the advantages of operating this type of store as part of a chain: costs cut by way of wholesale purchases, the reduction of inventories through the exchange of merchandise between stores, the possibility of developing intimate contacts with local residents, and so on.

The last page contained the list of merchandise, sales prospects, and the floor plan of a typical store. Part of the information in this portion was borrowed from the examples of convenience stores in the United States. The total area of the shop and residence was about 1,440 square feet.

It's too bad that the A-Electric Industry—a light electrical appliance maker with 80 billion yen in capital, and 4,000 employees—has to get into such a marginal retail business. A perplexed feeling passed through Tomita's mind. This wasn't the first time he had felt this way, either. In fact, the bewilderment kept coming back. Among other things, he feared that President Ohkura's clay-colored lips might let out an enraged bellow and blow away his hard-earned position in the A-Electric Company.

But, no, I can't be wrong . . . , Tomita told himself in an effort to calm down. He had done five months' hard thinking on this and had written it, with Yoshifuji's help, in the kind of language Ohkura liked.

II

Undoubtedly, Shigeki Tomita was exceptionally well-treated by the A-Electric Company. His luck began when he was appointed assistant executive secretary. That was six years ago, about ten years after he had entered the company straight out of the university. This was a top managerial position in the main office. In addition, the new position gave him ready access to the president and his favorite executive, Yoshifuji.

An assistant executive secretary, in a way, was a secretary's secretary. Opportunities to have direct contact with the president were few, but Tomita had plenty of miscellaneous work to do for him. Among other duties, he had to map out the president's schedule of activities, draw up rough drafts of presidential addresses and manuscripts for professional magazines, make plans for the president's golf matches with clients, arrange employment for relatives of bank executives and politicians, and get rid of petty sōkaiyas[2] who sought an audience with the president. He always had to be on top of these time-consuming and yet inconspicuous chores. A good performance was taken for granted and error was not tolerated.

Tomita had been at it for three years without making a serious mistake. His performance had cost him his personal happiness and home life. He reported to the office early in the morning, and went home late at night. He was summoned to join golf matches—which he never enjoyed—on Sundays and special holidays. Frequently, he spent weekends and holidays drafting papers at the office. When his wife gave birth to her second child, he couldn't even take time off to visit her in the hospital. His absence had made a rubble of his home life.

He was very much involved in company work, yet had fewer exchanges with the president than he had hoped. Rare and brief meetings took place only a couple of times a month. Sometimes he was instructed by the president on how to handle a specific project, or even more rarely, they spoke in the car. Always, Secretary Yoshifuji was around, attending to the president's needs more zealously than anyone else.

Tomita had been released from this post about three years ago, although not to take part in anything more exciting.

"As you are aware, we send outstanding young men to the provinces. This is a three-year project we started last year. Its purpose is to strengthen our branch store network." Yoshifuji had gone out of his way to preface Tomita's transfer order. His apparent intention was to motivate the man who had gone through the ordeal of being his assistant secretary. It didn't work. The assignment to be the supervisor of a small store's business office in Shikoku³ flatly disappointed Tomita.

Tomita was familiar with A-Electric's three-year plan to send two hundred qualified young employees to the provincial branch offices and agencies. This was an attempt to make up for the inefficiency of the national railroad and the postal system, while at the same time strengthening the company's local network. But to most staff, the assignment meant nothing beyond a step into rustication. A common practice had been that those who had worked as an assistant executive secretary were given the post of deputy section supervisor of the business office in the main office, or else sent abroad, unless they were found to be incompetent.

Fortunately, it didn't take long for Tomita to realize that the secretarial position had paid off after all. He was called back to Tokyo in two years and two months. His new position, the section supervisor of the president's Corporate Planning Office, was a temporary arrangement; nevertheless, Tomita was in the main office. Not only that, this was a very respectable promotion, compared to those such as deputy section chief, branch company section chief, assistant executive of an agency, and the like, which were assigned to his peers and his immediate seniors. Yoshifuji himself had been promoted from secretary to executive chief of the president's office. How highly President Ohkura regarded Tomita was unknown, but it seemed obvious enough that his immediate supervisor Yoshifuji was his strong supporter. That's what counted. For Yoshifuji—who had made it to the post of executive chief of the president's office at the age of forty-six—was second in line to succeed the president.

"Tomita is the first man in the Yoshifuji lineup." Gossip like this traveled, but didn't bother Tomita. He didn't go for the interpretation implying favoritism, but appreciated Yoshifuji's recognition of his three years of dedication. He swore to himself that he would answer Yoshifuji's good will with hard work.

For some reason, no big assignment came around after the promotion. His job was to make large investment plans and to draw sales plans for new products among other things, but there was no work in these lines. The Japanese economy, which had looked hopeful during the 1980s,[4] had plunged right back into a deep recession. So, the order to "draft a radical recovery plan which would irradicate all the existing problems" was just what Tomita needed. It came on a cold morning several months ago. At that time, he didn't dream of proposing a plan like the one he had just handed to the president. At the time, he was not fully aware of A-Electric's chronic problems.

III

"A Radical Recovery." This phrase was cant by now. Its popularity spread in the 1970s, and it had been used frequently for a good four years. The duration of its popularity underlined the scope of the problem and the absence of a remedy. "Radical recoveries" were really needed everywhere in present-day Japan: in the national economy, local governments, the management of a majority of businesses, the household economies of many families, and so on. Ten years after the high growth period, ubiquitous distortions and strains in the economy had become far too numerous for any quick fix.

Japan had achieved "miraculously" high growth in the twenty-eight years between the end of World War II and the Oil Shock. The growth rate of its second half (1960s through the early 1970s), above all, was "outrageous." Like a huge avalanche, which accumulates speed and size as it rolls downward, the Japanese economy grew year by year until it reached second place in the global GNP ranking.

"It looked as if nothing could stop the high growth of those times. . . ." Tomita looked back every now and then. He had stepped into the "real world" at the mid-point of the high growth period.

As the twig is bent, so the tree shall grow. Shigeki Tomita's generation was a product of the culture created by a high growth society. He grew up while Japan raced up the ladder of economic growth, subscribing to the futurologists' prediction that "the twenty-first century will be a Japanese century." It all came about while he was dumbfounded by the scale of the projection and outraged by the blind force of an economy that trampled over everything else. Companies furiously invested for the future, and individuals bought land to build houses. This was when "everyone feared missing out on the growth, but none feared the snowballing debts." Everyone believed that "tomorrow meant more prosperity and that next year would be an improvement over this year."

In retrospect, it had been unreasonable to hope for endless growth, and worse yet, to fall victim to the belief. As if to punish this shortsightedness, a small war in the distant Middle East brought an end to Japan's vast growth, quickly and effortlessly.

The aftermath of the Oil Shock and the subsequent global recession was jarring. At least people felt so at the time. It appeared to mark a finale to the Japanese high economic growth period. However, the impact must not have been felt severely enough. The high growth theory, which had reached every corner of Japan, was hardly reexamined. Little changed in the economic structure of national and local governments, deficit-based industrial management, lifetime employment and seniority systems, the education craze, or the frivolous and flamboyant consumer pattern. The slowest to change was the mental framework of those who had become accustomed to the high growth economy. Everyone talked about economic stabilization, but didn't rid themselves of the belief in a better tomorrow. It goes without saying that politicians, managers, and labor union leaders didn't dare to take away the pleasant dream of the public. No one put any effort into expounding upon the true meaning, or the concrete impact, of stable growth. And then, for better or worse, the Japanese economy found itself on the way to recovery beginning around 1976, never experiencing a total collapse.

This seemingly strong recovery restored in the minds of the Japanese people a trust in their own economic system. It is true that the precipitous, madcap inflation ended in only a year. Production picked up faster than predicted. But this didn't mean that those who had ascribed their "rely on others" type of economic recovery to uniquely Japanese systems and customs, or to the personality and ability of the Japanese people, could claim any of the credit. They were too conceited to admit that the growth of Japanese exports was helped by the United States and the Middle East. They were guilty of renewed praise for Japanese vitality, Japanese-style labor management, et cetera.

As an assistant executive secretary, Tomita had written a number of papers on this theme in Seizō Ohkura's name. A majority of them concluded with expressions like "The high growth period for the Japanese economy is definitely over. But there's no doubt that the Japanese economy has already skillfully placed itself in an orbit of stable growth. This orbit, I am confident, will lead the Japanese public to an even brighter future."

IV

Thinking back, that had been Seizō Ohkura's heyday. A-Electric's business grew steadily even during the 1974–76 recession. It did better than other companies during the economic recovery period. Although home electric appliances didn't sell, audio equipment—A-Electric's main product—sold remarkably well in both national and international markets.

The old president, seventy-three at the time, with twenty years of experience in management, gained influence and became convinced of his own worth. Others were just as happy to believe that Ohkura had single-handedly bailed his company out of the recession in its early stage by adjusting its major production to consumer demand. Whether or not proper management was the result of chance was nobody's concern. In the world of economics, results are what count. Explanations can be added afterward.

Naturally, the success magnified Okhura's power and self-esteem. Coming from a large trading company at the end of the 1950s, he had rebuilt the nearly collapsed A-Electric Industry into a giant despite a series of poor conditions. An extremist flattered Ohkura as "too great a manager to belong to a middle-size electric appliance manufacturer." Financial journals welcomed Ohkura's arrogant "humanitarian" economic philosophy. Had Ohkura retired then, his reputation would have remained unscathed. But old men puffed up with power and pride are not inclined to step down. And of course, his luck did not last forever. It died down, keeping pace with the shrinkage of the age group that was crazy about audio devices.

Tomita had returned to the Tokyo office last fall, and found it completely changed. "It's only been two years and two months . . . ," he lamented.

It was true that the Japanese economy had been sliding downward towards the end of his assistant executive secretary days, but he could at least feel there used to be some vitality left in his company. Ohkura used to be in high spirits. His instructions, "A company-wide campaign to increase sales," "Let's go, salesmen!" "Harness your skills and ideas," had boomed throughout the company like a military trumpet. The zeal had eroded while Tomita sweated blood, cutting minor expenses and supervising the inexperienced sales staff in his Shikoku branch store. The sales of audio equipment had slumped, indifferent to the old president's scolding and urging.

Ohkura kept on preaching, issuing one presidential instruction after another, sometimes sounding harsher than before and at other times appealing for sympathy. He also had goals and slogans posted everywhere. But they had no more power of persuasion than yesteryear's popular songs. All evaporated into thin air, leaving behind only an "end of the summer" atmosphere. No, it wasn't a matter of atmosphere. The "summer" of A-Electric was clearly over. The swollen population, which had generously expanded the market for audio equipment in the 1970s, had outgrown the consumer phase.

The Japanese population had multiplied to an unprecedented size from 1947 through 1949, just after World War II. Twenty percent more Japanese were born during these three years than the preceding years, and 26 percent more than the years that followed. This was an unusual distortion of an otherwise very stable demographic pattern. It critically affected the Japanese economy and society. There were shortages of school buildings and teachers when this generation reached school age. The generation left behind surplus facilities and instructors. The facility adjustments for the 20 percent population increase required more than a 20 percent increase in investment. Similar problems developed at high school and university levels. When this age group reached the upper teens, the consumer market fattened. When they reached the "young adult" stage, "young noise" blasted throughout Japan. And then in the early seventies, wedding halls had done a big business.

The baby boom generation constituted an invisible lump in Japanese society and created peculiar demands and vogues. Wherever it passed, it left the marks of surplus facilities and excessive competition. The growth of the audio equipment market in the seventies was no more than a by-product of this demographic event. When the population lump moved out of the business territory of A-Electric, it took the success of the company and its president with it. By now, the so-called postwar generation lump had grown out of its adolescence and had entered the age of worry over the family budget and the children's education. The younger brothers, fewer in number, were content with the record players their elder brothers handed down to them.

The same demographic problem brought about another crisis for A-Electric in a totally different manner. The sake-bottle-shaped graph on Tomita's second sheet of paper illustrated the situation. The document was titled "The Demographic Charts of Our Company Employees."

V

There were three graphs in this document. Each had horizontal bars, mounted one on top of another. All represented the number of employees in each age group between the ages of twenty-two and fifty-eight. The graph on the right represented all employees; the one in the middle, female employees; the one on the left, male employees. The bars spread wide at the bottom, although only slightly in the female graph. The other two swelled in the center. The male chart was unique in that it swelled disproportionately in the center, and looked more like a high-hipped flower vase than like a sake-bottle. The contortion was caused by the company's hiring procedure. The company had hired many university graduates each year during the high growth period, but had cut back widely after the Oil Shock.

The chart alluded to A-Electric's current problems. It also revealed one of the hidden reasons for the company's earlier success. The postwar baby boom generation had poured in a massive fresh labor force during the high growth period. This age group was lucky to hit the expanded job market. Looking at it another way, the booming economy was due to this enormous young labor force. The Japanese seniority system had taken advantage of this demographic flaw. Low wages of young employees—meaning a majority—had kept the mean salary and personnel expenses low.

Unfortunately, the equilibrium broke about the end of the 1970s. The postwar generation, once a synonym for youth, was now over thirty. What used to be a beautifully proportioned pyramid in the demographic chart of employees now swelled unpleasantly in the middle. The lump, which climbed steadily every year, sought higher salaries and ranks. Those who had found jobs during the high growth period would not give up the dream of "a better tomorrow."

This was as big a setback for A-Electric as it was elsewhere. Companies at an economic impasse were unable to pay the ever rising salaries or to give proportionately higher ranks to the increasing number of senior employees. Economic stagnation prevented an expansion of the system or the building of ancillary plants. A-Electric temporarily sought its way out of this problem by sending two hundred middle-ranking university graduates to the provinces with the slogan "give strength to district branch offices," but it prepared nothing to reward them when they returned.

They should have foreseen this problem a long time ago . . . , thought Tomita when he first became aware of it. As a member of the baby boom generation, Tomita found this discovery appalling. As best he could tell, the solution would be either a mass dismissal of his peers or a total cap on salary raises. So long as all other companies were suffering from the same syndrome, the surplus workers had no alternatives. The loss of a job in one's thirties was fatal. This problem, much more serious and imminent than the widely discussed financial viability of post-retirement life, was now falling on the baby boom generation.

The company must find a way to grow. It may just have to step into new business areas. This was the only conclusion Tomita could see while investigating ways for a "radical recovery." This was how he came to propose the installment of the convenience store chain.

VI

"So, a convenience store chain . . . ," muttered Seizō Ohkura once more, after spending a luxurious amount of time looking at the paper. He slowly exhaled his pipe smoke.

Tomita's heart started racing again. He noticed that the vertical wrinkles on Ohkura's forehead had disappeared. The change indicated that the old man had come out of his meditation.

"This may be a good idea, Yoshifuji-kun.[5] This is the time for 'Give a chance and wait for the result.'" Ohkura pointed a baggy-skinned finger at the top of an ornamental shelf.

There was a framed calligraphy—"Give a chance and wait for the result"— done by a certain high monk to whom Ohkura had shown his respects. The monk had passed away more than ten years ago, but the four ideograms in North Sung Dynasty style were very much alive. The saying, "Give a chance and wait for the result," expressed the crux of the "humanitarian management" the Meiji[6]-born president prided himself upon.

Tomita let out a sigh of relief. He wasn't sure exactly what kind of relationship the convenience store chain plan had with this philosophical saying, but he knew that the president was in a good mood whenever he brought the calligraphy to people's attention.

"Yoshifuji-kun, go ahead and try it." Ohkura ignored the proposer of the idea, Tomita, and continued talking to his henchman. "Outline concrete ways to go about this—financing, allocations, construction schedules, and a rough estimate of income—as soon as possible. Get everyone in the president's office involved, and if necessary, you may even want to ask staffs in other departments to help you. Don't forget to put it on the agenda of the department heads' meetings. It also needs the approval of the board of directors. You should let banks know ahead of time, too. You need someone well-informed to handle this; otherwise people will start saying all kinds of things about it." Out of a wish not to be called an autocrat, Ohkura made Yoshifuji follow normal procedures.

"Yes, sir." Yoshifuji bent his stubby body double in a show of gratitude. Tomita copied Yoshifuji, ducking his forehead between his knees. The thrill of success and the release from tension made bending difficult. The prospect that the autocratic president and his leading henchman would have more confidence in him from now on was exciting.

PART 2

I

The company launched the convenience store project that very day, right after the president's approval. Yoshifuji had a four-hour conference with Tomita, reexamining Tomita's ideas and American examples. His diligence and commitment were obvious. The prompt start and Ohkura's instruction to do it quickly, however, did not build up momentum. Yoshifuji first had to organize a committee to study the proposal, rather than acting directly on it. Diligent, motivated, and capable though Yoshifuji was, his abilities did not include innovative planning. He was better at coordinating people's opinions, mediating inconsequential communications, and keeping everyone happy. This was probably a trademark of the executives who were born in the late 1920s. They had joined large organizations in the 1950s and had enjoyed the benefits of the high growth period.

Yoshifuji spent the entire month of July talking with related department chiefs and organizing a "CS (Convenience Store) Planning Committee." This was staffed by the section chiefs of every department. There was nothing wrong with Yoshifuji making himself the chairman of the committee, but it amazed Tomita to find that the committee had more than thirty members. As one who honored harmonious communications and a balanced organization, Yoshifuji had staff members from every division which had even the remotest relationship to the project.

Committees like this present a façade of having tremendous potential, but in reality they are usually ineffectual. Most staff members showed up at meetings held once every 10 days or so. They asked questions and stated opinions to suit their whims, but left all the work to Tomita and his three assistants. All that this collection of people meant to Tomita was the distribution of more paper, more time spent explaining things, and a lot of busy work. But the inefficiency did not bother workaholic Yoshifuji, who prided himself on assiduousness. On the contrary, he was now about to build an executive superstructure, "Special Committee," atop the existing "Planning Committee."

Yoshifuji ran around among executives and department chiefs daily, took care of endless chores, and scrupulously examined the reports that were piled up on his desk. Without fail, he met with President Ohkura for at least three hours a day. Yoshifuji's office hours from 9 A.M. to 6 P.M. were always divided into small segments, and were clogged up with endless tasks. But these tasks did not seem to satisfy his hunger for something more to do. As a rule, he called Tomita after six o'clock to tell him something like, "Managing Director X said . . . today," or "I heard . . . at Department Chief Y's place just a while ago." All were more or less related to the convenience store plan, but rarely did Tomita gain anything from this chitchat. To begin with, it was highly unlikely that executives or department heads of an electrical appliance manufacturer knew much about convenience stores. To make matters worse, the chitchat was merely Yoshifuji's starting point. It usually developed into questions and requests for more work, sometimes keeping Tomita at it until midnight.

The company work was not Tomita's exclusive interest. He really resented having the long gossipy sermon take up his personal and family time. He was fed up with the cold restaurant dinners catered to his office. It was also a financial strain to take a taxi home once or twice a week. He could not charge the taxi fare to the company as Executive Yoshifuji did, nor was he paid overtime as managers were. Tomita's home life this summer consisted of guzzling down *ochazuke*,[7] taking a bath and going to bed, his wife's unhappy face, quick glances at his withdrawn children, savings that stopped increasing, and incurable exhaustion.

II

The first draft of the convenience store chain outline was completed in mid-September, and it was approved in principle by the Planning Committee and the Special Committee. Although the first draft was a large volume of 250 folio-size pages, most of it was a lengthy preface plus reference material culled from overseas. Major points were summarized in the first fifteen-page abstract. The abstract defined convenience stores: they operate between 8:30 A.M. and 9:00 P.M. An average store space is 70 to 90 square meters; it sells (1) canned food, packaged food, spices, snacks, and other preservable items; (2) basic clothing such as underwear, socks, and so forth; (3) detergent, soaps, papers, and other daily needs; (4) periodicals; and (5) inexpensive consumer electric goods such as light bulbs and batteries. An annotation read that a store could also carry cigarettes, alcohol, and drugs, if a permit was obtained. The report insisted on providing catalog sales[8] and electrical repair service. The latter would mobilize the existing technology of A-Electric, while coping, at the same time, with a shift in the consumer buying pattern from that of disposable goods to durable goods.

In short, the new draft was not much different from Tomita's July proposal, in spite of the long discussions and research conducted since then. Most of the new ideas and criticisms had been wiped out before maturation, either because of their unrealistic nature or by the force of conflicting viewpoints. One might also simply say that Tomita's original proposal had been well drafted.

Tomita concluded the summary with a note that a convenience store must not be a mini-supermarket. It should be like a supermarket in the sense that it carries a larger variety of merchandise than a traditional retail store. On the other hand, it should retain the charm of a traditional retail store where the shopkeeper lives in the store and has intimate contact with his customers. In brief, a major selling point of a convenience store should be accessibility and friendliness.

"This is pretty well written." President Ohkura was as happy as a clam when he summoned Yoshifuji and Tomita a day after the first draft was approved by the Special Committee.

"I thought of this myself a long time ago." Ohkura pressed the last paragraph of the abstract with his wrinkled finger. That portion of his copy was even underlined in red. "Really, we don't get friendliness in supermarkets. Shopping should be enjoyable. Japanese in particular seek intimacy. That's why mail order and self-service shopping centers with vending machines haven't taken root in Japan."

Ohkura was unusually talkative. He took the trouble of quoting technical information about retail stores whenever appropriate. In all likelihood, Ohkura had done his share of research on convenience stores.

"This plan is good in that respect. Ours will be a convenient, inexpensive, and friendly store. The shopkeeper will be a resident of the area. I bet we can get good catalog orders, too." Ohkura concluded by flattering Tomita, "It's great that we have a young man who comes up with a novel idea like this. Don't you think so, Yoshifuji-kun?"

Varying from his habit of making himself look obliged, Yoshifuji ventured this time to smile and pat Tomita's shoulder.

But after going through a series of compliments and jokes, Ohkura stiffened up and said, "However, the true battle hasn't started yet."

III

Ohkura pointed out the weaknesses of the plan with an astuteness abnormal for a seventy-seven-year-old man. He commented with amazing accuracy on serious problems pertaining to the site selections, site purchases, wholesale purchases, repair service, merchandise selection for the catalog sales, financing, bill collecting, the relationship between the shops and the distribution center, and the balance between the existing A-Electric retail stores and the new outfits.

"At any rate, I would like to build at least thirty chain stores before the bonus season next summer. And I would like a total of 300 stores by the end of the following three years. That will bring the annual income to 50 billion yen. The larger the scale, the larger the profit. So we should expand rapidly. Also, a nationwide network of these shops will make our company better known and will facilitate the sale of our products."

Ohkura's determination thrilled Tomita once again. The time schedule, the size of his sales plan, and the accuracy of Oh-kura's directions pleased Tomita. It was likely that his hard summer work would be rewarded sometime soon.

But Ohkura broke the brief silence, "The most important thing is to get this started right away. You know what kind of world we are living in." The cheerful expression had left his face and he had lapsed back to his lonely and worn old self. A-Electric had done very poorly in this summer's sales; it had made 18 percent less profit than the same period last year.

The Japanese economy was on its way down. The net GNP during the April–July months declined by 24 percent compared with the same time last year. The electric industry as a whole produced 7.8 percent less. A-Electric was in a more perilous condition than its competitors because it had fallen behind in the introduction of energy-saving devices and solar equipment which were now in great demand.

IV

Because the latter half of September had been spent "organizing," the second phase of the convenience store chain did not start until October.

The Planning Committee and the Special Committee were left intact, but a "CS Plan Promotion Headquarters" was set up inside the president's office, and active members were chosen from various departments. Unlike the first two, this new organization was strictly practical. It was divided into four units: General Planning Unit, Placement and Planning Unit, Facility Building and Repair Unit, and Management and Operations Unit. According to Yoshifuji's "Duty Assignment," the task of the General Planning Unit included overall management, obtaining licenses and permits, and seeking funds; that of the Placement and Planning Unit was planning store buildings and actually seeking sites; that of the Facility Building and Repair Unit was buying land, making rental agreements for buildings, building stores, and interior decorating; that of the Management and Operations Unit was purchase, distribution, repair crew, and catalog sales. Tomita was made in charge of the fourth unit. This meant that he now had the title "Chief of the CS Plan Promotion Headquarters, Management and Operations Unit" in addition to "Head of the Presidential Office Planning Section."

Tomita was satisfied with this arrangement. The leader of the General Planning Unit, Kiyoshi Arikawa, was five years his senior; he was a man of high caliber with a record of having served as a section supervisor in the General Business and Accounting Office. The leaders of the

Placement and Planning Unit and the Facility Building and Repair Unit
were veterans in management and industrial facility installment, respectively. Comparing his own background and age with those of these
selected few, there was no question but that Tomita was well recognized
by his company.

In Tomita's mind, the project gave him a firm standing in A-Electric.
He could picture himself taking a seat in an executive board meeting as
the "Department Chief of the CS Project Headquarters" some years
later. The project by then would have expanded into a huge organization of over 500 chain stores. He took a chance and shared his views
with his wife Sachié. Sachié listened to him with a glitter in her eyes,
calling off her often repeated complaints about his late returns from
work and about the little savings they had left.

Women are eager for everyday enjoyment and future dreams. While
being somewhat critical of his wife's attitude, Tomita was still happy.

There was a manpower shortage in the CS Plan Promotion Headquarters. In relation to the size of the system, the ratio of underlings to
unit leaders was small. There were only fifteen of them counting
Yoshifuji. And two of the fifteen were nearly fifty years old, each titled
the Coordinator and Attaché to the Headquarters Chief. This meant
that the structure was top heavy: one headquarters representative, two
coordinator attachés to the headquarters representative, four unit leaders, four chief clerks, two rankless men, and two female secretaries.
The structure mirrored the A-Electric employee demographic chart
with its bulging middle.

All the unit leaders labored at their duties. Yoshifuji now had too
many chores of his own to talk with Tomita during the day. The two
coordinators lacked ambition and vitality. The two female clerks had
families to take care of; they were sure to go home before six. The two
rankless men were ignorant and uncommitted. Consequently, the actual
work piled onto the unit leaders and chief clerks.

"If necessary, we can have other divisions help us. Don't hesi-
tate to ask me," repeated Yoshifuji, but the work load was not
something that could be reduced by cutting up and parceling out.
As is typical anywhere, the true work force in the organic system
consisted solely of those who were familiar with and responsible for
the entire process. Soon, pressure from work generated an unhealthy
atmosphere. At times it developed out of discrepancies in the
unit leaders' opinions and later deteriorated into deep-seated an-
tagonisms.

V

The first of these disputes cropped up in early December between Tomita and the leader of the Placement and Planning Unit, Kuroyanagi. It began with Tomita's violent objection to Kuroyanagi's site selection.

"Stores should be put in small cities outside the Tokyo and Osaka metropolitan areas," proposed Kuroyanagi.

Tomita's idea was to put them near housing blocks in the outskirts of the metropolitan areas. In particular, they should be at such places as the entrances to apartment developments and bus stops in the recently developed suburban residential zones.

Tomita argued vehemently, drawing examples from the United States. He insisted, "From the standpoint of wholesale purchases, group deliveries,[9] repair crews, and so on, it's impractical to scatter the stores in dispersed cities."

Kuroyanagi refuted on the basis of the effectiveness of the catalog sales, and the utilization of the preexisting A-Electric retail stores.

The dispute continued for nearly a week and was settled by Yoshifuji. "Both of you make sense. I am in agreement that we are wise to give serious considerations to the country if we want to expand this plan in the future." So saying, Yoshifuji cited the recent population migration, the growth in consumption and purchases, and the deterioration of the national railroad and mail services in the country. This was to save face for Kuroyanagi. Having done this, he concluded, "But it is also true that we would be unwise to build our stores in remote regions from the start, mostly because we won't have very many. So I would say that we probably ought to concentrate the first thirty stores for the next year in the Tokyo and Osaka regions."

This was apparently a compromise, but in essence it supported Tomita's position. It meant to Kuroyanagi that he had wasted time on extensive research, traveling all over the country four days a week for two solid months.

A similar argument ignited in late December between Tomita and the leader of the Facility Building and Repair Unit, Tanaka. Tanaka held that each store had to be decorated differently to suit the tastes of the consumers in the region, the available land, and the size and nature of the leased building. But Tomita demanded maximal uniformity in design. He believed that uniformity of shop design and merchandise worked advantageously for both wholesale purchases and image build-up.

"All the display shelves and the rest of the interior decorating material should be standardized as much as possible. That's how American chain stores are built," Tomita concluded.

Tomita's assertion cut deeply into architect Tanaka's professional pride. This quarrel was suspended by the coordinator's double-edged comment, "Well, we can decide after we get the actual plots and buildings." But it left hard feelings.

"Tomita is despotic because he thinks he is the originator of the plan."

"That guy gives himself airs under the shelter of President Ohkura and Executive Yoshifuji." These and other such statements were made, mostly in departments unrelated to Tomita's.

VI

The New Year and cold days deepened Tomita's frustration. Work and arguments multiplied. His work did not progress at all smoothly. The wholesale purchase negotiation, aiming for the large supermarket price range, added more problems. Most wholesalers and manufacturers distrusted the sales ability of the A-Electric convenience stores.

"We'll be happy to renegotiate the prices after you've sold as much as Supermarket Z." The future plans and estimates Tomita showed had no persuasive powers.

The same was true of the catalog sales. A good number of manufacturers and trading companies wanted to have their commodities printed in the catalog, but most asked to use full department store prices.

"It won't help to give an impression that we are high priced," said Tomita.

"We can't discount for a market we don't even know," the manufacturers retorted.

The most amazing development was A-Electric's refusal to discount its own products. Tomita felt totally betrayed.

"If we sold our products in a catalog, our commissioned retail stores would be all over us." A-Electric's business manager lost his temper.

"The printed discount prices will make our products look cheap," the head technician protested.

From late January through February, Tomita walked himself lame in unfamiliar food stores and everyday grocery suppliers. He flew at least once a week to Osaka, and negotiated with wholesalers and factories, only to learn that few would enter into business agreements under the conditions he proposed. Because of all this, Tomita was downright touched by the goodwill of a large wholesaler who pleasantly accepted the "large supermarket" price. But again, there was a repercussion to even this success: some talked behind his back, saying that Tomita stuck to business dealings with chosen dealers. Such uncalled-for talk hurt him, but there was no way to talk back.

There was another snag in February. One of the suppliers of canned goods offered to do business with Tomita on the condition that he be paid in cash or have a comparable financial arrangement. Obviously, all that A-Electric had to do was to conduct its transactions through the supplier's business bank. Tomita was happy to have found the solution until Arikawa, leader of the General Planning Unit yelled at him, bringing his senior authority to play, "Who are you to make arbitrary decisions like that?"

"I should be able to make some decisions," rebutted Tomita.

This time, Yoshifuji unwaveringly declared Arikawa the winner. Behind Arikawa was the M-Bank, A-Electric's host bank. Tomita had no choice but to revoke the entire contract with the canned goods dealer, only to be upbraided again. The sudden awareness of the complicated power mechanisms in the world of finance, and of the politics within the company crushed his confidence in himself.

Agony awaited him both at work and at home. His family life had lost meaning and warmth. No family enjoyed having its head routinely late or not returning at all. There was no celebration for Christmas or his daughter's birthday last year. The end-of-the-year bonus, which was very small because of the company's business doldrums, was reduced even more by accumulated taxi bills. His life in a public housing apartment was a far cry from affluence or relaxation. Life insurance was practically all he could manage to invest in. There were hardly any savings or securities investments. A private home was just a dream within a dream.

Tomita was worn out. For some time, it had become burdensome even to talk or play with his children. Nor could he keep his wife company. The so-called postwar generation had already turned thirty-nine years old.

How many more years do I have to live like this? Anxiety ate at him as he lay on the floor of his small Japanese-style apartment one Sunday afternoon. Although he was ahead of his peers in the company, an executive's chair was some distance away, and he wasn't sure if he would finally get there. And even if he did, it seemed all that was waiting at his destination were busy and uneasy days, the kind Yoshifuji led.

Was he really fortunate to be trusted by President Ohkura and Chief of the Presidential Office Yoshifuji? The question made his head swim. This was the first real sense of defeat felt by one who had climbed up the success ladder: first as an outstanding high school student, then as a serious student at a prestigious university, and now as a select member of a large company.

Beside Tomita, his wife Sachié kept talking like a broken record about their third grade son's report card and his work at a cram school.[10] She was blindly enthusiastic about reproducing the life-pattern of an outstanding high school student, a serious student at a prestigious university, and then a select member of a large company.

PART 3

I

After many twists and turns, the Convenience Store Chain Project suddenly got off the ground in March. The move ahead helped Tomita out of his winter depression. As is typical with a project organizer, Tomita's emotions were rather unstable. Joy and fear alternated with every step he took. But the project began walking on its own like a growing son. In March, the talks suddenly became concrete and the responsibilities of each unit became clear cut.

First came the problem of site selections. There were some forty prospective sites that the Placement and Planning Unit and the Facility Building and Repair Unit had nailed down through trust banks and local real estate agents. They were all different: wooden buildings, currently operating stores to be sold, a part of a large building, a section of the first floor in a condominium to be rented, and others. Most bore little resemblance to anything Tomita had in mind.

One was in a nice location in front of a large housing development, but the plot was small. Another was a nicely shaped spacious lot, but it was hidden in an unfrequented back alley. Then there was some fine land in a good location, but the street in front was closed to motor vehicles during the day. This last one would prove very inconvenient for large orders, group deliveries, and the electrical repair crew.

But the members of the two units preached with the torrential eloquence of a city realtor on how ideal each site was. They gave examples of how other shops had succeeded in such locations and land conditions. Given the time and budgetary restrictions, the A-Electric Company couldn't exactly be particular.

In any event, the site selection was no longer within the jurisdiction of the Management and Operation Unit leader. Tomita had to keep his internal dissatisfaction and disappointment in check. He could only comment on the forty odd sites from the viewpoint of merchandise delivery and the repair crew.

Luckily, Department Supervisor Yoshifuji and President Ohkura were very cautious. The president visited some of the prospective sites in person. The result was the purchase of only fifteen sites out of the possible forty. And because three of these fell through during negotiation, the project finally started with only twelve stores.

The trimming down of the project from the original thirty to only twelve shops required a thorough revision of the purchase agreements already made. What did not change was Tomita's and Ohkura's insistence on annexing the manager's residence to the shops. A residence connected to the shop had always been Tomita's first priority.

President Ohkura still supports my basic ideology, thought Tomita. And he pictured the life of a low-income hard-working young couple as store managers. They would work for their own profit and for the welfare of the local community. They would be thankful, meanwhile, to A-Electric Industry for giving them the home and shop. Tomita reveled in his dream plan and found General Planning Unit leader Arikawa's "CS Plan Management Guideline" ideal. It proposed a "Three-way Division Profit."

II

The "Three-way Division Profit" plan stipulated that all profits would be equally divided among the company, the shopkeeper, and the consumers. "On principle, each convenience store earns an independent income. The profit (the net profit after taxes) of each store will be divided in three ways. One will go to the parent company, one will be spent for lowering future prices, thereby contributing to the local community, and the remaining portion will go to the shopkeeper." Equality and harmony had always been major components of Ohkura's "humanitarian management" philosophy. Arikawa's document had converted these concepts into a realistic system.

"That should motivate the shopkeepers," said Tomita in agreement.

According to Tomita's calculations, if a store grossed 15 million yen per month, there should be a net profit of about 1.2 million yen per month, after taking out the salaries of the shopkeeper and two part-time workers, interest, refunds, heating bills, and other expenses. After paying the corporation and local taxes, there would be 700 thousand yen left. This would give the shopkeeper a 230 or 240 thousand yen income besides his salary, which would be a rather substantial sum even in these days of inflation.

"This extra benefit will attract a lot of outstanding young people." Tomita indulged in a bit of optimism.

But all that Yoshifuji did was to say "Do you think so?" and smile wryly.

There were more things to confuse Tomita. One of these was the "CS Project System Guideline." It said that two branch companies would be set up in Tokyo and Osaka to facilitate wholesale purchases, deliveries, catalog merchandise purchases, and mailing, and for the repair crews.

Why bother? thought Tomita. It made no sense to attach six (including the two wholesalers) intermediary companies to twelve retail stores whose annual income would not exceed about 200 billion yen. This puzzle was partially explainable in view of future plans for more shops. But the next puzzle in the "Guideline" was more difficult to unravel: "Each store building of the convenience store chain will be considered an independent branch company."

These days it was not unusual for greengrocers and variety shops to register themselves as joint-stock companies for tax and inheritance reasons. But there seemed to be no reason to take the twelve-store unit apart. It was also doubtful that the formation of such small companies would generate tax breaks. The gain and loss of individual stores can be balanced out for tax purposes only if they are registered as part of a company.

Tomita used this argument to try to change Arikawa's mind.

"It's to give independence to each store and to give substance to the divided income system," Arikawa answered lamely.

Yoshifuji, who overheard the exchange, injected, "This arrangement is essential to giving independence to each store. Our company owns the stores' shares, but each shopkeeper works independently." He spoke in an unusually forceful tone as if to stop any further debate. Tomita was still not convinced. He sensed something ominous in the system and in Yoshifuji's unusual reaction. And the bad news was not long in arriving.

III

In about the middle of April, a personnel rotation was posted. This was unannounced and totally unprecedented. A-Electric's rotations were usually announced at the end of March and April. The spring rotation had just been completed. It confused Tomita, who was told that he would remain in the same post until the CS Project made headway. It seemed strange that this special rotation applied only to the ranks of section supervisors of branch offices or to deputy section supervisors of the main office. These ranks belonged more or less in Tomita's age group. Normally, personnel rotations were like a chain reaction. Mr. B takes Mr. A's place, Mr. C takes Mr. B's place, then Mr. D, etc. In other words, the lower-ranked staff could move only if the higher-ups did. A sizable shift at the deputy section chief level suggested that a fairly large number of new posts had been created.

What's going on? Tomita's curiosity was aroused. *More than ten people received the written order to be "Attaché to Personnel. What's an attaché supposed to do? Does he go for training in a foreign country?* Tomita mulled it over, looking at his close friend Hiromasa Fukushima's name on the list. Fukushima joined the company with Tomita. *Come to think of it, Fukushima spoke some French; maybe he'll be sent to Africa or the Middle East.* Tomita felt like congratulating his friend who had worked in obscurity in northeastern Japan for three years. But he soon learned that his speculations were far from the truth.

That very day, Fukushima came to visit the CS Project Promotion Headquarters during Tomita's lunch break.

"I'm not sure if I can do this. I don't feel confident. . . ." Fukushima broached the subject. Worry and shock had made Fukushima's fair and handsome face look paler than usual. "I'm lost. In my family, my father was a salaryman, and there's no merchant even among my relatives. They have no advice to give me. . . ." Fukushima kept complaining to Tomita, who knew nothing of Fukushima's situation.

"What's happening?" Tomita interrupted.

Fukushima looked at Tomita warily and suspiciously. But by the time he had said "You didn't know about this either?" several seconds later, Fukushima was feeling flat again.

"I was told to be a shopkeeper of a convenience store or something like that," Fukushima said resignedly.

Fukushima had come to Tokyo the day before at the brief order of his branch office manager in the northeast who said no more than "Your post will be changing, so go to the Main Office and receive your orders." The new title given to him that morning was "Manager of a Convenience Store in Hannou in Saitama Prefecture."[11]

"I'm supposed to be trained for three months until the building is finished. The first month is for classroom instruction and the other two for hands-on training at supermarkets and elsewhere. Do you think a layman can learn the new trade in only three months?" So saying, Fukushima showed Tomita a booklet he had just acquired.

It was the "Outline of an A-Electric Convenience Store" that Tomita himself had written. *How could they do this to him?* Tomita was outraged. He had never dreamed until this moment that an A-Electric employee and, worse yet, a university graduate and a middle-ranking staff member would be made into a convenience storekeeper. In the bright and hopeful plan that Tomita had imagined, a shopkeeper was a young and friendly man, born a shopkeeper, whose healthy, simple-minded wife worked with him. Fukushima in his mid-career wasn't one of those. Tomita's store was supposed to be more cheerful and hopeful.

"It seems that I have to live where the shop is. Because the store is open from eight thirty in the morning till nine at night. . . ." Fukushima's voice dropped lower.

"I know . . . ," Tomita answered morosely, recalling his own plan. The anger switched to sympathy, and sympathy grew into regret.

IV

Tomita's heart sank deeper and deeper from that day on. The spring sun had grown brighter every day. New leaves became greener and glossier, but nothing lifted his spirits. There was no romantic vision or passion attached to the convenience stores any more. They were overshadowed by his feelings for Fukushima and the rest of the twelve middle-ranked employees, who must be practicing "Welcome" and "Thank you very much" in some conference room. Obviously there was no way out of it. Depression and anger didn't help. If he wanted to stay in the company, he simply had to keep working on the project. So far, President Ohkura and Chief of the Presidential Office Yoshifuji were supportive. But a single rebellious act would mean the end of his career. Falling off the success ladder was synonymous with the loss of A-Electric employee status. Carnivores starve when they stop fighting.

The convenience store chain project progressed steadily, indifferent to the changes in Tomita's feelings. The Facility Building and Repair Unit became livelier every day. They already displayed the floor plans and sketches of the twelve stores.

What a crummy design! thought Tomita.

Probably in an attempt to create uniformity for shops in different localities and plot sizes, each shop sported an awning of yellow and green stripes with a red "A-Electric CS Chain" on its lower end. This design reduced the stores to cheap variety stores, completely different from the American examples Tomita had collected at the beginning of this project.

Employees of building contractors walked between room dividers which had floor maps and sketches pasted all over them. They were builders of homes and shops in the localities of the twelve different stores. They knew how to build what A-Electric wanted. They were also contact people in the community. But they knew nothing of aesthetics.

Even if this is temporary, it's something A-Electric is doing. The company shouldn't risk its own reputation. . . . This was basic to Tomita's belief.

Arikawa's "Management Guideline" made no more sense. The salary guidelines struck him as demoralizing. Each shopkeeper's salary was set at nearly 10 percent less than that of a new university graduate.

"It's not really that low," Arikawa explained, showing a detailed statement of accounts. "To begin with, rent is free and electricity is part of the store cost. Right there you save 60 to 70 thousand yen more than living in public housing. On top of that, the shopkeeper's wife, as an assistant, gets paid 40 percent of his salary."

Of course his wife gets paid if she works. Forty percent of the shopkeeper's salary is less than a part-time high school student's wage, thought Tomita, but Arikawa nonchalantly went on with the simple arithmetic.

"And the major portion of their income comes from the profit sharing you know of. The company takes only half. Forty-five percent of the net profit goes to the shopkeepers in the first two years. If things go as planned, a shopkeeper will earn about 2 million in the first year, and 4 million in the second year. All in all, he earns more than a section chief in the Main Office."

"If the store makes a profit, that is." Tomita tried to sound sarcastic, but couldn't impress Arikawa.

"Of course, the store has to make a profit. We are counting on your bulk order strategy." Arikawa turned the sword tip around.

You don't have to tell me that . . . , thought Tomita. As a matter of fact, the wholesale purchases and catalog arrangements were well under way, in spite of the decrease in the number of stores and the delay of the opening date. And Yoshifuji had complimented him about it just the other day.

The news that the stores were actually being built, although they numbered only twelve, put some pressure on wholesalers and manufacturers. They were nursing the romantic vision that A-Electric would "do something big," large company that it was. No one had told them that the middle-aged staff were about to be converted into shopkeepers.

V

". . . Akihiko Suzuki-kun." A voice from a loudspeaker called in a high-pitched ending. Sporadic applause echoed forlornly in the large hall. Ornate chandeliers glittered and formally attired waitresses wove among the guests. The hall was packed with people, but they lacked spirit or unity. It was late July at a hotel in central Tokyo.

"Ryōji Inoue-kun to Toride City, in Ibaragi Prefecture . . ." The microphone voice cried again. As before, the announcement was wiped out by the gabbing of uninterested guests. About ten men filed across the platform in front. Each wore a large man-made flower on his chest and stood up as straight as he could, but they all looked despondent and worried. One of them took a step forward, bowed deeply, and listened to more sporadic clapping. Hung above his head was a long sign board which said "A-Electric Convenience Store Chain Inauguration Ceremony."

Those lined up on the platform were the company employees now appointed as storekeepers of the convenience stores. They were thirty-six- to forty-year-old university graduates of middle-level rank. Watching them from the hall entrance, Tomita found himself counting them. *Eleven . . . ,* he thought. There was no reason to count. He knew already that there were only eleven. The twelfth man had left the company just two days ago on the pretext of a "lack of confidence."

That makes four. . . . Tomita was saddened. Three out of the original twelve nominees had resigned in April and they were immediately replaced.

"Saitama Prefecture, Hannou City, Iwasawa Store Manager, Hiromasa Fukushima-kun." The voice rang out again. Fukushima, in a dark suit, stepped forward from the line and bowed. The clapping was fainter than before.

"Good for him!" Tomita muttered.

Fukushima had vacillated about this appointment. He had also visited Tomita twice for consultation since his first return from the northeast.

"My wife won't have it . . . ," he once said.

Tomita knew that Fukushima's wife was a good-looking woman who had graduated from a Christian college in Tokyo. She was not the type to humor uneducated housewives as the mistress of a small retail store.

"I don't think I can do it," he kept whimpering at another time. "I'm training at a supermarket now but I can't memorize the names of the merchandise. I'm all thumbs when it comes to wrapping things. When a man reaches thirty-eight years old, I'm afraid both his brains and hands slow down."

It was obvious that the economist, who had spent many years at A-Electric as an accountant, had lost his aptitude for manual labor. It was impressive that Fukushima didn't leave the company.

"My wife gave in. We shall see what we can do. If I do well, they may put me back in the Main Office. If things go wrong, they'll replace me soon enough," said Fukushima, trying to sound hopeful. "When it comes right down to it, starvation is worse than shame." He smiled sadly.

To Tomita's eyes, Fukushima's bloodless face, as he stood rigid on the platform, was proof of this last sentence.

What a dull celebration this is! Tomita was beginning to feel weighted down.

Yoshifuji stood next to Tomita, wearing an extra-large red man-made flower on his chest. He curried favor with guests who were going home early.

"What do you know! We're embarrassed to get in this silly business, but it doesn't mean we are forgetting our proper trade. . . ." Yoshifuji was talking to an elderly man, most likely an executive in a large company. A ribbon with "A-Electric CS Chain Company, Vice-President" dangled below his large man-made flower. He was now the vice-president of the wholesale company for the convenience stores.

PART 4

I

"I'm sure you aren't all that keen about it, but please agree to do this, Tomita-kun." President Ohkura lowered his huge bald head, although only slightly.

The October evening sun, glowing through the shaded glass, lit the bald head in a shade of nauseating russet.

Tomita stiffened. He had never in his life imagined that the old president would kowtow to him. But Yoshifuji, in the seat next to the president, languidly slumped down and didn't so much as sit up.

"You know very well that our company is in a fix. And the convenience store chain, which we started in hopes of a business upturn, hasn't even seen daylight yet." Ohkura spoke in an agitated voice.

He's fallen apart with age. . . . The discovery startled Tomita.

In a matter of one year, Ohkura's skin had lost elasticity, his voice had become oppressively shaky, and his eyes were clouded gray as if they were set on a far away target.

"We've spent 1,800 million yen altogether: 800 million on the buildings, 700 million on circulation and repair crews, plus office expenses, research costs, and advertisement, but the revenue since the opening is below half our estimate."

Ohkura quoted detailed figures. The clarity of his thinking offset the waning strength of his body. His passion for the convenience stores seemed intact but the pitiful figures revealed his defeat.

"What is particularly bad is that there's no sign of recovery. And even worse is the instability of the store managers."

There was good reason for concern. Four out of the original twelve appointees had resigned before the opening. During the past three months, three had given up and left the company and two were hospitalized. This meant that in a matter of three months, eight stores had changed managers and three stores sat closed due to two consecutive departures of managers.

The situation destroyed the image of a "convenience store frequented by local housewives." Needless to say, sales were weak and some inventories were miserably wasted. Other supplies, the delivery system, and the repair crew for thirty stores, lay idle. Worse yet, the shortfall of the first twelve stores had eliminated the possibility of finding new volunteer store managers.

"Some say that I started the silly project to get rid of unwanted employees," Ohkura continued despondently, "but I had no such intention; I really did it in the spirit of 'Give a chance and wait for the result.' I wanted to give as many of our people as possible a chance to prove their ability. But nobody understood me. I couldn't believe it. There were times when I lost my temper. As they say, children don't know how their parents feel. But, you know, parents make mistakes, too. I puzzled over what was wrong and what went wrong. . . .''

This was the first time Tomita had heard that Ohkura had intended from the beginning to turn his staff into storekeepers. The difference between the prewar companyman's mentality—who had wandered around throughout Southeast Asia—and that of a contemporary salaryman with university degrees painfully took on meaning in Tomita's mind.

Ohkura's talk was finally getting to the heart of the matter. If the president asked for suggestions, Tomita decided to propose that A-Electric stop sending company staff to the stores and start recruiting young people who were genuinely interested in operating small stores.

''I finally figured it out the other day,'' continued the president, ''we gave those people stores and merchandise, but we didn't give them souls. I mean, we built the facility, but didn't teach what to dream. This is precisely what they mean by 'you made a statue of Buddha, but forgot to put a soul in it.' '' Ohkura stopped there and began packing tobacco in his pipe. The slow motion of his fingers reflected the speaker's remorse and grief.

''We need a dream at work,'' continued Ohkura, ''particularly when we are starting on a new project. It's important that one have a goal, a model, and a rival. It was the same when I first came to this company. National Electric and Sanyō Electric were my goals, models, and rivals. My wish to be like them, no, my belief that I could be as good as they were, bolstered me. But there's none of that for our store project. This is why nobody has found a dream or a goal. Most felt abandoned the moment they were appointed store manager.'' Ohkura was blowing out from his brick-colored lips a mixture of purple smoke and words of self-justification. His talk now seemed to be veering in another direction.

''It dawned on me that I should have selected the company's very best employee. I should have asked him to be the model, a successful example for our convenience store. I should have thought of this earlier. I don't think it's too late to correct my mistake.''

Tomita felt a chill run through his body. He thought that Ohkura's face had flared red. He missed his last words. Whatever he might have said, it was all decided. Yoshifuji rudely thrust a sheet of paper at him. It read, ''I transfer you to Osaka Kawachinagano[12] CS Company, Inc. as its Store Manager, Director.''

II

"Is Kawachinagano close to the Naniwa Middle School?" This was Sachié's first reaction to Tomita's report of his transfer. Her son's future education concerned her the most even at the moment when her family's life and her husband's future were at stake.

"It couldn't be. Naniwa Middle School is in Kōbe. Kawachinagano is on the southern edge of Osaka," Tomita answered impatiently.

"Oh." Sachié took a deep breath. "I don't think I would like it."

She got angry first and then started making rambling protests. She had neither experience nor interest in working in a store. She was a poor talker and not exactly sociable. It was onerous for her to make friends with neighborhood housewives. The irregular work hours would exert a bad influence on the family's physical and mental health. In fact, she had been feeling weak lately and her little girl was in delicate health. Her husband didn't seem fit for the trade. Wasn't there anyone in A-Electric who had better judgment? She kept every appearance of being extremely cool-headed and logical. "I'm sure your company would understand if you talk sense as I do. Why don't you explain to Yoshifuji-san tomorrow and ask him to reverse his decision?" she finally declared.

Sachié's suggestion was totally out of place. Tomita had already considered it. He had taken a chance by saying, "I am not prepared to be a model manager." But it didn't work. He knew that the company, which had let go so many employees for the same reason, would never consider withdrawing the written order of transfer. Tomita told this to his wife, but she wouldn't listen.

"You're always left holding the bag because you aren't aggressive enough." She was keyed up. "I married you because you were a promising companyman out of a prestigious university. I would have married a young store master with fifty employees had I known that I would have to turn myself into a shopkeeper's wife," the "educated woman" who had gone to school in the United States yelled.

Shall I leave the company? The thought flashed in Tomita's mind. Momentarily, Fukushima's sorrowful face revisited his memory with the remark, "Starvation is worse than shame." He had received a long letter from Fukushima only a few days ago, griping about the hardships and complications of a convenience storekeeper's life.

III

It was in late November of the same year that Tomita, his wife, and their two children moved to the Kawachinagano store in Osaka. So that the store could be reopened before the end-of-the-year sale, Tomita underwent only four weeks' hands-on training at a supermarket in Tokyo. The company had skipped the classroom training, saying that the man in charge of the project from its start had no need for it.

"As you all know, Tomita-kun is our company's hope and the father of our convenience store," announced Yoshifuji at Tomita's farewell party. "I have no doubt but that Tomita-kun will soon make a triumphant return to our Main Office as the savior and foster father of the CS Chain."

A majority of the listeners did not take Yoshifuji seriously. Rumor had gone around in the company, "Tomita's days are numbered now that he is being sent away as a storekeeper."

I'm different from others. I was personally asked by President Ohkura. Tomita himself did not give up hope.

That hope didn't spare him from the disappointment he felt at the first sight of the A-Electric CS Chain Kawachinagano Store. The two-story wooden building, standing against the magnificent Mount Kongō, was much smaller and shabbier than the conceptualized drawing that hung on the Main Office wall. The store had been closed for over six weeks since the departure of the previous manager. The interior was filthy. Rats and cockroaches had built nests inside the bags of sweets and toilet paper. The inexpensive plastic tile floor was covered with a mixture of detergent spilled out of torn boxes, underwear which had dropped from shelves, and broken glass from tipped over electric floor lamps. The stench from these filled the damp store space as well as the dust-laden residence rooms.

While Sachié complained and wailed, Tomita spent four days cleaning up the building and stocking new merchandise. He spent the entire one million yen "New Store Preparation Fund" loan from A-Electric for advertisements, matches, and other mementos to distribute at the Grand Opening Sale. He also hired a part-time high school student and a middle-aged widow from the neighborhood. The two, who had worked for a nearby supermarket, were to help cope with the end of the year rush. In short, Tomita did everything he could for the "Refurbished Reopening."

Perhaps because of the thorough preparation, earnings were fairly good from the first business day in early December. He earned 500 thousand yen on the first day, 620 thousand on the second day, and 480 thousand yen on the third day (Sunday) of business. In fact, the store ran out of mementos.

If things go at this rate, I can make at least 12 million yen a month. That will make a profitable business. Tomita did figures till late every night, tapping on a desk calculator.

Going like this, I'll have 1.5 million yen per month a year from now. The day of 'triumphant return to the Main Office' Yoshifuji had mentioned may not be that far away. He began to feel optimistic.

But his optimism died out after the third day. Customers disappeared. The daily earnings gradually dropped: 330 thousand yen, 280 thousand yen, 220 thousand yen, 250 thousand yen, 200 thousand yen. From the third week on, it wasn't unusual to earn less than 200 thousand yen a day. Tomita learned the hard way that the shrewd Osaka housewives had only come for the opening sale and mementos.

This will give me only 5 million yen a month, groaned Tomita.

Tomita's depression and Sachié's nagging increased in inverse proportion to the number of customers.

IV

There were many additional problems. A couple of times a day a housewife would yell at Tomita for selling defective merchandise. Unpriced items often confused the checkers. At other times, broken merchandise and falling shelves made chaos of the store. And then there was the time when a checker caught a female shoplifter. Tomita didn't know what to do with her. Another time, the cash was ten thousand yen short. Tomita suspected the widow checker and questioned his own fairness.

Most unpleasant was the ordering and sending back of merchandise. It was arranged so that the wholesale purchases were made via the company Tomita himself had set up. But the items that were delivered to him did not always agree with the consumer tastes of the area. And many were priced higher than those in the Dobuike and Matsuya areas. Tomita was indignant about this situation because he had made sure that the wholesale prices were compatible with those of the large supermarkets. But the A-Electric Osaka Wholesale Company refused to consider

a discount. The costs of transportation, storage, and interest charges
had to be included. The primary problem was slow turnover. Business
expenses had fattened the per item price.

Return shipments caused more problems. The wholesale company
made an issue of damaged or stained merchandise. Refunds had to be
negotiated every time. Tomita tried to get his way but was never very
successful. His stockpiles multiplied; mountains of them rapidly took
over his home of three small rooms.

As anticipated, business was strong in late December despite these
problems. There were three or four days when a day's gross exceeded
500 thousand yen. These few days kept Tomita and Sachié busy but
happy. But January took customers away, and so did February. Tomita
started hearing unfavorable remarks like "People are unfriendly in that
store," and "They think nothing of selling spoiled things." Efforts to
disassociate himself from these problems didn't work. Meanwhile, he
tried to economize on maintenance costs by using the part-time helpers
only on weekend afternoons and turning off lights during the day. These
efforts had the reverse effect, making the store look deserted. He lost
customers.

The idea of making ends meet, let alone showing how a convenience
store should be run, started looking absurd. Tomita stood in front of his
empty store, gazed at the snow-capped Mount Kongō, and sighed. The
magnificent mountain stood there, like an unfeeling wall separating
him from his protected company life and his dream for the future.

I wish I could get back to the salaryman's life . . . , thought Tomita.

More and more often he felt like following his predecessors by
sending a letter of resignation to the company, and returning to Tokyo.
The only reason to hang onto the store was the slim hope that the
company might take him back someday. But a big blow to this hope
came on a cold day in late February. He happened to read a small
newspaper article captioned "A-Electric Industry President Seizō Ohkura Resigns."

V

The snow had melted, and the mountain was now shrouded in thick
green. Six months had passed since Tomita had moved to Kawachinagano. A token sign of recovery showed in the long-depressed Japanese
economy and perked up Tomita's store a little. His son, a fifth grader,

became an outstanding student in the elementary school nearby and had picked up a fluent Osaka dialect. Sachié stopped complaining. It became her habit to push up the grillwork of the store after she saw her children off to their schools. She had acquired the art of passing out a compliment or two to her customers. She also bought foreign-made foodstuffs and craft work and put them on the display shelves. The items did not have a large market, but helped make the store look more interesting. These changes in Sachié may have been the cause for the small improvement in business.

Nonetheless, Tomita's worries and depressions were not about to go away. The income from the shop barely provided for wages and other expenses. It did not return even half of the interest on the investment. It was very unlikely that he would receive any "divided benefit." His family economy suffered. The news that Seizō Ohkura was gone worried him to death. Ohkura's resignation had weakened the bond between him and A-Electric. Still, Tomita was not quite ready to discard the hope of returning to the Main Office. He resisted as best he could the idea that Ohkura's departure would lead to the jettisoning of the president's promises into the nearest wastebasket. After all, Yoshifuji, one closer to Tomita than Ohkura, was still going strong. Junji Yoshifuji was promoted to be the first executive in charge of General Business and Personnel at the executive board re-election following Ohkura's resignation. According to an amusing account in an economics magazine, Ohkura's resignation was the result of a kind of coup d'etat carried out by an intrigue between rebels in the company and A-Electric's main bank. The reason was given as bad management. Amazingly, the hidden choreographer was Yoshifuji.

On a fair day in late May, Yoshifuji surprised Tomita with a phone call. He asked Tomita to report to the A-Electric Osaka Headquarters.

VI

"Oh, hello! It's been a while since I saw you last. How have you been? . . . Oh, I'm glad to hear that." Yoshifuji stood up from his chair with a friendly smile. He welcomed Tomita in the guest room of the Osaka Headquarters.

"There are a lot of things I want to go over with you, but I don't have the time," began Yoshifuji in a businesslike tone of voice after he had listened to a brief report of Tomita's recent situation.

"To be honest, our company is still in bad shape. We haven't gotten the strength to expand the convenience store chain. It's a shame that we put you to so much trouble, but the whole thing was really no more than old Ohkura's hobby, you know."

Tomita had come with great expectations, but now felt that a wet blanket had been thrown over him. Yet a hidden joy softened the feeling of victimization. It was a hope built on the belief that he could return to the Main Office if the company disbanded the convenience store plan and if his present assignment were called off. But Yoshifuji said something totally different.

"So this is what we decided: We'll ask the present store managers to keep their stores. That is, they will buy the stores they manage and operate them on their own."

Tomita didn't understand right away. But Yoshifuji's intent soon became clear. Currently the manager of each store was the staff of an independent branch company. Technically, he was not an employee of A-Electric. The company had been keeping their retirement benefits only to leave the possibility open for their return to the main company. Yoshifuji wanted Tomita to take charge of the shop and the residence in exchange for the retirement benefits.

"I'm not forcing this on you. We can pay your retirement benefit in cash if you would rather. If you take the store and the home, you only have to pay 80 percent of the original acquisition cost. And the difference will be converted to a ten-year loan. You definitely gain that way." Yoshifuji rattled on as he opened a file folder on the table. The document said that Tomita only had 1.2 million yen per year to pay for ten years.

Tomita got back to the two-story store/residence in Kawachinagano while the sun was still high. The tremendous shock delivered by Yoshifuji had totally disoriented him. He had no recollection of how he had reached home. All he knew was that the sole reward for the long arduous struggle since his graduation from the university was this tiny building burdened with a substantial debt. His lifetime destination was a dingy retail store in a new housing development. He wanted to scream.

"What did Yoshifuji-san have to say?" Sachié was at the shop. She asked in a whisper, probably because she was shaken by the gloomy look Tomita had on his face.

"I'm fired."

Sachié was panic stricken, although she had thought that she had steeled herself against any bad news.

"And what about this store?"

"This thing?" Tomita glanced around disgustedly. "He's giving it to us instead of my retirement benefit," he spit out.

Sachié's reaction was beyond belief. "How wonderful! This will be ours then." So exclaiming, she walked up to his back and gently pulled off Tomita's suit coat. "Some people say that they feel uncomfortable shopping with us because you wear a suit," she whispered into his ear.

Tomita wordlessly looked at the dark suit in Sachié's hands. The glimmer from the silver A-Electric pin hurt his eyes.

Notes

The section translated here is the first "Episode" (*Dai ichiwa*) named "Give a Chance and Wait for the Outcome" (Yoki taika) in *The Baby Boom Generation* (Dankai no Sedai) published by Bunshun Bunko, 1984, pp. 7–67.

1. The shape of a sake bottle is narrow on top and wider from about a third of the way down.

2. For definition, see Shiroyama's "Kinjō the Corporate Bouncer," translated in this collection.

3. Shikoku is the smallest of the four major islands in Japan, located between the largest, Honshū, and the southernmost, Kyūshū.

4. This is a near-future novel staged in the late 1980s.

5. This *-kun* suffix indicates a superior's intimacy with his junior staff.

6. The Meiji period was the time of the Meiji Emperor's reign between 1868 and 1912.

7. *Ochazuke* is cooked rice mixed in tea or soup.

8. In this sales system, the catalog is kept in the retail stores and at the homes of clients, and orders are made to the retail stores; it is slightly different from the American mail order system.

9. This is a system whereby goods are delivered to a house that represents a group of other houses.

10. Cram school, or *juku*, is a private school of various sizes, where supplementary instructions are given on certain hours of the day, or a few times a week. The subjects of teaching vary depending on the *juku* or the class one takes.

11. Saitama Prefecture is a northern neighbor of Tokyo. Hannou is a tourist town.

12. This is a residential area within 40 km of Osaka.

Giants and Toys

Takeshi Kaikō

I

The Samson's Candies building is located in the center of Tokyo. Because it faces a train station, throngs of people walk through its front yard during commuter hours. Also, because the station exit is clogged with cars, Samson's front yard serves as a station plaza, a buffer zone. This piece of land is valuable, but is made available by the company as a sidewalk. The sidewalk runs right along the front windows. Behind the glass panels is a huge display chamber. It shows all year round countless kinds of Samson products, ranging from chewing gum to *marrons glacés*. Pedestrians are bound to peek in the window as they walk by. In other words, it is for advertisement purposes that Samson offers its plaza to the public. The sidewalk is comfortably spacious and roofed. Many benches and flower beds give it the feeling of a small park. Samson's architectural layout also conveniently frees the neighborhood from pedestrian congestion caused by the station. For this reason, Samson sits well with the area.

I have a full view of the plaza from my office window on the second floor. People float outside the glass wall day and night, like a rolling ocean. Twice daily, large currents go up and down. These are the sad processions of commuters. The walkers' heads always hang down, because the sun is too bright in the morning, and the people are hungry and tired in the evening. Only their legs are restlessly busy. As they are vomited out of old iron boxes, they drift in unison into this plaza, pace along the glass wall, and are quietly siphoned into various colored cement walls here and there. The sounds from the numerous footsteps resonate like the sea and echo inside me.

The plaza is never empty. The glass wall vibrates all day long. After the commuters come various other people: fashion models, photographers, sightseeing groups from the country, followers of new religions, housewives, students, traders, the unemployed, pairs of destitute lovers on Saturday afternoons, laborers and the police on May Day. People of every profession and every age eddy by, sometimes drenched in rain and at other times bathed in dust. I am always conscious of the presence of the throng behind me. One of them, who never came back, was Kyōko. She stepped aside from the crowd, squinting and smiling at the April sun, and stood in front of the window.

One Monday afternoon in April, I was called by Section Chief Aida and went down to the coffee shop on the first floor. The coffee shop is right next to the showroom. At its entrance is a candy store; deeper inside is a dining hall. Because it was the lunch hour, it was packed with people. I saw Aida by a window in a corner, talking with a girl. I took a seat by him and listened to their conversation.

The girl sat in the sun. Two decayed and chipped teeth showed when she smiled. Her eyes were round, her eyebrows were thick, and her nose tipped cheerfully upward. A worn checkered duffle bag, like a carpenter's tool bag with its opening drawn shut, lay neglected on the table. It was obvious from the girl's face that the bag contained nothing better than a film or fashion magazine with its cover ripped, or a plastic makeup kit with a broken clasp. The girl's nail polish was chipped in places. Her shoes were dirty. She was the kind easily found in the nearest sewing or cooking school.

Aida told me later that he had happened to find her on the other side of the show window, while replacing display merchandise. That day, the company had installed a new automatic wrapping machine imported from England, and had a public wrapping demonstration. The spectators were thrilled by the turning motor pushing the conveyer belt forward and the dizzily flying metal hands wrapping Samson candies handsomely in pink vinyl acetate sheets. One of the girls pressed her nose against the window and kept on laughing and marveling. Aida was fascinated by her expressions. Before I met her, Aida had talked with her about a Walt Disney movie, as intimately as if they were uncle and niece. I have no idea how he managed to bring this stranger to the coffee shop. He must have had faith in the magical charm of his gray hair, the deep wrinkles in the corners of his eyes, and his new light gray suit.

He gossiped about jazz singers and movie stars for some time. The girl laughed a guileless laugh, looked amazed, or acted shocked at each anecdote. Aida asked the name and telephone number of the company she worked for at the end of the chat and wrote them down in his memo book. She turned out to be a bookkeeper at a small trading company nearby. She said that she also did things like waitressing. As ordered by Aida, I bought a box of chocolate from the candy store and handed it to her.

"Thank you. This is great. This saves my money for the three o'clock snack pool." She casually thanked Aida, tossed the box in her duffle bag, slung the sack over her shoulder, and smiled. The sun hit her lips momentarily. Her downy hair glistened like the shadow of fish in the bottom of the sea. This was the only charm I could find in her. Aida asked my opinion of her as soon as she left. My answer didn't please him very well.

"She may look cute in a photograph," he muttered. With some effort, he lit a cigarette with a lighter he had nicknamed "gunpowder," then left the table.

Aida is a dedicated, energetic worker, but he has a couple of strange hobbies, namely model toys and women. He picks up either one on the street. He is quite professional when it comes to model toy building. He builds cars, ships, jet planes, and whatnot. He builds them in exact proportion to their originals, using paper, wood, and plastic chips. Airplanes and cars, along with glue and wood chips, keep cropping up from piles of paper on his desk. He steals time out of work to build them. If it so happens that he comes across a set that takes his fancy, he may stay behind at work almost until the hour for the last train of the day. A gray-haired man over fifty years old, hell-bent on model toy building, is a rare sight, but I'm too used to it to be surprised.

Aida's hobby with women is more closely related to his work. His enthusiasm for work prompts him. Aida is the advertising section chief but, on the side, he also works as an art director for designers and commercial writers. When the company makes a poster, designers do the detailed work, but Aida decides things like whom to choose for a model and where to have the poster printed. And he ends up recruiting models. He always keeps his eyes on women, be it in a theater, on a train, or in a crowd. Once he sees a woman that interests him, he follows her, watches her closely from all angles, in different lighting, and in all possible expressions. Then, he talks to her and brings her to our company. Our company takes sample shots, most of which are useless. Aida's drawers are full of pictures of women who never got hired as models. Although cautious, he still errs. Once he followed a woman for three hours by train and bus. When he finally talked to her, she took him to be a kidnapper and ran away. Unfortunately he had already given his calling card, and the girl's mother came to the company the next day to complain. Aida was bawled out by a manager, which is embarrassing for someone of his age. This incident hasn't changed his way of doing things, however. His legs go after women of their own accord. There's no stopping them, he says.

Kyōko was another case in point. A couple of days after we met her in the coffee shop, Aida called me on the sly and told me to get a taxi. As I got a taxi and waited at the exit of the plaza, he brought Kyōko out of the coffee shop. I hadn't the slightest idea how he got her over there. It turned out that she had been called by telephone out of the blue that day, then put a bookmark in her account book, and slipped out of her company. She flushed when Aida told her about the sample shooting. She became more restless in the car when she heard the photographer's name—Harukawa. She complained and protested that she had not fixed her clothes, hair, or makeup for the occasion. She almost burst into tears. She wriggled her body, pushed Aida's shoulder, and kicked the floor, protesting somewhat like a kitten. Aida took it all with a calm smile and gallantly recited his often-repeated lines.

"You leave your clothes and makeup alone. Harukawa-kun's[1] studio has cocktail dresses, Max Factor, you name it. So all you have to do is ignore the camera, look like you've just eaten caramel for the first time in your life, and stick out your tongue or do something like that with an expression of *Gosh, how delicious!* Just be natural. Harukawa-kun will take care of the rest." Aida kept saying this sort of thing, not at all taking Kyōko seriously.

Harukawa is Aida's old friend and a celebrated photographer. One of the things he specialized in during his youth was romantic pictures, using soft focus amber lenses and other special equipment. Lately he has been concentrating on women's portraits. He doesn't take genre pictures. His strong sell is quirky editing and acrid observation. He seeks out popular actresses, and, between their armament of professional pauses, snatches vanity, loneliness, and wrinkles. He once published the greasy skin of an artless debutant actress and was sued by the film company. On another occasion, he snapped a fashion model in evening dress biting into a roasted sweet potato behind the stage curtain. He lives surrounded by scandals. He is past his middle years, but still single, and has an ugly middle-age spread. The strangest thing is that the more harshly he treats his models, the better they like him.

Harukawa was expecting us because Aida had called ahead of time. His assistants and lighting equipment were all set to go. Harukawa's face was ravaged by cut-like wrinkles, gashed by fatigue. Below his eyes hung bags which made people wonder if he was beaten black and blue. Standing close by, I could smell last night's cognac. He flashed a sharp glance at Kyōko, then combed back his unkempt salt-and-pepper hair with his fingers. Kyōko hunched her shoulders in fright. Because her reaction was so childish, Harukawa let out a complaint for Aida's ears only as he walked up his studio steps, "More trash!"

Aida seems to have stayed with the girl until she was allowed to go home, but I lost interest before the first shot was taken. I went back to work. From past experience, I knew that Aida was not eyeing the girl with personal curiosity or taste. Still, she looked too plain to be useful. She was too scared of Harukawa to utter a word even when dunked under the merciless studio lights. When Harukawa commanded her to pause in a certain way, she stared stone-stiff at the camera, like a country girl. I was just beginning to take note of the peculiarities of her face that Aida seemed to have recognized, but the stiffened girl had lost them all. Throughout, I just couldn't help seeing Aida as a man of bizarre taste. I didn't realize till later that I was seeing her with my naked eyes only.

Harukawa came to our company about a week later. Aida and I met him in the coffee shop. As always, his face was marked with corruption and emaciation. Only his eyes sparkled brightly in the heavy leftover scent of alcohol. As soon as he had taken a seat, he threw a thick envelope on the table and said with a grin, "I'll take that girl." He wiped the crud in the corners of his eyes with the back of his hand.

Harukawa's envelope contained about one hundred photographs. Aida sorted them into two piles, checking each photo very carefully but swiftly. His face beamed with satisfaction when he put down the last photo. He lit a cigarette, and fingered the smaller pile as he spoke to Harukawa, "Not bad."

"Not too bad, are they?" Harukawa smiled.

"That girl is photogenic, though her real face is hopeless." Aida waved his hand in the air and grinned cynically.

"She's got a huge mouth. You can stuff a bun in there when she smiles."

"She's such a bumpkin. She stuck her tongue out and licked the tip of her nose. That caught me off guard. She says that's her special talent."

Harukawa went home after gabbing about the trifles of life and discussing payment for the shooting. Handing me the pictures, Aida asked me to keep them. I took them to my office, and after checking through them, put them in my desk drawer and locked it. It was queer how Aida paid Harukawa an exorbitant amount out of a confidential budget but never mentioned the pictures or Kyōko again.

I didn't see Harukawa or Kyōko for a good while. How the two had spent their time became evident only after the next month's photography magazine, Camera Eye, came out. Harukawa's work on Kyōko was in there. The editor had given it the title, "Oh, Teenage!" and the subtitle, "An Ordinary Girl's Special Day." It was an ambitious work of six pages of large photographs. It became the talk of the other weekly magazines. Camera Eye sold the largest number of copies ever. The article rammed it home that Aida and Harukawa had succeeded in uncovering a new type of woman. The lens had changed Kyōko into another person.

"Oh, Teenage!" was about a girl of humble means. Harukawa had followed Kyōko around like a policeman, from the time she got up until she went to bed, and he portrayed her day with dramatization and documentation. He sorted out different qualities of Kyōko's. He painstakingly studied every part of her poverty, solitude, small vanities, lonely happiness, and selected the shots that best expressed her personality while alluding, at the same time, to several million other teenage girls. An editorial comment said that it cost Harukawa six hundred negatives to come up with the twelve pictures.

Kyōko was a girl of mediocrity, as the title indicated. Her life typically comprised crowded trains, a collection of movie stars' photographs, sunbathing on the rooftop, the three o'clock snack, window shopping at clothing stores, waiting in a long line for admission to an on-stage recording, eating ramen noodles at an outdoor wagon at night, walking by a smelly gutter in front of a public bath, and her younger brother jumping down from a closet shelf with a blanket over his shoulders, pretending to be Superman.

"She keeps tadpoles in a goldfish bowl, in a corner of her company's kitchen. They aren't small ones. They are the tadpoles of edible frogs, with faces like swellfish. She says that dried and grated bonito is the best feed. That's about the only way she's different from other girls,"

Harukawa answered brusquely when reporters interviewed him.

A close look at "Oh Teenage!" brought home, for the first time, Kyōko's special features: oversize eyes, oversize mouth, bushy eyebrows, and upturned nose. In no way was she good-looking, but these defects strangely accented her face. This is what Harukawa meant by photogenic. Youthfulness, expressiveness, and freshness filled her funny face and made her charming. This laughing girl with decayed teeth bore little resemblance to the tactless and wary girl I had seen at the test shooting. Here, she roamed about freely and accosted her audience eloquently. How did Harukawa get her to do all this? What power of persuasion lurks in that lipidic body, a good likeness of melting butter with only two eyes glittering? How much had Aida known when he brought Kyōko to him? All I could do was marvel at the outcome and discredit my own visual judgment.

About a month passed after the test shooting. During this time, the issue of *Camera Eye* came out, weekly magazines responded to it, and newspapers also made comments. Aida bore an air of indifference throughout. He had made both Kyōko and Harukawa swear that they'd never mention him as the discoverer of Kyōko. It turned out that this span of time was part of Aida's secret plan. The plan didn't even enter my mind, although I was in a position to know his predilections better than anyone else. Aida would wait out a delaying strategy and then hack his opponents with the axe of "time out."

In our company, each section meets at a general assembly, sometime after the tenth of every month. This particular month's meeting was exceptional, however, in that its special agendum was a big sales campaign scheduled for mid-June. Branch managers and the heads of agencies convened from different parts of the country. Executives in charge of this project were all present for the final confirmation of the campaign strategy which had previously been discussed, unofficially agreed upon, and outlined three months before. Basic issues—what prizes to give, what kinds of cards to insert in the caramel boxes, how high the special commission for wholesalers and retailers should be, which hot springs they should be invited to during the special sale period—had been settled. Our factories had already increased production proportionately.

Things were working right on schedule, except for one thing. The unsolved question had been raised at many meetings during the past three months but had gone up in smoke and gotten nowhere. It concerned the choice of the "trade character," or model, for newspaper advertisements and campaign posters. Aida was responsible for the selection, but he kept turning down the young girl singers and boy actors the executives had proposed at these meetings. His reason was that popular stars were "commercially overexposed." Aida's unusual stubbornness rendered the meetings turbulent. Not a single poster was printed, with the impending campaign only a month away.

Aida turned down all the children's-song singers, boy actors, baseball players, jazz singers, sumo wrestlers, and so on, who seemed to appeal to young people. At the mention of a champion professional wrestler, he swiftly pulled out a newspaper or two to prove that he was already under contract with an electric razor company and a television manufacturer. When a fashion model was suggested, he shook his head, "No way! She's already taken by a juice company and a lipstick company." The Osaka dialect[2] was deliberately thrown in as a shock absorber whenever he protested to executives.

It has been Aida's common practice to hide behind the shield of the Osaka dialect at trade negotiations and political maneuverings, never laying himself open to attack. The dialect is never part of his speech when he discusses the works of Shawn and Roypin with designers, but he uses it throughout his negotiations with trade agents. When salesmen come from broadcasting companies to sell sponsorship of certain programs, Aida lets them have it with biting criticism. Just before an agreement is made and prices are to be negotiated, Aida starts brandishing his abacus in the air hollering, "Here we go. Are you ready to have it out?" and breaks into a nasty grin. It is my conviction that nobody can guard himself completely against his Osaka dialect.

The last meeting was no exception. Former meetings were recalled, and the names of once-entombed stars and heroes were reviewed one after another, but Aida sifted them all out through the screen of his placement test. The heroes were disqualified not by Aida's distaste for their readiness to serve whatever company that paid them, or anything of that sort, but rather, strictly on the basis of their commercial value.

Aida's argument was something like: if the image of a "lipstick seller" is transferred to a "caramel seller," the public loses the ability to separate lipstick from caramels, and the impression of each will be only half as strong.

"You may have a point there, but don't stars have fans? The fans remember the stars well and look at them tirelessly. They are loyal to their stars."

Aida nodded deeply and politely when a manager came up with this statement, but he didn't alter his position. He first paid courtesy to the manager by highly accrediting the stars' ability to attract fans, and then gently gagged him to death by disclosing the nature of fans' interest, that is, fans look at posters to eye the face of a star; they pay little attention to the product the star recommends.

"Samson will do well as a poster company, but . . ."

The executive knitted his eyebrows and became quiet.

From shortly after noon until nearly three, Aida combatted the "heroes" singlehandedly, and murdered them with sophistry, tricks, and cunning oratory of one kind or another. So successful was he in building this foundation that it took no time for him to defend Kyōko after three o'clock. His prosecutors were totally confused, exhausted, and resigned. Some division heads and section chiefs started dozing in the cradle of the May sun and cigarette smoke.

"Essentially, you are saying that a new face, even if not well known, is best, right?" An executive disengaged the war.

"Yeah, I guess. I guess that's what I mean." Aida stepped down after he made sure that his opponents were sufficiently injured.

The executive sent back a sour smile at Aida's feigned ignorance.

"That's enough. Come on, bring it out. Don't waste our time." At someone's interjection, Aida calmly took from his briefcase the issue of *Camera Eye* and another weekly magazine. I got up from my seat at this point to fetch the test shooting pictures from my desk drawer. Back in the conference, I found Aida surveying the room, his chest proudly pushed forward, and his back barring the sunny window.

A representative from western Japan took a close look at Kyōko's pictures, and hit on something Aida, Harukawa, and I had all vaguely felt but were unable to capture in one word: "Heavens! This kid is like a water imp."[3]

The two magazines traveled through the hands of the executives, division heads, section chiefs, branch managers, and agency heads. These people's interest was not in the "Oh, Teenage!" pictures. Rather, it was in the magazine that summed up all the criticism and responses to "Oh, Teenage!" and described Kyōko's background. One wistful prosecutor raised his eyes from the magazine, ready to fire against the new proposal, but quickly swung his glance away, noticing that Aida's lips were twitching with an urge to shoot out the Osaka dialect.

Only after a bout of silence, an executive gently raised his face and asked, "So, am I correct in assuming that no company has taken this girl yet?"

As if to say, "There you go!" Aida spilled the contents of my envelope all over the conference table.

"I'm the one who found her," exclaimed Aida, and he elaborated on how he had discovered Kyōko, and how the test shots were taken in Harukawa's studio. He footnoted that he had forbidden Kyōko from taking any other sponsor until Samson had made up its mind.

The match was over. The high executive mumbled, averting his eyes from Aida to keep his temper to himself.

"What can we do? We don't have much time left anyway."

There was no time for voting. Aida, who had pushed away one piece of driftwood after another from the shipwrecked people, helped himself to the only weapon—time—and threw overboard only one lifesaving buoy. With less than a month remaining, it was unrealistic to run from theaters to studios to negotiate with stars, settle the terms of the contract, take pictures, and print them. Aida's time scheme had won him a smashing victory.

Aida telephoned Harukawa right after the meeting that day. He officially ordered a poster photograph, and set up the date for the shooting. After that, he called Kyōko at work in a nearby building and asked her out to a bar. Because it was just five o'clock, time to go home, Kyōko cried in agreement on the spot. Aida and I went to pick her up. Upon hearing about the exclusive contract and the amount of honorarium, Kyōko squealed excitedly, "I want to eat some rice crackers." She said that she wanted to eat the kind that were wrapped in thick seaweed and baked with plenty of soy sauce.

II

The staff in the advertisement section are drifters. For the past several years, we've been waging war against a certain anxiety. We've dedicated a vast fund and effort to it, all to no consequence. Some years ago, our anxiety was only a matter of figures and premonitions. But now we have it inside us, like our own intestines. The words we exchange are ill and feeble. Aida began to take refuge in model toy construction, away from this foul stench.

For some reason, caramels stopped selling. That's that. The big gun, who keeps shooting out harsh orders from his air-conditioned, quiet room, does not like to admit this. The proud official will take us to the window to show the incessant departure of loaded trucks from the underground warehouse. We also see the throng coming and going from the candy store. We hear the whisper of a throaty voice in our ears and feel the light tap of a dry, warm hand on our shoulder. It says, "Our business is all right. We can get by as it is. But wouldn't it be better if we sold more? That's all I'm saying. Can't you come up with a brilliant idea?" This voice is shoddy. It is filled with pretentious friendliness. The old man is trying to cover the chart on the wall with his back.

Yes indeed, trucks go off to towns, heavy with our product, footsteps clatter in the candy shop all day long, empty boxes scatter all over parks, the dust in the zoo smells sweet on Sundays, and girls must be keeping their fingers busy unwrapping the wax or paraffin paper as they read in bed. These are credible facts. Caramels are selling.

But I have a sheet of paper on my desk. It's a settlement of accounts. The trucks, footsteps, sweet dust, and the girls' fingers all fall dead right over this piece of paper. This paper lets me know, when I walk away from the window, the presence of a hushed fear waiting to whisper into my ears. I pick up the monthly business report and add to the graph on the wall a short line. The line grows slightly downward and is a synopsis of the happenings over the past several years. The long curved line has been flowing downstream ever since it reached a peak quite a while ago. We are neither hiking on the plains nor climbing a hill. Other than small ups and downs, we are definitely heading toward the sea.

If you add up the factory's facility improvement costs, advertisement fees, and personnel expenses, and compute the return ratio and put it against this line, you'll have a clearer picture of how serious Samson's condition is. There's no need to stand by the window again. The figures and the line, rather than the mob in the plaza, are what we must deal with. And to be honest, Samson is not the only one wounded. The market is shrinking for Apollo and Hercules—including all their subsidiary factories—and for caramel itself. What has happened to children's tongues?

We tried all kinds of theories. The salesmen were the first people to speak up. These friendly, slick-talking, capitalist knights, who would rather believe that they are selling the candies by themselves, consoled our seniors one day with their passionate lies.

"This month was unusual. It rained through the extended weekend. The long-awaited 'Golden Week'[4] went down the drain. Rain called off the extra shipment for picnics. Good weather will rectify the situation. This is how all the large wholesalers are looking at the situation, too. I met an Apollo salesman during my business trip. He complained the same way. We said to each other that the bean jam[5] business isn't the only one to suffer the effects of the rain. I don't think you should worry.''

Actually, this salesman had a point. It's true that we are working in an ultramodern building. Walls are painted in the best color for work efficiency; the production process is automated; waltzes are played to relax workers during rest hours. But amidst this modern setting, unfortunately, we experience joy and sorrow in quick alternation in accordance with the weather pattern. A weather station to Samson is a lighthouse. A rainy holiday stops the circulation of a great quantity of caramel, so long as mothers of limited means buy candies only for outings. The elders nodded halfheartedly but decided to overlook the falling figures.

The sad thing was that the ''uncontrollable force'' stayed strong in later months as well. The salesmen busied themselves each month thinking up good excuses for the tumbling business. The National Railways had a strike when the weather was good; a ferryboat sank when there was no strike; and, of course, there were typhoons, floods, and fires when the trains didn't stop and ferries didn't sink. A good search always hit on a reason or two to discourage people on this small island nation from peacefully eating caramel. In a month when no easy excuse was to be found, the salesmen made up the theory that the good fruit crop had robbed the children of their appetite for caramel. On absolutely unexcusable months, they criticized the enforcement of the set-price policy and the forty-day billing system as an unreasonable pressure on retail stores. All were true, but none was the sole cause of any given circumstance.

On the other hand, the production section, which is in a position to investigate the public's preference in flavor, presented another viewpoint. Those people candidly reasoned to their elders that the times were different. In later Meiji and early Taishō,[6] when people's tongues were unsophisticated, the exotic flavor of caramel—a combination of butter, milk, syrup, and European spices—had a strong appeal. Folks who knew nothing beyond the starchy Japanese sweets felt enlightened by the ''nutritious and tasty'' propaganda. Apollo creatively adopted the idea of ''nutrition'' as a means to sell candies. Having witnessed Apollo's success, two other companies put up their symbols of brawny Samson and Hercules respectively. In those days, impoverished Japanese people craved even the illusion of nutrition in every food they ate.

They were eager to overcome their inferiority complex about their physical build. Caramels made one big hit after another. Even after trisecting the market, each company enjoyed a tremendous profit.

The new flavors the giants introduced to the nation continued to expand and grow. To applause, the treats of European middle-class people—chocolate, cookies, marshmallows, bonbons, and even *marrons glacés*—joined the Japanese delights of *miso* and *takuan*.[7] The new exoticism was swiftly digested and became firmly rooted. The crisis transpired only when the Western flavor became incorporated into Japanese culture. The masses' tastes shifted slowly but surely. After the long break brought by World War II, there followed another brief caramel boom. But by then the people had already gone past us. That is, people those days bought caramel because they were hungry for sweets, or because they were nostalgic for the prewar lifestyle. As soon as their living conditions and social order were restored to the prewar level, and when people's skin turned nice and moist again, caramel lost its charm. Our merchandise became boring. About this time, the graph line on the wall started to take a downward plunge. So, we counted on the public's naive and forlorn instinct to imitate others; we sold the kind of chewing gum the war victors chewed. We managed to gain popularity. But this profit by itself was far from augmenting a capital gain. Once again, we faced the need to invent a radical sales plan as well as new flavors. Men in the lab made various experimental items and introduced some to the market: almond caramel for exoticism, pepsin gum for digestion, antiplaque candy for oral hygiene, two-layered caramel to accentuate the traditionally favored saltiness with sweetness. Each company used every means to please the tongues of the masses, but none had much of a business increase. The seniors sighed deeply in the forest of spice jars.

During the war, Samson, Hercules, and Apollo concurrently started making crackers, field rations, and high calorie food for the benefit of the military and the destitute. The war took away or gravely crippled everyone's factories, but when the postwar candy boom came about, the devastation proved advantageous. Nothing stood in the way of installing mass production facilities. Each company either tore down or abandoned its old factories. And after spending some years planning, each built new factories for new machines. Soon, mixers started spinning, boilers started bubbling, and ovens started sending out heat. The renovation made it possible to produce 650 pieces of caramel every minute, one ton of cookies per hour, and six tons of candy drops a day.

The flood of candies made us run. After the boom, during the leveling off period, we still couldn't afford to sit still. The flood did not ease even at the sign of bad times coming up.

Hysteria erupted in the advertisement section, in addition to the fretfulness of the sales section and the exhaustion of the production section. We were made to stand in front of a gate without a key, so to speak. In order to sell caramel, we continued prize-giving sales. During the past several years, it's been air rifles, 8 mm movie cameras, and regular cameras, not the smell of butter or milk, that's been making children run to candy shops. And there have also been bicycles, tropical fish, deerskins, baseball equipment. . . . The three giants have turned themselves into variety shops.

Not all of our plans failed. Some proved better than others. The line on our wall showed nervous convulsions every time new capital was poured in. The salesmen sometimes offered thanks to the production section's helpful innovations but at other times cried in anger and pain. Every so often, Samson left the two other runners far behind into an easy victory. But no matter how successful, all that the special sales did was to temporarily implant a demand instinct in the public. It was no more than a kind of toxicosis. By its nature, one stimulant needed to be stronger than the one before. The giants frantically packed new cards in boxes, printed new dreams, and watched for an opportunity, with all their brains and resources put together, to strike at the others' blind spots. Each battle left, in cities and villages, numerous skeptics, distraught mouths, and millions of betrayed children. In spite of all this, the voice that came out from the bright and quiet room had only one thing to say, "Sell more!" Selling ceased to be simple propaganda. It was the giant's confusion, full of contradictions.

There's a parable which leads us to examine ourselves. During the war, three billboards were built along a highway in the flatlands of Tennessee. The first one had a picture of two donkeys pulling hard toward different haystacks. Because their necks were roped together, the two beasts, pulling away from each other, got nowhere. In the second picture, the donkeys had realized that they should cooperate and walk side by side. By doing so, they finally reached a haystack. In the third board, the two donkeys enjoyed a haystack larger than the two they had initially tried to reach. That's all there was to the billboards. There was neither an explanation nor a command. But the pictures had a goal—to preach the advantage of cooperative labor for the war effort. Sartre was not an authority on advertising, but he found a deeper meaning below the surface of the parable. He analyzed: "These posters encourage viewers to draw their own conclusions. Problem solving is a creative process which makes the original proposition more convincing than if a plain answer is given."

Americans are gifted at grasping mob psychology. They have figured out that advertising funds are best invested in the workings of the subconscious. We Japanese have also enjoyed the benefit of this strategy during our better years. Aida trained his designers and drafters to advertise the joy and sweetness of caramel, rather than forcing, entreating, or abetting consumers. He sold feelings instead of commodities. Consumers, more often than not, have a deep-seated distrust of advertisements. Being aware that people were most unhappy to be hounded by advertisements, we tried nothing beyond extolling happiness in front of masses that aimlessly roamed about in a wilderness of flavors. We left mothers to enjoy the self-respect of willfully selecting merchandise. We simply hoped that Samson's image loomed larger than those of Apollo or Hercules in their dim subconscious. Aida and the rest of us shared this view. This was the period when Samson's designers produced their best. In those days, our elders had nothing to think about other than the pleasant long arc of a golf ball in the blue sky.

In retrospect, our good time was no more than an optimistic whim drifting in the peaceful air. At least it ended up that way. It took only the first sign of a weak economy to show that we were no better than rabble-rousers. The mountains of boys' magazines crowding our desks recount the situation. Horrendous sales competitions drained companies who made speculators out of children. Now we were caught in a shower of attacks by PTAs and women's organizations. The bitter experience forced representatives from the three companies to sign a self-regulation treaty at the end of last year. But early this year, in January, disquieting rumors took to the air, and the treaty instantly lost power. We were again ordered to create new dreams.

I started my research in early February. First, I gathered as many boys' magazines and books as I could find, then broke down the special features of children's stories—including cartoons and biographies of great people—into categories, and finally made a chart. In order to learn what interested them the most, I also went to amusement parks, cartoon movies, children's picture shows, amd playgrounds to closely observe the children's actions and voices from morning till night. Even if my company had fallen into hysteria, I wanted to direct my energy towards worthy causes. Since I've never been good with my horse sense, speculations, or gambles, I relied on systematic investigation of children's tastes and inclinations. Vertically and horizontally, I studied sample towns in Tokyo and a certain prefecture. I paid considerable fees to news agencies and retailers to purchase their figures and charts about children. The unprecedented meticulousness of my research, in a way, spoke frankly for the profundity of the current recession.

While I was steeped in cartoons like "Gamma Line Man," "Hydro Troop," and "Jungle Ken-chan," Aida made a tour of toy stores and souvenir shops and rummaged through all kinds of junk. The advertising office soon gained the likeness of a toy warehouse. Gun belts, paired shotguns, and a ten-gallon hat hung on the walls. On the floor, a wireless remote control tractor ran, and robots walked around. On a desk, there was a tank of tropical fish and model boats. Aida randomly bought these to carefully inspect them by dismantling and reassembling. When preoccupied, he worked the wireless car, his face less than an inch above the floor.

His favorite was an American toy gun. The design of a spur was printed on its square handle. It was stone heavy and looked real. The gun hammer snugly sprang up as the trigger was pulled and the cylinder rotated. The only unreal thing about it was that it did not shoot bullets. Aida gloated over it.

"This gun has a long barrel. This is what they call the Wyatt Earp style. I love it! Look at this precision. This is something a very caring adult would make for children. Since only one out of 500,000 or a million gets a prize, I would like to give something this good."

It wasn't that he was all taken up by the American Westerns. Having me take care of the mathematics, he bought from foreign bookstores a quantity of science fiction, future stories, and space cartoons. He never read them. He just cut out illustrations, photographs, and designs. Not only did he collect foreign books, but he also collected from Japanese boys' magazines any pictures related to space science. When it came to fantasy films, he saw them on the first day of their release. He didn't mind traveling any distance to catch one. My guess was that he was studying space suits. Space helmets and space guns were not available in Japan as yet, not even in toy stores. But Aida's bulky secret scrapbooks were littered with queer sketches of space suits.

Aida had used a silly and dangerous trick when he tried to sell the nameless homely girl, Kyōko, to the board members; but with the spacesuit, he resorted to the more traditional tools of numbers and factual data. He did this because he had more confidence in his choice of prizes. The directors' meeting was held a month before his discovery of Kyōko. My role there was not to present ideas but to report the results of my research with the aid of a map. Aida then used my data to steer the drifters toward his goal. Why Aida had never sought prior consultation with me was beyond me, but that was the way it was. Most likely, he was too sure of himself.

I read off the results of my research that showed which children's programs on television and radio were the most popular, what stories appeared most frequently in boys' magazines, which films were hits, and what elements moved children the most. I further summoned children's heroes, supermen, and idols from underground dungeons, airports, river valleys, and skies to introduce them to older generations. The end of my report marked the opening gambit of a most diversified discussion as to what kind of prize should be given. The board meeting was another toy fair. Baseball nuts brought an entire baseball outfit, science fans recommended a microscope, sports fishermen opted for a fishnet, someone who was sufficiently intimidated by women's groups from earlier experiences had consulted a publisher and suggested giving an encyclopedia. But none could reasonably satisfy the overall requirement that the prize should be respectable as well as interesting and healthy, even though speculative. Aida silently watched them argue and patiently waited for fatigue to set in. He kept perfect composure, convinced by my report that his judgment was on the right track.

When finally his opinion was sought, he stood up, and circulated many scrapbooks to the directors. He then explained the details of the space suit and made me stand up again to reiterate the portion of my report that told how popular space stories were. I checked through my file, cited the percentage of space stories used in children's newspapers, magazines, radio and television programs, and films, and sat down. Obviously, the senior staff's silence meant Aida's victory.

Aida talked at length. Space helmets and space guns are ordinary toys for American children, but their Japanese counterparts have seen them only in drawings. They are unique and eye-catching for sure. They are timely in that newspaper companies are planning to sponsor a space show in an attempt to expand knowledge of artificial satellites and space rockets. A Walt Disney space film will be released concurrently. If Samson takes part in this space campaign, we can save advertisement funds and still enjoy good feedback. To protect ourselves from the criticism that Samson's prize would only stir up the children's gambling spirit and actually corrupt them, the lowest prize can be generously expanded as a free admission to the space show and planetarium. He went on to lecture that Samson could also capture the hearts of parents if it serialized a space story in children's newspapers and magazines, independent of its advertisements, during the three months' special sales period. If a physicist and a novelist put their effort together, they might come up with a scientific and yet entertaining story.

"From the foregoing, I have the feeling that this idea, which may sound outrageous at first, is more promising than you think. . . . And it may just do the trick." He equivocated the ending in a soft voice, and sat down.

I told myself that this was Aida's favorite technique. So confident was he of his own proposal, he didn't bother to finish the sentence. Without sounding assertive, he had coaxed an agreement. Quite skillful! The ultimate responsibility was thrown in the face of whoever approved his idea. The choreography would protect him when things went wrong and peevish seniors started picking a quarrel with him. I saw the barbed wire casually pitched on the tail of his diction.

The directors were at first befuddled by the inventiveness of Aida's idea. They kept examining the pictures in the scrapbooks. But my statistical information and Aida's editorials managed to enthrall them. Eventually, one of them asked, "What would you make this helmet from?"

"I'd say plastic. I think that injection molding produces better results than vacuum molding. Here's the estimate by a certain company." Aida handed an estimate slip made by a plastic molder. He had also brought estimates from a toy manufacturer and a work-clothes maker. I was flabbergasted by his forehandedness.

"Did you design the emblem on this whatever you call it?"

"Yes, I superimposed the designs of the Gamma Line Man in *Boys' Club* onto Mr. Comet in *Space Fan*."

"What if we put the Samson mark?"

Aida scratched his head, acknowledging his oversight.

"I'm not convinced. I'm not sure if Japanese children would go for something on the basis of its popularity among American children. What do you think?" asked another man.

This voice was immediately wiped out by Aida's citation of the figures explaining the popularity of space stories and by the voices of a majority of the directors who by now supported Aida, but it drove a wedge in my heart. The latter half of the day's meeting was focused on Aida's proposal. Although no resolution was reached, things were working in Aida's favor. The meeting was adjourned with the agreement to make a definite plan for the special sales within a week and meanwhile to kick around the realistic possibilities of joining the space show, the Disney film, and the serialized story.

The final proposal violated the three companies' gentlemen's agreement. But it made no difference in the end, for we learned before the end of the day that Apollo and Hercules had also been compelled to do the same. The two companies would start their special sales on more or less the same day in mid-June. Aida came back with the report from the boardroom, handed it to me, and thumped down on his swivel chair. His note outlined Apollo's and Hercules' confidential special sales plans. Heaven only knows from where information leaked, but we could reasonably suspect, judging from the way things were going, that the two other companies had also gotten hold of our plan by then. Be that as it may, the time for diplomatic rhetoric and hypocrisy was clearly over. I read Aida's note to find that the two other companies were no more innocent than ourselves. After a good amount of deliberation, Hercules had decided to give live animals for prizes. Pocket monkeys, guinea pigs, and squirrels were listed. I wasn't surprised. To me, live animals are attractive and a realistic equivalent of the fantastic space outfit. I could tell that Hercules was also desperate.

But Apollo Confectionery's plan shocked me into taking a second look at the note. There was only one line on it, but it said everything I needed to know about Apollo's design: "The Special Prize: Scholarship for Elementary School through University."

I looked up. Aida was fumbling with a model airplane, speechless. He didn't turn around to answer my stare. I knew he saw his own clumsiness. I interpreted his silence as his suffering. Apollo's idea was definitely extraordinary. Apollo had given up fighting with children and decided to approach their mothers. They hit our blind spot dead center. Hadn't Samson been shot right in the heart while it was totally hung up on children's dreams?

"They did it." I gave Aida the note back with this comment.

Aida lit a cigarette, took a deep breath, and nodded. I let out a gasp and swung my eyes toward the darkening window. The evening turmoil at the station plaza shook our glass wall. I could tell that we were in for a hopeless competition. We had spread too many epidemics of apathy with too many unrewarding prizes. This cannot be denied. Children and parents have gotten weary of dreams. Apollo's sweet newspaper commercials must have practically no appeal to them. Yet if parents are coached by their children to buy caramel, and if they compare the three companies' advertisements, they will sadly smile and pick Apollo. And the mother will go out once more, secretly, without being asked by her child. To me, Apollo's idea was that appealing.

Aida was silent, all pent-up. He put glue on an emblem of a model jet airplane, placed it on a wing, and carefully smoothed out the wrinkles.

"Apollo's president is Christian, isn't he? Didn't he once forbid the production of whiskey bonbon and baba? Don't you think his religion has something to do with this?" Baba was sponge cake soaked in rum. It was commonly understood that Apollo's president barred the production of these for religious reasons. I reminded Aida of this.

Aida winced at the cigarette smoke and shook his head.

"I doubt it," he objected flatly. "Whiskey bonbons don't sell as fast as caramel. That's why. That's all." Speaking over his shoulder, Aida finally lifted his lifeless eyes from the model airplane, his shoulders lowered. There was no vestige of his readiness and dauntlessness of this afternoon.

"They really did it." He droned in a new tone of voice, combed his silver hair upward with his fingers, and slowly creased the corners of his eyes. His neck suddenly looked thinner. "There are some brains over there."

We smoked for a while in silence. The rumbling of the massed pedestrians echoed in the room and reverberated endlessly. Cars drove and trains creaked.

"They are certainly one step ahead of us." I put my cigarette ash in an ashtray. "Not much ahead, though. Only one out of a million gets the prize."

Aida lifted his head. He looked at me with probing eyes. "Of course. We aren't a scholarship society," he snapped. He got up, dropped his cigarette on the floor and crushed it under his shoe. A moment later, his back sprang up straight, his shoulders pulled back, and he was over with the depression.

"That's the rule of the game." He was all charged up. He had a calm smile on his face but spoke as sharply as a razor blade.

III

We call the effect of posters "visual scandal." People's brains are impaired by the colors, sounds, and letters of advertisements and are afflicted by mental elephantiasis. Already, viewers are made incurably thick-skinned by distrust and fatigue. But as is often the case with toxicosis, their nervous systems are still amazingly sensitive. They repel unpleasant things and resist mediocrity. Advertisers must wage a war against their pupils. We must awaken, with our lively and over-flowing scandals, those unfriendly eyes which have been dulled by hammering stimulations.

Our poster this time was an unprecedented hit compared to numer-ous others we had printed in the past several years. Aida made daily trips to the plastic molding factory to have the best possible space helmet made within the capacity of available technology. He put it over Kyōko's head and told her to smile, exposing her cavitied teeth. Har-ukawa staged it and took pictures. The smashing success was a result of Aida's violation of all conventions. For one thing, he highlighted the cavitied teeth for a candy commercial. Secondly, Kyōko was neither good-looking nor well known. He let a girl wear a boy's outfit. And he used a professional portrait photographer's work in a commercial. Just one of them could choke a man of common sense to death. In prepara-tion for the executives' objections, Aida cautiously and surreptitiously prepared a poster with a boy star. But by the time this was ready, Kyōko's poster, which had come out one step ahead, had gained a smashing popularity. The boy's poster was put away unknown.

People are interested in other people's faces. Everyone's face has drama. One may be more telling than another, but they all have drama. Since faces attract more attention than anything else, Aida took pride in the idea that he could create, through the art of editing and printing, a face more captivating than one in the flesh. His approach was consis-tent. From the instant he saw Kyōko, laughing in the sun on the yonder side of the glass wall, he had measured her face solely in terms of the triangular relationship among the lens, the printer, and Harukawa's editing ability.

"That face survives through any number of retouchings by a printer. But no matter how funny-faced Kyōko may be, her everyday smile has no commercial value. Only Harukawa can make it marketable," Aida had explained to me.

We received many compliments on Kyōko's poster, but the predomi-nant ones were: youthful, fresh, extraordinarily expressive, atypically charming. These coincided with the reactions to Harukawa's "Oh, Teenage!" Kyōko's cavitied teeth fascinated people before they had a

chance to be warned of the harm candies can bring. The public identified itself with the poverty, youth, and laughter Kyōko represented.
The charm stemmed, that is, from the sense of intimacy. Aida's further
accomplishment was that he had elevated the caramel to something
beyond a category of food. He had imprinted caramel, in the mind of
the public, as a daily necessity which would bring a fresh sensation to
life. He revived the atrophied flavor by dint of visual freshness.

We sent Kyōko all over the place. She laughed on walls, in stations,
candy shops, theaters, and zoos. She tickled people with droll gestures.
Her poster decorated towns a month after "Oh, Teenage!" A fashion
magazine editor was the one to make the first association between the
poster girl and the one who kept tadpoles. After that, Aida received
many telephone calls. Aida's trips with Kyōko extended to many publishers. At his suggestion, Kyōko carried Harukawa's recommendation
along with her pictures. She sent about thirty vitae to magazines and
fashion photographers. By the third week, she was so well off that she
no longer needed the bookkeeping job. Agents from fashion magazines
and fashion shows followed her, invited her, and ordered her to pose for
them. Everywhere she went, Kyōko made the same expression and the
same pose taught by Aida and Harukawa. She used it as her style.

The strength of a poster shouldn't be measured by how popular the
model has become. Rather, its power ought to be measured in terms of
how deeply her impression penetrates the viewers' subliminality. But
strictly speaking, the latter is impossible to measure. All we can do is to
observe and analyze the reactions of selected informants and surmise
the whole scope of things from this piecemeal research. After that, the
best we can do is to keep faith in statistics and their numerical results.

Inasmuch as Kyōko's popularity enhanced the effect of her poster,
Aida begrudged no effort to make her famous. At the same time, he
gave a very binding kind of exclusive contract to her. He made her
swear not to appear in commercials of any other company or industry,
while allowing her every freedom to appear in any number of shows or
magazines. A generous fee was expected to make up for the rigidity of
this contract. Aida introduced her voice and face to radio, television,
handouts, and all other means of mass communication, including
newspapers and magazines, only after he had ascertained her success as
a poster model.

Kyōko soon forgot about her tadpoles and threadbare dufflebag. She
threw out her denim pants and ripped sandals. She dyed her hair with
Oxyfull, and got acquainted with corset hoops. She chewed gum, but

never again gave a thought to the automatic wrapping machine. She disappeared from the station plaza, and put out of her mind men's iron ribs in sardine-packed commuter trains. She bathed in lights, slinked in camera lenses, and rode over the sweet waltz which was luxuriously seasoned with volatile lyricism. And she inhaled the stares, body odor, and applause of women milling in semidarkness. On stage, she smiled in a glittering river of lights, breathed in hot dust, trotted along forming numerous little swirls around her, bowed, and went away. Her name pervaded the minds of teenage girls; it was recited at offices, coffee shops, and everywhere else.

On the night of her first appearance in a fashion show, I took her out on Aida's behalf. Over the after-dinner coffee, she talked about her wish to study jazz. She dwelled on this long-standing dream. When I told her that she ought to learn English in that case, she said she wanted to buy a dictionary. Since this was something we could try right away, we walked over to a bookstore as a way of working off the meal. The bookstore had rows of dictionaries with golden titles on their bindings, ranging from pocket dictionaries for college entrance examinations to an Oxford edition. I pulled them out one by one, flipped through the pages, explained the strengths and weaknesses of each, and suggested that she compare their contents with the prices. She cogitated for a while, in front of piles of books, and raised her confused face.

"Can you tell me the difference between English-Japanese and Japanese-English?" she asked in a whisper. Her widely opened, unblinking eyes gaped in my face. Obviously she really didn't know the difference.

In astonishment, I put down the copy I was showing her.

"What did you learn in middle school?" I asked, finally coming back to myself.

A stormy cloud passed over her cheerful face.

"I don't want to buy one today." With a little squeak, she did an about-face, and walked out of the store. Before I knew it, she was gone in a taxi.

The obscurity of her cultural background pounded at my brain. I must have tripped a girl who was just getting ready to crawl up the social ladder. I felt in my flesh her little stomach convulsing in great pain. I returned all the dictionaries to the shelves and bought a beginner's pocket dictionary which annotated English words with Japanese katakana.[8] I then bought a beginner's language record at a music store, and had the clerk send the two items to Kyōko's home.

The special sale competition started in June, as scheduled. A spate of merry outcries decorated the newspapers. Each company disguised its agony and desperation in busy optimism and fantasy. Nevertheless, the kind of lonely regret one would experience as he walks into a badly attended theater affected him. Skies and forests suddenly popped open before children. Mothers and fathers, their faces mixed with contrived grins and headaches, gazed at the giant who beamed with an expression of charity.

Samson, before anyone else, filled newspapers with fantasies. Our grand prize was a complete space travel outfit; first prize, a helmet and gun; second prize, a rocket packed with caramel; third prize, the choice between a visit to the planetarium or a Disney film. Also, one caramel box would let one in the space show. Hercules made a frontal attack on this. It assembled a parade of prizes, led by a pocket monkey and running along in the order of squirrels, Angora rabbits, and guinea pigs. During the sales period, it sponsored a children's theater at the zoo. The ticket to this, as expected, was a box of caramels. The repertoire included "Dr. Doolittle Goes to Africa," "Honeybee Maya," "The Jungle Book," and others. These two giants followed each other's travel routes, grappled on all fours, and watched for their chance to win.

Compared to ours, Apollo's voice was far more persuasive and prudent. The company would give the scholarship to ten victors, without ranking them; nothing more, nothing less. It declared that, for the sake of fairness, it would establish an "Apollo Scholarship Fund" corporation for the delivery of the monthly scholarship. Also, it declared that the prizes were not a temporal stimulus for chancy speculators. They were part of a semi-permanent system to be renewed yearly, regardless of business conditions.

"You hypocrites!" The announcement made Aida grit his teeth in chagrin.

Apollo did not adorn the papers with exclamation marks and smiles. Instead, it published one long message entitled "To Mothers" which sensitively vindicated and stressed how unmercantile the company's intentions were. It laid open its healthy business record and gave the public a glimpse of the interior of a gate of happiness.

Reactions were clear-cut. All the women's organizations, educational institutions, religious corporations, and countless letters lauded Apollo. Samson and Hercules were skinned alive. Housewives excavated, tinkered with, and compared Apollo's way with the two companies' impudence, lewdness, and clamorous optimism apparent in such phrases as "Oh, it squeezes me!" and "Go, quick, to a candy store!" The two giants were injured all over their bodies, if you will. Apollo managed to receive the kinds of responses from the types of people it had anticipated. They fawned on adults instead of children. Children do not write letters to newspapers. We were well penalized.

Although Samson and Hercules suffered this murderous blow just when they were preparing to thrash out a game, the two giants did their best in the swamp of hysteria. Battle cries were heard and flags were hoisted in cities during June. I gave up my research and ran around on a variety of missions requested by the advertisement section. Following the newspaper ads, the space outfit appeared in the sky. That is, gigantic advertising balloons rose in the skies over parks and zoos, and they were lit up at night. A statue was built in the Samson building plaza. Aida hired a man, put the space suit on him, and made him stand like a statue on a pedestal. People were greeted by future space travelers at the doorway to the exhibition hall and at various display floors. Electric billboards flashed up, down, and sideways. The radio carried Kyōko's exclamations. We filled advertisement trucks with sample prizes to deliver to candy shops. On Sundays, helicopters dropped leaflets. Kyōko's smiles shone in the sun and then got trampled on, eventually to be absorbed into the soil.

It didn't take long for her rival to show up. Hercules contracted a professional wrestler. Driven out of its wits, the company dressed the wrestler exactly like their trademark. The "nutritious and wholesome" champion wore leopard-skin pants, leather sandals, a pocket monkey perched on his arm, and tramped across the stage of the outdoor theater. To get louder applause, he would jump down off the stage, walk through the little Sunday audience, and distribute boxes of caramels. Olive oil, rubbed on his whole body, did him up as a burly bronze statue. His nerves twitched, muscles heaved, and arteries swelled every time he made the smallest motion. The impression I got from this figure was that he looked unnecessarily barbaric. Wildness and deformed robustness spilled out from the edges of his controlled behavior and face-filling smiles. The wrestler, in fact, called to mind a tragic slave.

I took a walk through the park after watching the wrestler and "Dr. Doolittle Goes to Africa." The park was Hercules territory. Its trademark was ubiquitous on benches, sign boards, trash bins, gift stands, and wherever. There was not a hint of Kyōko's smile. Hercules showed its prize animals and birds at the entrance to the amusement park and on the side of the outdoor theater. When swarmed by children, those spots looked like little zoos. I looked around and found some empty caramel boxes but no prize cards. Children were running around, steaming in the sun, covered with dirt, and emitting a straw-like odor from the tops of their heads.

Up against the background of early summer cumulus clouds, an American Windmill and an Octopus Ride—together with a merry-go-round and a Monkey Island—whirled carnival-like raptures up in the sky and down on the ground. I paused in front of a water chute. A long line of children and adults waited their turns in the boiling heat. Two box-shaped boats took turns climbing up a sharp slope and plunging down into a pond. Each boat had a guide standing on the deck. One was young and the other middle-aged. The younger man's total concentration on his work arrested my curiosity.

The boat was pushed back with a bamboo pole onto a stand and pulled from there up to the top of the slope. The younger man brought out two buckets of water, after a new group of children got on the boat at the top, and blew a whistle on the deck. As the boat slid down the sharp incline, he bent forward at the bow and slowly spilled the two buckets of water on the railing. This was done while the boat moved at a tremendous speed. His trousers flapped in the billowing wind, and he challenged the moment of the boat's plunge into the pond by lifting the buckets high in the air.

The young man probably had to jump up in order to avoid the impact of the boat hitting the water. The middle-aged man did the same but just enough to parry the shock. He jumped ever so slightly, and started poling back to the shore right afterward, with a weary expression on his face, not at all like the lad with Don Cossack's legs. At one time, the youngster lifted the buckets. At another time, he swished the bamboo pole in the air. Yet other times, he wildly clapped above his head and even tried to kick his feet together a couple of times above the floor. Sparse clapping did not discourage him. He tried one thing after another, quietly but eagerly.

I was impressed by his enthusiasm. He had no muscles to speak of, but his movements were terse and his energy effectively consumed. He seemed to know children better than the wrestler at the zoo. He was serving them out of his unsolicited and unforced volition. He would probably not argue, even if his coworker called his enthusiasm a wasted effort, in the shed after the children had gone home. Next day, he would be standing on the tip of the water chute slope with the same bamboo pole, ready to repeat similar tricks. There was something childish about how he acted, but to me he seemed to be doing the right thing. Children don't clap, but this lad will be there when water splashes again in the murky interior of the children's memories. Both Aida and I may have his diligence, but I'm not sure if we are using our energy as effectively as he does. It was my long-standing fatigue that made me prostrate in front of the youngster's simplest action. As I walked away from the amusement park, I was trying to force this interpretation on myself.

Aida was gradually consumed. Every morning he came back to work exhausted. Bags, very much like Harukawa's, started to form below his eyes. They looked like shadows at first, then turned into stains before long, and now they unmistakably remained as stains. Looking back, I think the best time for him was when Kyōko's poster came out. He's been wasted away by fatigue ever since. He's been too busy. He doesn't have the time to glue a wheel on a model car. Every day, he goes to the exhibition hall, gives directions to the advertising cars, and carefully inspects the activities of Apollo and Hercules so that he can figure out business countermeasures. He also has to look over the pictures, the drafts, and the layouts of the originals the designers show him. At night, he has to watch television and listen to the radio to check on Kyōko's performance and voice. In the waiting room, newspaper and magazine advertisement salesmen with bloodshot eyes hang around trying to sell their columns and pages. Aida argues, coaxes, threatens, plays possum with each of these people, using his Osaka dialect, and bargains them down. Sunk low and sloppily in his armchair, he listens to their praises made of half flattery and half honesty about Kyōko, then cuts off their smiles as soon as they finish talking. "Don't call me a movie maker, you son-of-a-bitch." This, mind you, comes after a treacherous business negotiation. There's no rebutting him.

The scenes before the negotiations make you sick in the stomach. His single-track wish to get a good deal drives him to talk turkey with wrinkles all around his eyes. "Oh brother, you make me feel so good. I've been dying to hear a thing like that. You look so sharp, by the way. I can't get over it." So saying, he would raise his exhausted body and rub and shake the agitated salesman's shoulders, practically embracing him.

I'm skeptical about the economic feasibility of this sort of lip service. If we just look at the end result, it's true that Aida always had his way in business deals, bought columns and show time at amazingly good prices; but I have no way of telling how much of that is owing to his business strategy. Newspaper companies, magazines, and radio companies bleed in front of Aida because they are under the pressure of a stagnant economy, the summer slump, and television's monopolization of potential sponsors. Up against these economic undercurrents, Aida's talent means nothing.

It was not Aida alone who was worn out. Factories and offices worked overtime continuously from day one of the special sale to keep up with the rush orders. The seniors explained statistically the company's strained circumstances. They exchanged a temporal contract with the labor union concerning their overtime work within the legal limit of the law. This caused a female worker to faint in the factory, an accountant to fall asleep at his office calculator, and a salesman to crack his ribs in a motorcycle accident. A blood sedimentation test detected a number of people who required medical treatment. Many men asked for tranquilizers at the medical room. This is how the children's dream robbed sleep from adults.

I had a strange experience on the street. I was on my way back to the office, after discussing with a physicist a space story serialized in a boy's magazine. Crossing a railroad track, I was about to enter an open space. Because the traffic light was red, I stopped on the sidewalk at an intersection. My throat was parched, my legs were heavy, and my forehead was covered with thick dust. It being late in the day, the thin blue night was starting to drift over the sidewalk, mixed with the smell of gasoline. The flow of cars looked like a river of metal and glass. Many kinds of cars hurtled by with high shrieks, hustling and pushing one another. Right then, a felt hat came flying by. A gust of wind kept it rolling on the pavement. It looked like a spotless, brand new light gray felt hat where it landed, sheltered from squeaking wheels. It looked soft and light and seemed to have a remarkably tender touch. It was brightly vivid as if this spot on the street had dissolved all the tar, gasoline, rag, and other stains. But just as I took a deep breath, a car brushed past me, and the hat was squashed flat under a wheel. The disappearance of the original shape startled me. A car had reduced the hat to a flat sheet of cloth clinging to the pavement.

I raised my eyes to see the people around me. They were walking in the twilight noisily and unmindfully. I felt that only I was in a strange world. It bothered me. I couldn't understand why the hat neither screamed nor spilled blood when it was run over. Why didn't I hear the crunch of bones, why didn't the car stop, and why didn't a policeman rush over? Something had really happened. Strength escaped me. I sensed something collapse deep inside me, and I was utterly spent. Where in the city did my energy stray to, outside my skin? The city was getting dark; it was dusty, noisy, and obstinate. While pacing in the plaza, I had the sensation that all kinds of people, cars, buildings, and monuments were flying through my body. I was won over by the deep exhaustion.

IV

Something interesting happened, although it didn't take any load off my back. One of the giants dropped out. Apollo, the most intelligent of the three, disqualified on account of a most unexpected break. This brought to Apollo mass anxiety and threats.

One July day, an elementary school student returned from a dragon-fly hunt and took a nap. When his mother tried to wake him up in the evening, he was found unconscious. His face was pale, and his dry teeth bit his lower lip. A doctor diagnosed the cause to be food poisoning. The injection of an antidote restored him, but the boy complained of a severe headache and could not get up. After some search, Apollo's drops were found in the pocket of the pants he had taken off.

This was the beginning of Apollo's fall. The doctor, acting for the mother, sent a letter to the local newspaper. By the afternoon of that same day, the newspaper company had received many other letters reporting similar conditions. An investigation was started right away. One newswriter got hold of the drops and ran over to Apollo. Apollo verified the production date from the serial number and took the drops to its factory. Because drops are made of glucose, sweetener, spices, and food coloring, the head technician performed a microscopic analy-sis of each ingredient and detected an unusual reaction with the food coloring.

Apollo wrote an apology in that day's evening paper, frankly admit-ting negligence in its quality control procedures. The analysis chart it published perfectly matched the datum given by the Industrial Testing Center. Apollo must have held an all-night board meeting. The compa-ny warned consumers in the next day's morning paper not to buy its drops until the defective batch had been recalled from retail stores. Apollo's trucks scrambled around the country to collect the drops from wholesale and retail stores, but it was too late. Starting with that day's evening paper, for two weeks, the second and fourth pages of the morning and evening issues of every newspaper printed victims' photographs and articles. The articles brimmed with complaints, shrieks, and curses. By now the same people who had complimented the scholarship program were ready to fire fierce attacks. The voices of accusation and panic appeared in children's newspapers, women's magazines, and weeklies. Mothers whispered to one another, and candy shop keepers turned touchy.

Upon the realization of how critical the situation was, Apollo published another "To Mothers" article wherein it candidly explained the situation, admitted its technical failure, avowed compensation to victims, and advised the public to buy other companies' drops until another notification was made. In addition, it discontinued the caramel prizes as a way of avoiding misunderstanding. It said that there was no relationship between the drops and caramels but that this was Apollo's expression of apology. The article further told the disappointed mothers that just for this year, the "Apollo Scholarship" fund would be equally distributed among the victims as compensation and scholarships. All of Apollo's advertisement efforts terminated on the evening this statement came out. Neon lights were turned off, balloons were pulled down, and there were no more radio, television, or newspaper advertisements. Aida groaned, watching how Apollo had put, one by one, every promise it had made in its second "To Mothers" article into practice; but he made no comments.

It was our salesmen who clapped to the giant's swoon. They recovered vitality at the thought of expanding their narrow market. The time was bad enough without the competition. Wholesalers were fighting to collect cash. The small market had been divided by three elbowing companies. Slow circulation had made a mountain of stock in the retailers' warehouses. Apollo's sales network was strong, but who would buy the unadvertised caramel with no prizes? Was it too early to deem Apollo insolvent? The company had thrust its hand into its own wound and shed blood. Our salesmen encouraged each other, saying in chorus that a path had been opened for them. Color came back to their cheeks. They became friendlier. Laughter filled their office. Apollo's miasma was reported at each end-of-the-week departmental meeting. Our reporters gesticulated, showing how abjectly Apollo's salesmen entreated wholesalers to stock up on their products. These reports were progressively abridged and exaggerated as they traveled up from the salesmen, head salesman, section chief, department chief, and further up to directors and the president.

I observed this process with bewilderment. I resented the way people abandoned themselves to the Darwinian rule of survival. The public had already lost interest in our products. Aren't the space suit, the pocket monkey, and the scholarship the only things that bind the children and their mothers to our merchandise? I couldn't imagine that the mothers who were cut off from the scholarship would walk into the worlds of space suits and pocket monkeys. True, they may reach out for Samson and Hercules at their children's request, but this kind of reluctant choice would not bring us a big business. Without the begging, the mothers would not buy.

The terrifying thing is that the giants hadn't realized that they had hanged themselves with their own investment and effort. In other words, they had fostered large herds of skeptics. Apollo wasn't the only one tearing open its own wound. Samson, Hercules, and everyone else were strangling themselves with their own hands. Isn't it an ugly mistake to forget about the apathy we've fed the public and cry for a positive return just because Apollo has faltered? I lost patience with our salesmen's gleefulness.

The survivors, Samson and Hercules, were equal matches. Our space suit does not have the realism of wild animals, but it has scarcity value. Hercules' children's theater does not turn into a newspaper topic as does the space show, but it absorbs a lot of children during the summer vacation. While we work with newspaper companies, they go around shaking hands with PTAs and education committees. Kyōko appeals to adults, but the wrestler is a children's hero. Hercules' counterpart to our magazine space story is a jungle adventure. When the Disney film was released, a documentary film on Africa showed up.

Hacking fights went on in the sales arena also. As long as commodities flow from producers to wholesalers, and from wholesalers to retailers, the producers keep their hands on the wholesalers, and the wholesalers on the retailers. Taking advantage of this system, the two giants mobilized another prize system akin to the ones used for the children. Samson and Hercules offered special rebates to wholesalers. Each company inserted a card in every ten-dozen caramel cartons. The card was a cash prize added to the regular profit margin. It also served as a lottery ticket for an additional prize ranging between one thousand yen and one hundred thousand yen. Our salesmen started running madly day and night for this game as well. They soon realized that more needed to be done beyond the expansion of the wholesalers' profit ratio, additional rebates, and dangling the bait of cash prizes in front of their eyes. They took the wholesale and retail store owners to spas. Samson traveled to Hokkaido and Hercules drowned in the hot springs of Atami. Sake was poured and women danced for them.

In the face of this superficial conviviality, disquieting news started to arrive in August: smaller candy factories went bankrupt. The problem was that they had to sell the same caramel without the provision for prizes and bonuses to give away. Wholesalers refused to take the small producers' merchandise on account of their backlogs of merchandise from the giants. The small companies entreated the wholesalers, in panic, to accept their products below the fixed price. Their hope was to turn even one more box into cash. The summer drought of cash was unruly. But the result was as if the smaller companies drowned when they opened their mouths for a breath of air. At the first discovery that one middle-size producer accepted a price cut, all wholesalers quickly got on the backs of smaller companies. Like a forest fire, dumping, discounting, and bankruptcy spread through the whole country. It became the norm to see several small factory managers' names among the newspaper's listing of suicides. There were tragedies in the shallow market of limited hope. This was a territorial war fought in a confined area. Space helmets smothered and pocket monkeys bit off the smaller companies' arteries, in a manner of speaking.

Salesmen did not applaud this time. The fierce "invitation war" went on, but it was as meaningless as cats dancing on a hot tin roof. Sake started tasting bitter and the orgies became woeful. Cans and boxes were piled in retailers' closets. Wholesalers' warehouse floors became invisible. And presently, the symptom of price cuts spread to the giants' products as well. The overstock needed to be cashed in. Retailers in various regions started selling Samson and Hercules caramels at half price, or with extras. They broke open the dormant boxes in their warehouses and pulled out the prize cards to give them to their young customers. This was a kind of avalanche, something nobody could stop once it started rolling. All that the shopkeepers did in response to the supplicating or lecturing salesmen was to look down or yell back. Their bloodshot eyes never smiled again. The pity of the matter was that all the maneuvering was not so much for profit as merely to make ends meet.

In the end, the giants and wholesalers cut off these local infections in a resolute surgery. Venom would spread through the body if left alone;

Samson and Hercules agreed perfectly on this point for a change. Representatives from both companies invited major retailers and wholesalers to a hotel. They threatened to discontinue business with those who discounted or dumped their products. They then granted an extension of the settlement date for outstanding accounts, as a way of preventing a dealers' revenge. They told the stores to relax a little during the forty extra days. They also offered emergency loans to weak stores. Food was served and a party went on after the business talk. But the attendants' sighs soon spoiled, and their whispers clouded the cool scent of liqueur which permeated the banquet room. Only the salesmen's hollow guffaws reverberated.

The pessimism of reports arriving from branch offices and agencies became more clearly contrastive to the joviality of the advertisements. Aida no longer hid his pained look when he compared the reports from the sales department against the one from the factory. Fatigue from arduous work had deepened the crinkles at the corners of his eyes, and age spots had spread to his cheeks. He petulantly paced up and down the room, his rumpled silver hair flying every which way, and unsparingly bashed the wings of his jet planes. He didn't need words to let us know how he was bearing up within himself under tremendous pressure. The mounting pressure, nevertheless, never reached the point of tearing him away from his dream. He kept on fighting, no matter how poisoned he was by the reported figures. He commuted to the exhibition site to walk restlessly among the crowd and to politely give his staff precise instructions. Unaffected by the August sun, dust, or melting asphalt, he assiduously strewed his dream throughout the city in broad daylight. I trekked after him, day in and day out, to newspaper companies, to broadcasting companies, and to the physicist, and occupied myself with the task of giving a final polish to the details of his dream.

Even then, Samson received a heavy blow. A wholesaler wound up issuing a bad check. The wholesaler happened to be Samson's close associate from the time it was founded. In the past, Murata Store was sure to rescue us every time we fell into a slump. The Murata Store had so much power that one might even say it monopolized the dealership of Samson's products. The intimacy between the producer and the wholesaler, extending from the loan of capital to the exchange of employees, had a good reputation among our colleagues.

It wasn't that we knew nothing about Murata Store's latent problems, but they hadn't sounded any worse than many others we had gotten used to hearing about. Anyhow, in my mind, it concerned the business department, not our advertisement department. Still, when Murata announced its debt of one hundred million yen, and issuance of a ten million yen rubber check, Samson's beautiful walls shook from the basement to the roof. The news traveled between desks, up the stairs, streamed through hallways, windows, and all the rooms, and set in to stay. We were hit in the stomach. We congregated in threes and fives here and there and engaged in anxious discussions. The rumor was that the Murata Store's wreckage was due to its new investment in the production of canned food and juices, not to an overstock of Samson goods. An official-sounding report came from the directors after a while, and slowly and waveringly it wandered about on each floor, retracing the path of the earlier rumor. People listened to it only indifferently, with dismal and suspicious faces. They tasted the pungent satisfaction that their own premonitions had hit the mark. They argued their hearts out and found no solution but to drag their heavy feet back to their desks.

It was night when Aida and I got back to the company after watching Hercules' children's theater. A salesman met us in the entrance hall to inform us what had happened. Aida ran up to the boardroom. The room was brightly lit, and a high-pitched discussion was pouring into the corridor. I waited for Aida in our office. Upon his return, Aida dropped his exhausted body onto his chair, as if it were a sandbag. He then succinctly outlined Samson's decision: Samson will distribute Murata's quota to its affiliated wholesalers and do business directly with them; we will assume Murata's debts for the time being and send one of our directors to manage its business.

"What do you think is the real cause, canned food or caramel?" I asked.

Aida acted as if he didn't hear me. He started cleaning up his desk, picking up one sheet of paper at a time. He sighed heavily with his shoulders, as his hands tore and crumpled paper. Presently, he looked up and looked out the window. Convulsively, his torso stretched straight and his eyes twinkled. He let go of the half torn paper, got to his feet, and stuck his head far out the window to gaze at the dark sky.

"The lights are off!"

Behind him, our space man's night balloon, which was sent up from our roof, drifted like a giant jellyfish all dissolved in the darkness. Aida turned his body around, walked back to his desk, as impatient as ever, reciting the telephone number for the lighting equipment contractor. I was touched by a distant view of his figure.

This man is fighting a lonely war. . . .

Aida telephoned a fashion model agency a couple of days later to have Kyōko over to our company. Kyōko arrived in a magazine company's car, carrying a sheaf of music under her arm. By now, I had let many days go by without seeing her, on account of all the other things I had to do. On her part, Kyōko hardly came to Samson any more. We only saw her twice a week in a television commercial during the program sponsored by us. Actually, there was no need to call her for newspaper pictures and magazine advertisements. We still had plenty of extra pictures left from the time of the poster making. Radio commercials were also taken care of by her earlier recordings. In fact, it was in Aida's interest to free up Kyōko from Samson's work so that she could make herself famous elsewhere. She had spent most of her time going around as an independent fashion model. She had bound herself to her contract and stayed away from other companies' commercials, but as a model, she had made herself one of the best known. Nowadays, just about every single poster for shows had her name on it. Professional photography magazines, weekly magazines, other picture magazines, and fashion magazines ungrudgingly offered space on the front cover and photogravure pages for the cavity-toothed smile. One fashion designer dared to call Kyōko ''one face out of two million.''

As usual, we met her in the coffee shop on the first floor. I found her completely changed in a matter of two or three months. She still had the habit of putting a straw between her cavitied teeth, but now she wore nail polish and eyeshadow. Her downy hair was hidden under thin layers of makeup creams whose names I had no clue to. It was as if she had put an oddly shiny mask over her face. The trace of the girl who had happily asked for rice crackers was no more. Her shoulders had become rounded, and the contour of her body had gotten sharper, but her skin, burned by lights, was amazingly bumpy.

Aida asked about her recent activities as we drank coffee and later brought up his request. He elaborated how a stronger sale was necessary now that the closing date of the special sale was approaching, and finally asked her to hand out caramel at the space exhibition center in competition with the Hercules sales campaign.

''I have one condition to put on this.'' He shoved his coffee cup away and pushed his shoulders forward. ''I want you to wear the space suit at that time. In other words, I want you to look the way you do in the poster and on television.'' Aida then put a smile on his careworn face and leaned back on the seat.

Kyōko looked down and remained quiet for a while, but soon lifted her face with a deep breath.

"How long does it go?"

Aida innocently raised both hands and showed ten fingers. "For ten days." He then dropped one hand with a smile. "No, just five. Five days will do. Ten days will be too many to ask from you, or from your magazine companies. So, won't you be kind enough to help us for five days? From ten in the morning till four in the afternoon. Of course, you'll have plenty of time to rest in between."

"I have a problem." Kyōko cut in with a low but distinct voice. "They can take magazine pictures at night, but for recording, my voice collapses when I'm tired. . . ."

"Recording?" Aida shrieked as if he were attacked unguarded.

Kyōko nodded and pulled out a thick sheaf of music from under the table and said that she was practicing jazz at a studio every day because a musical instrument store had asked her to try it. Aida groaned at the realization that, while watching her every day on television, he had failed to stretch his imagination that far. It was too late. When Aida launched on an attack, quoting the exclusive contract, Kyōko looked him full in the face, to his consternation. She listed every item in the contract and answered that she had promised to appear in magazines, newspapers, and radio and television shows but not to work as a street saleswoman. This was unexpected, but she had a point. In business terms, what she said was perfectly correct. Aida panicked. This time he wielded humanitarian logic, reminding her of the effort made by the fellow who had sent her out into the world. He looked cheap. Kyōko listened to his words carefully and responded to each of his conclusions with a defensive but determined silence. The wall around her had the hardness of a shut-up clam.

"All right then." Aida tapped on the table distraughtly. "Let's forget about the exclusive contract. I'll revoke it as soon as the space show is over, but I want you to put up with us only this once. You can do jazz after that, can't you?" He folded his arms firmly on the table, cast his eyes downward with his head slightly drooped, and waited for her reply.

Kyōko watched him in that posture with the eyes of an onlooker, curious but a bit lost. She soon pulled a memo pad from her makeup bag, unhesitatingly wrote a figure, and slowly put it in front of Aida. Aida first took a quick glance at it, then raised his head, and glared at it for a second time.

"Whose idea is this!"

Kyōko sympathetically looked away but remained wordless.

Aida slowly ripped the pad, crushed it in his hand, and threw it on the floor. His tightly shut lips and drooping head trembled in the bright sun.

I got up, leaving the two behind. I inhaled the air in the plaza, went back in the building, and went to a bathroom. When I stepped into the restroom to wash my hands, I heard a deep sigh on the other side of the divider. Turning back on my way out, I saw Kyōko leaning against a mirror, her face almost touching it. She was pale, her eyes were shut, and her head bowed down deep as if she had fainted. Her maturity, unknown to me before, showed outwardly on her rough-skinned nape. She stayed that way and didn't budge.

I didn't go out for the rest of the day. I had no urge for loitering. All was over. Sitting by the bright second floor window, I kept at my work for the day. My desk top was a pile of scraps. There were research data, boys' magazines, and the space suit. Pictures of squatting pocket monkeys and international flags at the space show flapped. I tore and threw out newspapers and photographs in the order I lay my hand on them. The sun was strong, but the breeze was cool. Every now and then, the odor of hot dust joined the breeze, but I could work without sweating much.

I rested my hands after five o'clock. An anemic human current flowed in the plaza. The usual throng, the hungry, tired people, dragged their feet toward the station. From nowhere, a man in a plastic helmet appeared and stood on a stone pedestal in the center of the plaza. It ruined the aesthetics of the place. He had no power to stabilize the air or the things about him. He was left out, like a rock in a stream, by the plaza, by the buildings, and by the mob. No one lifted his eyes or rested his feet for the man. When the sun completely sank below the horizon, he got off the pedestal and disappeared.

The mob's continuous footsteps shook the wall. Our windows vibrated. I felt that a machine was moving. In the ruins, lit up by light green walls, machines didn't stop operating. I had drawn projection charts and lateral view charts about children's personalities and activities on my desk, and Aida had built his dream on top of them. As a result, a girl smiled, rotary presses turned, and a physicist used his brain. Mothers were disappointed, small candy-makers committed suicide, and a wholesaler went broke. Kyōko sold well but caramel didn't. Sweet scent was rotting in the gloom of towns and villages. Where did the thirty million yen investment and the daily-harnessed one thousand manpower go to? Did we leave only an elusive shadow in the dim consciousness of children, and nothing else?

I smoked by the window, tasting a tremendous amount of wasted effort. A noise made me turn around. It was Aida standing at the doorway. He grinned tightly on seeing me but walked in without a word. He was neither drunk nor spent to death. He tossed his flax suit on top of his desk, pulled down his trousers, and kept only his undershirt and underpants on. What he pulled out, under the light, from the glass cabinet, gave me a wretched pang. He put on a silver suit with a bright emblem of a giant on its chest.

"Wow! Great! This fits me perfectly!" He then put on the plastic helmet. "I'm going to walk around in these!" He shouted merrily inside the space helmet, flipped the antennas two or three times, and circled around the room.

I got up from my seat and went to the hallway, leaving him in the office by himself. Aida's loud voice, asking the weather bureau by telephone about tomorrow's weather, chased after me. By the time I started walking down the stairs, the voice had turned to sad laughter. As I walked in darkness, it dawned on me that there was only one instance in my life when all my power crystallized. It was only once, but it was critical. When I saw the hat flattened in the middle of the road, I was all for throwing my body on the pavement. At that time, I wanted to hear my own shriek and the sound of my cracking skull. I crawled out of the dead cement and scampered into the crowd in the polluted August night.

Notes

This story was originally published in a monthly magazine, *World of Literature* (Bungakukai), October 1957. This is a translation of "Kyōjin to omacha" in *Collected Works of Takeshi Kaikō*: Novels 2 (Kaikō Takeshi zen sakuhin-shū: Shōsetsu 2) (Tokyo: Shinchō-sha, 1973), pp. 72–110.

1. *Kun* in this case means "Mr." with a sense of intimacy.

2. The Osaka dialect is more blunt, yet friendlier than standard Japanese.

3. *Kappa*, translated as water imp, is an imaginary animal that lives in water. It has a dish on top of its head, hair around it, a human-like but scaled green body with webbed fingers, and a large, beaked mouth.

4. *Renkyū*, or the Golden Week, occurs when a weekend comes close to a national holiday, creating consecutive holidays.

5. *Anko* is cooked lentil beans sweetened with a lot of sugar.

6. The Meiji era was from 1868 to 1912 and the Taishō era was from 1912 to 1926.

7. *Miso* is salty beanpaste and *takuan* is pickled long radish.

8. *Katakana* is an alphabet often used to phoneticize foreign words.

A graduate of the State University of New York at Binghamton, TAMAE K. PRINDLE received her Ph.D. in modern Japanese literature from Cornell University. Since 1986 she has been Dana Faculty Fellow and Assistant Professor of East Asian Studies at Colby College.